# WITHDRAWN
## UTSA Libraries

# The Wealth Transfer of Inflation: How to Compute It, Account for It, And Profit From It

Harry M. Hansen

INSTITUTE FOR BUSINESS PLANNING, INC.
IBP Plaza, Englewood Cliffs, New Jersey 07632

This publication is designed to provide accurate and authoritative information in regard to the subject matter covered. It is sold with the understanding that the publisher is not engaged in rendering legal, accounting or other professional service. If legal advice or other expert assistance is required, the services of a competent professional person should be sought.

*—From a Declaration of Principles jointly adopted by a Committee of the American Bar Association and a Committee of Publishers and Associations.*

©Copyright 1981, by Institute for Business Planning, Inc.
IBP Plaza, Englewood Cliffs, NJ 07632

*All rights reserved. No part of this publication may be reproduced in any form, or by any means, without permission in writing from the publisher. Printed in U.S.A.*

**Library of Congress Cataloging in Publication Data**

Hansen, Harry M. (Harry Morris)
  The wealth transfer of inflation.

  Includes bibliographical and index.
  1. Accounting—Effect of inflation on.  I. Title.
HF5658.5.H36           657'.48           81-6250
ISBN 0-87624-014-7                       AACR2

# Dedication

*To the Franks and to the Hansens*

# About The Author

Harry M. Hansen served as an adviser on taxation to various governments in South America and Asia. These were countries of high inflation. It was this experience that gave Mr. Hansen an insight into inflation's ability to substitute semblance for fact in accounting and taxation. Mr. Hansen is a Certified Public Accountant and a financial consultant for small- to medium-sized businesses. He writes on tax and accounting subjects, and is a lecturer for the American Institute of Banking.

# What This Book Will Do For You

This book is written for the firms and people I deal with daily—firms in the medium and small-class, both incorporated and unincorporated, closely held and listed; for people who invest, manage, lend, and give credit. It is, of course, written for fellow professionals engaged in advising business clients.

This is the first book that treats the subject of the analysis of inflation-distorted financial statements and cash flow accounting. It is also the first book that treats inflation as a wealth transfer—not as a chase—a chase of too much money pursuing too few goods. It will help you perceive the subtle, almost imperceptible, wealth transfer of inflation, from your business, and to your business; from and to you personally.

Inflation does not create wealth. Its sole function is to transfer it. It indiscriminately takes wealth from those who do not understand inflation and gives it to those who do. Inflation transfers wealth from the unorganized to the organized, from the taxpayer to the government, from those who have the "money illusion" to those who do not. It transfers wealth without the wealth owner's permission. Its annual toll is approximately 100 billion dollars. Yet conventional accounting does not perceive it. This book will help you to detect this mass movement of wealth and to deal with it.

Take a test: How much interest does an individual, in the the 50% marginal tax bracket, have to earn in order to receive a 6% return on capital, in real terms, in a year of 10% inflation? Answer: 32%.

Another inflation question: The owner of a closely held corporation wishes to maintain the purchasing power of his $100,000 capital investment. In a year of 10% inflation, what rate of return on capital must the corporation produce *just* to maintain the original purchasing power of capital invested? Answer: 33.33%. This assumes a corporate tax rate of 40% and a stockholder's tax rate of 50%.

This book shows you how to make these computations. It also demonstrates how to compute the inflation factor to be added to your markup on goods held for sale. In addition, there are detailed, various inflation strategies a firm or individual can adopt to diminish inflation's bite on your capital and earnings.

But first one must learn where fiscal reality lies. Historic Cost Accounting, the system of accounting in current use, has the money illusion. Its perception of fiscal reality is that prices are rising, but the value of accounting's measuring rod—the dollar—remains stable and fixed at all times. As a consequence, it fails to report not only inflation's wealth *loss*, but inflation's wealth *gains*. Firms experience both.

This book maps out where to find approximate fiscal reality. It discusses the seven measurement errors of Historic Cost Accounting. Some of these are:

- Sales appear to increase over the prior year because no adjustment is made for the decline in the value of the standard of measurement dollar. A method for computing sales in real terms is given.

- Income is understated because gain from the reduction in the dollar value of debt is not reported. Debt is a widely used inflation strategy. This book tells when debt results in gain—an increase in the ability to consume—and when it does not. It gives the formula of how to compute interest paid on debt in real terms. Can the lender or creditor anticipate inflation and charge for it in his interest rate? The answer is "seldom."

- Losses from the reduction in the dollar value of monetary assets—cash, accounts receivable, etc.—are not reported. This book shows how to compute a monthly loss on the value of the monetary assets held by your firm. This will enable you to better manage your quick assets. Also discussed are the inflation strategies for creditor—savers.

- Historic Cost's understatement of the cost inventory and depreciation, causes an illusory infla-profit to be reported. These infla-profits are taxed, thus causing a wealth transfer from the firm to the taxing authority. Is the LIFO method of inventory a reliable method for reducing the phantom profits on inventory? It is a super tax strategy.

The errors detailed and others not listed here cause accounting to erroneously report the financial condition of an enterprise. What can those who must use the accounting statements prepared by accountants do to bring reality into financial reporting? This book gives a simple method for converting inflation-distorted Historic Cost Profit and Loss Statements and Balance Sheets into a distortion-free Cash-Flow Accounting Statement. Furthermore, the Cash-Flow Statement will tell you whether the firm is able to meet its debt, pay its loans, and reward its owners. Many firms are now earning profits, but no cash. Cash-Flow Accounting will show why this inflation-caused anomaly exists. Those who lend money, give credit, or invest, will find Cash-Flow Statements to be of great value. Actual illustrations for adjusting financial statements to show cash flow are also given.

Finally, there is an explanation of two inflation accounting systems: Constant Dollar and Current Cost Accounting. These systems are now being used on an experimental basis by the large corporations. Inflation will ultimately force their general use.

## Grateful Acknowledgments

First, I'd like to thank the generous and knowledgeable Ron Cowan for reading my manuscript and for the many suggestions he gave me. I hasten to add that reading a manuscript does not imply approval of what is written.

I owe a heavy debt of gratitude to the American Institute of Banking, San Francisco. John Corr of that organization gave me the opportunity to develop and test out my explanation of the various infla-distortions found in Historic Cost financial statements.

Finally, in expressing thankfulness, I would like to emulate the example of a composer who won an "Oscar" for the best musical score used in a movie. If you have watched a Motion Picture Academy Awards affair, you will have heard the award winners thank everyone from the producer to the dishwasher in the company's cafeteria. The composer dispensed with these amenities. He got right to the point. He said: "I want to thank Chopin, Liszt, Tchaikovsky and Debussy, for the beautiful melodies they gave me."

In the same vein, I would like to thank the following persons, accounting organizations, and accounting magazines for the leitmotifs they gave me. These are the infla-accounting pioneers, Ralph Coughenour Jones (Constant Dollar Accounting), Edwards and Bell (Current Cost Accounting), and G. H. Lawson (Cash-Flow Accounting). The accounting organizations and journals which gave currency to ideas concerning infla-accounting were the American Accounting Association and their excellent journal, *The Accounting Review;* The Sandilands Commission, the prestigious English magazine, *Accountancy;* and the Financial Accounting Standards Board.

I owe a lot of gratitude to other people and publications for ideas I've appropriated. I've tried to indicate who these are in the NOTES. Memory chides me to thank my professors at the University of Washington. They taught me how to question and analyze established ideas. Quite a gift, and I'm grateful.

# Contents

**About The Author** v
**What This Book Will Do For You** vii

### Part 1:
### What You Ought To Know About Inflation's Wealth Transfer And Its Impact On Accounting  1

### CHAPTER 1:
### THE BASIS FOR TODAY'S INFLATION STRATEGY  3

Why Inflation Is Considered A Wealth Transfer  4
Inflation Strategy: How To Win Inflation's Redistribution
　Of The Wealth Game  6
Money Is A Messenger  6
Money's Role In The Economy  7
The Accounting Roles of Money  7
Currency Must Have a Predictable Value For The Accounting
　Roles Of Money To Function  8
The Great Epoch Of Wealth Redistribution  9
Tying Together The Concepts Of The Role Of Money In The
　Economy During A Period Of Inflation  11

### CHAPTER 2:
### WHAT IS ACCOUNTING'S PERPLEXING PROBLEM?  13

Accounting Is A Measurement Of Art  13
Monetary Units Must Be Dated  14

**Part 2:**
**How To Detect And Measure The Hidden Wealth Transfer Of Inflation: Business Strategies For Minimizing Wealth Loss And For Gaining The Wealth Transfer** 17

**CHAPTER 3:**
**WHAT IS HISTORIC COST'S MEASUREMENT PROBLEM?** 19

Why Historic Cost Accounting Does Not Report Fiscal Reality  20
What Causes The Reporting Error?  21

**CHAPTER 4:**
**HISTORIC COST ACCOUNTING DOES NOT REPORT THE WEALTH TRANSFER OF DEBT: STRATEGIES FOR MAINTAINING THE WEALTH IN THE FIRM** 23

HCA Does Not Report The Wealth Transfer Of Debt:
 Therefore, Income Is Understated Or Overstated  23
How To Profit From Debt  25
Lenders Must Not Anticipate The Inflation And Charge For It  25
How Lender Must Compute Interest On Loan Whose Term
 Is For A Period Of More Than One Year  26
Lenders Have Not Been Able To Anticipate Inflation In Their
 Interest Charge  28
Holding Gain From Debt Will Be Realized If Revenue Is Increased
 By The Amount Of The Wealth Transfer  28
Holding Gain From Debt Is Taxable Income  30
How To Determine The Effective Rate Of Interest Paid On Debt  30
How To Determine Interest Costs On Long-Term Debt: Advantages  31
Facts of Figure 4-5  31
The Advantage Of Funding With Debt Instead Of Equity During
 A Period of Monetary Inflation  33
Comparison Of The Profit Earned By A Company Funded By Debt
 With One Funded By Equity Capital—Polonius Was Half Right  34
Inflation Will Increase Your Debt To Equity Ratio—How To Convince
 Your Banker Not To Worry About It  36
What Debt Yields The Highest Holding Gain? How To Shake
 The Money Tree  39
Deferral Of Paying Accounts Payable—Another Much Abused,
 Interest-Free, Or Partially Interest-Free Loan  41

Small Business Administration Loan—The Best, Low-Cost, 8¼% Loan For Small And Medium-Sized Businesses  **41**
Preferred Stock—A Loan Forever  **42**
Bonds And Mortgages Have The Inestimable Advantage Of Being Long-Term Debt  **42**

## CHAPTER 5:
## HISTORIC COST ACCOUNTING DOES NOT REPORT LOSSES FROM HOLDING MONETARY ASSETS OF THE FIRM: HOW TO PREVENT AND COMPUTE THE LOSS  **47**

Strategy For Offsetting Holding Gains From Monetary Liabilities Against Holding Losses From Monetary Assets  **48**
Strategy For Reducing Loss From Holding Cash  **49**
How To Determine The Amount Of The Holding Loss  **50**
How To Compute The Combined Costs Of Holding Money  **51**
How To Determine The Monthly Loss From Holding Cash  **52**
How To Compute The Holding Loss On Accounts Receivable  **53**
Strategies For Reducing The Holding Loss From Accounts Receivable  **54**
Monetary Holding Losses Can Be Materially Reduced By Inserting Gold Or Foreign Money Clauses Into Contracts  **55**
Indexing Long-Term Contracts To Commodity And Labor Indexes  **56**
How To Compute Your Net Holding Gain Or Loss From Monetary Items  **57**

## CHAPTER 6:
## HISTORIC COST ACCOUNTING WILL TRANSFER YOUR WEALTH BY INCORRECTLY MEASURING YOUR COST OF GOODS SOLD  **61**

HCA Understates The Cost Of Goods Sold, Thus Creating An Illusory Profit On Which Taxes Must Be Paid  **61**
Not All Inventory Profits Are Illusory  **64**

## CHAPTER 7:
## IS HISTORIC COST ACCOUNTING'S UNDERSTATEMENT OF DEPRECIATION DEFINANCING YOUR BUSINESS?

HCA Understates The Cost Of Depreciation And, Therefore, Overstates Profit  **70**

## CHAPTER 8:
## HISTORIC COST ACCOUNTING PROFIT AND LOSS STATEMENTS LACK COMPARABILITY: HOW TO DETERMINE WHETHER A FIRM IS INCREASING SALES IN REAL TERMS  75

How To Measure Sales In Constant Terms: Conversion Process  76
Alternative Method For Measuring Sales In Constant Terms  77

## CHAPTER 9:
## MEASUREMENT ERRORS APPEARING ON THE HISTORIC COST ACCOUNTING BALANCE SHEET  79

HCA Will Understate The Value Of Fixed Assets  79
The Understatement Of The Worth Of Fixed Assets May Misinform Bankers And Creditors  80
The Second Balance Sheet Error Of HCA  80
A "Quick and Dirty" Method For Computing The Infla-Income, The Infla-Tax, And The Approximate Inflation-Adjusted Earnings And Capital Of A Firm  81
Example Of How To Remove Inflation's Distortion From Profit And Equity  82
What The Grady Method For Computing The Infla-Loss Of Equity Does and Does Not Do  82
The Grady Infla-Accounting Method Has An Important Application To The Accumulated Earnings Penalty of Section 531, I.R.C.  87
Are The Seven Reporting Errors Of HCA Important To Managers?  87

## CHAPTER 10:
## HOW TO DETERMINE HOW A FIRM IS FUNDING THE COST OF INFLATION'S WEALTH TRANSFER. ALSO, THE USES AND LIMITATIONS OF HCA FINANCIAL STATEMENTS  91

Can You Predict Future Financial Performance By Analyzing Prior Years' Historic Cost Financial Statements  92
Historic Cost Statements Accurately Predict Short-Term Liquidity  94
The Long-Term Predictive Ability of HC Financial Statements Is Notoriously Inaccurate—But Useful  95
Why The Inflation Factor Is Important To Financial Analysis  95

How The Wealth Transfer Of Inflation Will Affect Future Net
    Cash Inflow  **96**
How To Determine The Source Of Funds A Firm Has Used To
    Finance Inflation's Demand On Cash  **96**
How To Make A Common Size Analysis  **97**
How To Make An Index Trend Analysis  **100**

## CHAPTER 11:
### THE LIFO CONVENTION OF INVENTORY: ZANY, BUT IT MAY SAVE YOU MONEY. IT MAY ALSO BE AN ACCOUNTING "SHUCK AND A SHAM." WILL THE LIFO (Last-in, First-out) INVENTORY METHOD SAVE YOU MONEY?  **105**

LIFO Is An Attempt To Correct Problem "A" While Creating
    Problems "B" and "C"  **106**
LIFO Is Premised On A Zany Idea  **106**
A LIFO Inventory May Report Goods On Hand That Were Sold  **108**
LIFO Errs In Stating The Value Of Inventory On The
    Balance Sheet  **109**
The Accounting Justification For LIFO—When Does LIFO Report
    Inventory Costs At Current Prices?  **110**
LIFO May Reduce Your Income Taxes  **112**
LIFO Will Report A Greater Profit Than FIFO When Prices
    Are Falling  **118**
How The LIFO Tail May Wag The Business Dog—LIFO Is Costly To
    Maintain In Both Time and Money  **118**
How LIFO Offers The Unscrupulous An Opportunity To Manipulate
    Earnings  **120**

## CHAPTER 12:
### THE ACCOUNTANT'S DUTY TO CLIENTS, TO THE PUBLIC AND TO THE GOVERNMENT  **123**

Are There Two Different Definitions Of Income?  **123**
Examples of TAXSPEAK  **124**
The Cost of TAXSPEAK  **125**

**Part 3:
Step-By-Step Illustrations For Adjusting Financial Statements For Price Level Changes 129**

## CHAPTER 13:
## CASH-FLOW ACCOUNTING: HOW IT WORKS AND HOW TO USE IT 131

Business Managers Are Cash-Flow Accountants 131
Why Managers Should Be Judged On Their Ability To Produce Cash Profits 132
Cash-Flow Analysis Provides Very Useful Information To Investors, Creditors, And Lenders 132
What Is Cash-Flow Accounting? 133
Cash-Flow Accounting Is Accomplished By The Preparation Of A Cash-Flow Analysis Statement 133
How To Convert A HCA Profit And Loss Statement Into A Cash-Flow Analysis Statement 133
Cash-Flow Analysis requires That We Make A Study Of The Current Year And Two Prior Years. In Addition, We Should Make A Cash-Flow Forecast For The Ensuing Year 142
What's Wrong With Cash-Flow Accounting? 142

## CHAPTER 14:
## PLANNING CASH FLOW FOR BUSINESS AND INVESTMENT TRANSACTIONS 147

How Do We Assimilate The Incredible Factors Of Inflation In Forecasting Cash Flow? 148
How Inflation Distorts Cash-Flow Planning 149
How To Provide For The Inflation Factor In Planning Cash Flow From A Fixed Dollar Investment 149
The Case Of My Neighbor And Yours, Mr. Fred Jason 150
The State And Federal Government's Cash Flow From The Wealth Transfer Of The Infla-Tax 152
An Example Of How Fred Should Have Planned The Cash Inflow From His Fixed Dollar Investment 153
Conclusions Concerning Planning Cash Flow From Fixed Dollar Investments 156

How The Inflation Factor Affects The Net Cash Flow From
   The Operation Machine. A Corporate Case  **156**
How To Compute The Inflation Factor For Payment Of Dividends
   And Return Of Capital In Constant Value Dollars  **158**
How To Compute The Inflation Factor To Provide The Cash Flow
   For The Payment Of Dividends In Constant Terms  **158**
How To Compute The Inflation Factor For the Return Of Capital
   In Constant Terms  **159**
The Wealth Transfer Of Capital Must Be Provided For In Cash Flow,
   Even Though The Stockholders' Investment Is Not Returned  **161**
Inflation Strategies' "Fashions Incorporated" Might Use To Offset
   The Wealth Transfer Of Inflation  **163**
Strategy Of Electing To Be Taxed As A Subchapter S Corporation  **167**
Conclusions In The Case Of Fashions Inc.  **166**
Savings From Electing To Be Taxed As A Sub S Corporation  **167**
How To Compute The Weighted Inflation Factor For Planning The
   Cash Inflow From The Manufacture And Sale Of A Product  **168**
Step-By-Step Explanation Of How To Compute The Weighted Inflation
   Factor For Product X  **168**
Forecasting The Price Trend For The Insignificant Many  **171**
How Far Ahead Should You Plan?  **171**
Example Of How To Compute The Weighted Inflation Factor For A
   Monthly Cash-Flow Plan  **172**
How To Prepare A Cash Flow Plan  **176**

## CHAPTER 15:
## INFLA-ACCOUNTING SOLUTIONS:
## CONSTANT DOLLAR ACCOUNTING (CDA) AND
## CURRENT COST ACCOUNTING (CCA)  **181**

With Which Dollar Should Accounting Measure? Can It Be Adjusted
   To Perform Its Accounting Roles?  **182**
Different Units Of Measure Produce Different Statements
   Of Income  **182**
Comparison Of How The Accounting Systems Differ: Examples Of
   How They Differ  **183**
Explanation Of Adjustments Appearing On Schedule I, The Beginning
   Balance Sheet  **185**

Explanation Of Adjustments Appearing On Schedule II, Computation Of Holding Loss From Monetary Assets  **191**
Explanation Of Adjustments Appearing On Schedule III, Comparative Profit And Loss Statement  **192**
Characteristics Of Monetary Holding Gains And Losses And Cost Savings In Financial Statements  **197**
Advantages And Disadvantages Of The Infla-Accounting Solutions  **198**
Do Constant Dollar Accounting And Current Cost Accounting Correct The Seven Measurement Errors Of Historic Cost Accounting?  **203**
The Combination Of Constant Dollar Accounting With Current Cost Accounting—An Alternative Solution  **205**

CHAPTER 16:
IN CONCLUSION: ACCOUNTING'S ROLE IN INFLATION  **209**

APPENDIX  **211**

INDEX  **249**

# Part 1

## What You Ought To Know About Inflation's Wealth Transfer And Its Impact On Accounting

# 1

## The Basis For Today's Inflation Strategy

Accounting has failed to report the fiscal effects of inflation, because it has misperceived the problem. The inflation issue has been defined as "too much money chasing too few goods." But that is like defining burglary as one person chasing another. It is possible that after a burglary one person may chase another, but that doesn't describe the crime—the taking of wealth, surreptitiously, without the wealth owner's permission. Wouldn't it be ludicrous to try to solve the problem of burglary by preventing the wealth owner from chasing the burglar? That's the equivalent of price control!

Therefore, to define inflation in terms of a chase is to misperceive the problem. That doesn't describe the act of inflation. It, too, is a transfer of wealth without the wealth owner's permission. Money will chase goods after the act, but not before.

The problem that accounting must solve is: How do you account for the wealth transfer of inflation? The questions that must be asked are: Who gains from the decline in the value of money? Who loses? How much wealth is gained, and how much lost? These are the right questions derived from having identified the right problem.

When you have read Chapter 1, you will understand how inflation adds to and subtracts from your personal wealth, and from the income and capital of your enterprise. You will also understand the general strategy needed to deal with inflation, and whom inflation rewards, and whom it punishes.

# WHY INFLATION IS CONSIDERED A WEALTH TRANSFER

The description of inflation as a transfer of wealth is more accurate and useful than the traditonal definition "too much money chasing too few goods" which describes a symptom of inflation. It does not tell of its effect. Governments create inflation to transfer wealth from its citizens to itself. But once the government lets the genie out of the bottle, it cannot control it.

The genie of inflation will not restrict its transfer of wealth from the private sector to the government. It will also, indiscriminately and perversely, transfer wealth within the private sector. Some firms and individuals will gain, while others will lose.

The success of inflation's annual multibillion dollar transfer of income and capital depends on one of two conditions:

1. The property owner must not detect his or her loss.
2. In the event the property owner discovers the loss, the law must offer no remedy for the recoupment of the property.

**Here Is An Example When The Loss Of Wealth Is Not Detected**

On January 2, 1970, Swenson, a businessman, lends the government $10,000, for ten years certain. He makes the loan by purchasing a bond due in 1980. The government, true to its word, in 1980 repays Swenson $10,000.

During the ten-year term of the loan, the rate of inflation averages 7% per year. This caused the general purchasing power of the dollar to decline by 50%. Consequently, it required 20,000 1980 dollars to purchase what 10,000 dollars bought in 1970. In effect, the government repaid Swenson one-half the value he had loaned.

Swenson does not perceive his loss, because he has the "money illusion." His perception of the transaction is that he loaned $10,000 and was repaid $10,000. "That's fair and square," says Swenson.

*How Historic Cost Accounting would report the loan transaction:* Historic Cost Accounting, the method of accounting in current use, would assure Swenson that his perception of the loan transaction is correct. It would say to Swenson:

>     You loaned ........................... 10,000 1970 dollars
>     and you were repaid ................... 10,000 1980 dollars
>     Since a 1980 dollar will purchase the same quantity of goods and services as a 1970 dollar, you have been fully repaid. No gain. No loss.

What is illustrated here is the role that accountancy has played in the long period of our inflation. It has blinded the eye of the wealth owner to his or her loss. Accounting and Swenson suffer from the same misperception of money. They believe that prices rise in a period of inflation, but that the value of money remains stable.

There are systems of accounting which can perceive and report the wealth transfer of inflation. These inflationary accounting systems—I call them systems of infla-accounting—are: Cash-Flow Accounting, Constant Dollar Accounting, and Current Cost Accounting. These infla-accounting systems are discussed in Part 3 of this book.

**Here Is An Example When The Loss Of Property Is Detected**

*How the law would view the loan transaction:* Supposing Swenson wakes in the night to hear clear-eyed Logic whispering in his ear. Logic informs Swenson that the loan transaction cannot be computed in terms of dollars. It must be computed in terms of the ability to consume.

"You didn't lend money, Swenson; you lent goods. Money is a symbol of goods. The government should have repaid you 20,000 1980 dollars, not 10,000 1980 dollars. If they had, they would have returned the same purchasing power you lent them."

Swenson sees the light. The next morning he files a lawsuit against the government for the payment of an additional 10,000 1980 dollars. Will the Federal Court hear his complaint? The answer is no. Nor would the court hear Swenson if he had lent his money to a private borrower instead of the government. It is settled law that a debt can be discharged, dollar for dollar, in what Congress has declared to be legal tender, i.e., paper bills and coins. (See *Norman v. Baltimore O.R. Co.,* 55 S Ct.) Thus, it is the role of law in a time of inflation not to offer a remedy to those whose wealth is transferred by the government's debasement of money. Both Historic Cost Accounting and the law perceive the value of a business transaction as being determined forever by the number of dollars exchanged at the date of the loan or sale. The value of a loan is eternally fixed by the number of dollars originally exchanged. The number of dollars paid for an item is its eternal cost.

This misconstruction of fiscal reality, exists with the cooperation of blind accountants and accommodating judges.

## INFLATION STRATEGY: HOW TO WIN INFLATION'S REDISTRIBUTION OF THE WEALTH GAME

The Inflation game is the redistribution of wealth. When the game has been played, there is no more wealth than when the game started. But there are winners who walk off the field with more wealth than they had at the game's start; and there are losers who walk off with less.

The strategy for winning is simple: Raise your prices and wages at a rate greater than your neighbors do. Borrow money and pay back less value than you received. Finally, gag the insatiable iron maw of taxation with tax-free income, capital gains, tax deferrals etc.

Accounting, the fiscal scorekeeper, cannot tally inflation's game. Accounting measures economic activity with money. Its measurement of gain and loss is premised on the supposition that the accounting roles of currency will continue to play their part in the economy. But inflation cripples money's ability to play these roles. As a result, Historic Cost Accounting—conventional accounting—is invalidated. To better understand this, let's review the roles money plays in the economy and in accounting.

### The Accounting Roles of Money
### Money Is A Messenger[1]

That intrinsically worthless dollar bill you have in your pocket bears a message. It states that you have produced a good whose value measures one dollar; that the value of the good has not been consumed; and that the United States government guarantees the message to be true and correct. You can take your dollar bill almost any place in the world and exchange it for a good or service whose value you and the seller agree is worth one dollar. The person who takes your money does not know what you produced, nor does he care. The seller takes your money on trust that you did produce a good, and that he will be able to exchange the dollar bill for something he wants.

Most money in circulation is not printed or minted. It is credit largely stored in the banking system, and evidenced by nothing more than bookkeeping entries. But currency of whatever form, bears the same message of goods produced, of measurement of value, and the assurance that the goods have not been consumed. Incredibly, all this rests on trust. Money is one of our most useful and astonishing inventions. Astonishing, because the world has so much faith in its message.

## Money's Role In The Economy

Money's role in the economy is to make the exchange of goods efficient and convenient. In a nonmonetary society, the person with two hams, who wants ten chickens, must search out the person with ten chickens who is willing to exchange them for two hams—a time-consuming, wearying transaction.

Currency permits the person with hams to make an immediate exchange of hams for money. The money received can then be exchanged for chickens. What we have just described is one of the roles of money in the economy. That is, to act as a medium of exchange for immediately completed transactions.

However, while currency supplanted barter, it did not eliminate the requirement that there be an exchange of goods—symbolically. Money is a symbol of goods. It represents objects, services, and rights. The person who has not produced a good has no money unless he or she got it by gift. In that case, the donor produced the good represented by the money.

Many governments, ancient and modern, have attempted to give their currency an inherent worth. At the end of each attempt, it was revealed that money had value only if it represented goods; otherwise it was worthless.

## The Accounting Roles of Money

Money in our complex society has other roles than that of a medium of exchange for immediately completed transactions. It also symbolizes the exchange of goods over time. We enter into contractual relationships in which we say: "I will give you a good, service, or right now, and you will pay me later." Money in this role is a standard of value for long-term transactions.

Another contractual role of money, involving time, is for currency to act as a store of value for savings and investments. The saving of money in a bank is the act of storing goods for future use. We say to our banker: "I will store these goods (money) with you, and you will return them to me when I need them." Or we purchase stock in which we say to the corporate officers: "I'll invest in your corporation. You will wisely use my money so that when I need to sell my shares I will get back what I stored with you."

These long-term uses of currency are termed the accounting roles of money because they are not completed by an immediate exchange of money for goods, but are completed by the exchange of goods for an accounting record, such as an executed contract or a signed invoice.

**Currency Must Have A Predictable Value  
For The Accounting Roles  
Of Money To Function**

When either of the two accounting roles of money is employed in commerce, there is a mutual understanding by the parties involved that the sum of money stored, or the sum of money agreed on in the long-term contract, will have a predictable value. The persons who consummate a long-term contract expect the debtor to pay, and the creditor to receive, the identical value agreed on. Similarly, the saver or investor expects to get back the exact value stored.

At the making of these contracts of savings, or the selling of goods, services, or rights, it is also assumed that neither of the contracting parties, nor the government, will deliberately manipulate the value of the money agreed on. The money roles of a standard of value for long-term contracts, and a store of value for savings and investments rests on the integrity of the contracting parties and on the government in whose money the contract is denominated.

If either of the contracting parties or the government tampers with the value of the currency, which measures the value of the contract, then its worth becomes unpredictable. The accounting or contractual roles of money are destroyed.

When money loses its ability to perform its contractual roles, the Historic Cost accrual method of accounting also loses its ability to function. It cannot report fiscal verity because it is premised on the proposition that money will symbolize a fixed value of goods and services in the past, present, and future. Thus, it is the primary assumption of conventional accounting—Historic Cost Accrual Accounting—that the number of dollars paid for an item determines its cost forever. An item purchased in 1981 for $100,000 will bear that cost until kingdom come. A machine purchased for $20,000 in 1981, with a useful life of 10 years, will have its depreciation computed on that cost until its useful life expires in 1991.

This is logical so long as money performs its role as a fixed standard of value for long-term transactions. But it is illogical when it doesn't.

The logic of Historic Cost Accounting is further undermined when money can no longer act as a long-term repository of value. Historic Cost Accounting assumes that the value of a monetary asset, a monetary liability, or the capital equity of an enterprise is fixed at the date of acquisition. If the stockholders contribute $100,000 to a firm, accounting will report that number of dollars in the equity section of the balance sheet, from here to eternity, or until the company expires, whichever occurs first. Similarly, $200,000 in cash, held for a year, in which the purchasing power of money declines by 10%, will be assumed to have the same command over goods and services as it had at the beginning of the year. The loss of purchasing power of cash will not be reported. It is in this fertile field of illusion that the wealth transfer of inflation luxuriates.

## THE GREAT EPOCH OF WEALTH REDISTRIBUTION

Our long epoch of inflation's wealth redistribution began in the year 1968. The rate of inflation attained the level of 4½%. In contrast, the inflation rate averaged only 2.3% per annum during the entire decade preceding 1968 (1959-1968).

In the ensuing decade, 1969 to 1978, the average inflation rate tripled to 6.3%. This caused the value of the dollar to decline by 50%.

The impressive characteristic of our inflation has been its ability to accelerate. Prices rose from 4.5% in 1968, to 13.9% in 1979. The average rate of inflation for the six-year period 1973 to 1978 was 8.1%. The importance of a relativley mild 8% rise in the Consumer Price Index can be seen in its effect on the purchasing power of the dollar. If prices increase at an average rate of 8%, the dollar will decline in value by approximately one-third in six years, 50% in ten years, and 66% in 15 years. See Figures 1-1 and 1-2. They show the rate at which the dollar will decline in value at various rates of inflation: (Also see Appendix A and B.)

Figure 1-1 shows how the value of the dollar measures less and less goods with each year of inflation. Those who lend, save, or invest money should commit Figure 1-1 to memory. Those who borrow money have an equal reason for knowing the facts of Figure 1-1.

The information in Figure 1-2 is the information presented in Figure 1-1, but now showing how inflation causes prices to rise or appear to rise. Figure 1-2 is useful in predicting replacement costs, but it should be

**THIS TABLE SHOWS THE DECLINE IN PURCHASING POWER OF THE DOLLAR AT VARIOUS RATES OF INFLATION**

| Yearly Rate of Inflation | Money Will Decline in Value By | | | |
|---|---|---|---|---|
| | 33% in: | 50% in: | 66% in: | 75% in: |
| 6% | 7 yrs | 12 yrs | 19 yrs | 24 yrs |
| 7% | 6 yrs | 11 yrs | 17 yrs | 21 yrs |
| 8% | 6 yrs + | 10 yrs | 15 yrs | 19 yrs |
| 9% | 5 yrs | 9 yrs | 13 yrs | 17 yrs |
| 10% | 4 yrs | 8 yrs | 12 yrs | 15 yrs |
| 12% | 4 yrs | 7 yrs | 10 yrs | 13 yrs |

**FIGURE 1-1**

**THIS TABLE SHOWS THE RATE AT WHICH PRICES WILL INCREASE AT VARIOUS RATES OF INFLATION**

| Yearly Rate of Inflation | Prices Will Double in: | Prices Will Triple in: | Prices Will Quadruple in: |
|---|---|---|---|
| 6% | 12 yrs | 19 yrs | 24 yrs |
| 7% | 11 yrs | 17 yrs | 21 yrs |
| 8% | 10 yrs | 15 yrs | 19 yrs |
| 9% | 9 yrs | 13 yrs | 17 yrs |
| 10% | 8 yrs | 12 yrs | 15 yrs |
| 12% | 7 yrs | 10 yrs | 13 yrs |

**FIGURE 1-2**

understood that monetary inflation does not cause prices to rise. Rather, it causes the value of money to decline.

The erosion of the value of money, as shown in Figures 1-1 and 1-2, is an important factor in both business and personal planning. Many companies plan ahead five to ten years. Loans are made for 20 to 30 years. Individuals make long-range plans also for 20 to 30 years in advance to provide for a pension, buy a home, or make provisions for the family in case of death.

## Tying Together The Concepts Of The Role Of Money In The Economy During A Period Of Inflation

Two conclusions can be made concerning our discussion of the roles of money. First, it is certain the dollar does not have a predictable value. Therefore, the vital accounting roles of money do not function. As a result, the conventional system of accounting, Historic Cost Accounting, is invalidated because it is premised on the proposition that money will function as a store and a fixed standard of value.

Second, the inability of money to act as a repository of value and as a standard of value for long-term transactions has caused a massive redistribution of wealth. The evidence of the great wealth transfer can be seen, for example, in the collapse of the bond market in 1980. Bonds issued in the 50s, 60s, and 70s are now quoted at a fraction of their original issue price. The transfer of the bondholder's wealth without right or permission rests on the legal doctrine that a debt can be discharged, dollar for dollar, in what Congress has declared to be legal tender.

Consider, now, the specific purchasing power losses and gains that conventional accounting fails to report, and the strategies for gaining inflation's wealth transfer, and the means for staunching its outflow from business. Chapter 3 begins this discussion.

Chapter 2 treats the fundamental and vexing problem of accounting: "How do you measure income and acquisition costs with the inconstant measuring rod, the dollar?" It is the problem that tortures the minds of accountants and economists, and it underlies all of the problems and solutions we shall discuss.

## NOTES

1. S. Herbert Frankel, *Two Philosophies of Money: The Conflict of Trust and Authority,* Chapter 11, St. Martin's Press Inc., 1977. I have drawn heavily on this exceptional work in discussing the various roles of money.

# 2

## What Is Accounting's Perplexing Problem?

In Chapter 1, we told you that inflation destroys the accounting roles of money, and that this causes a transfer of wealth. Conventional accounting, Historic Cost Accounting (HCA) cannot detect and report who gains and who loses from the wealth transfer because it does not see that its measuring rod, money, measures less and less value.

So, if money cannot fulfill its accounting roles, as a standard of value for long-term transactions, and as a store of value for savings and investments, why not find another standard that will play these roles? This chapter explains why only monetary units can be used as a standard of measurement for gauging economic activity.

### ACCOUNTING IS A MEASUREMENT ART

Accountants attempt to state the true financial condition of an enterprise as of a particular date on a balance sheet, and the operating result for a particular period on a profit and loss statement. They accomplish their objective by measuring economic activity. That is, they measure the income and acquisition costs of a business.

If you want to measure something, you use a standard of measurement.

An accountant could measure the economic gains or losses of a business in terms of product and service units. For example:

The Sly Typewriter Company
Profit And Loss Statement
For The Year Ended December 31, 1979

| | |
|---|---|
| Sly Company sold | 100 typewriters |
| Your accountant estimates two typewriters won't be paid for | − 2 |
| Net Sales | 98 typewriters |
| Subtract Cost of Goods Sold: | 1 ton of steel |
| | 100 motors |
| | 1000 man hours of labor |
| | 1000 hours of depreciation |
| Net Profit | ? |

Product and service units appear to be a superior standard of measurement because, unlike the dollar, their values are constant. The quantity values of product and service units do not change with time. A ton of steel in 1980 weighs no more, nor less, than a ton of steel did in 1967. A man-hour has the same time length in any year.

However, product and service units fail to guage value because, usually, they cannot express quality. What type of steel did the Sly Company use? We do not know.

Furthermore, product and service units cannot be mathematically manipulated to determine whether the firm is or is not profitable. You can't subtract one ton of steel, 100 motors, etc. from 98 typewriters to determine the profit or loss of Sly Company.

What is needed is a common denominator that will convert tons of steel, typewriters, etc. into a common expression which can be mathematically manipulated. Unfortunately, there is only one common denominator that will express these diverse items. That is MONEY and only MONEY.

## MONETARY UNITS MUST BE DATED

Money is a flawed standard of measurement because during a period of inflation, its value changes. Generally, it measures less and less goods and services. Therefore, the dollar of one year is a different standard of measurement than the dollar of another year. To properly express a value measured in dollars, we must date the dollar, so we know what standards of measurement we are using.

If I want to state the following equation in terms of money:

> One ton of bar steel purchased in 1974 equals
> One ton of bar steel purchased in 1979.

I must state the above equation as follows:

> 240 Jan. 1, 1974 dollars worth of bar steel equals
> 360 Sept. 1, 1979 dollars worth of bar steel.

*Note:* in order to state the equation with precision I must date the dollar in terms of day, month, and year.

This example shows the problem of measuring a ton of bar steel, or any other good or service, with the monetary unit—the dollar. It is an inconstant and flawed standard of measurement whose value is identified by date of measurement.

## Conclusion

Accounting is a measurement of art. Accounting measures economic activity in terms of money. The monetary unit, the dollar, is a unique and flawed standard of measurement, whose value measures different quantities of goods and services at different times. The central problem of accounting, in a time of inflation is: how do you accurately measure income and acquisition costs with the variable measuring rod—the dollar? Stated differently—accounting's perplexing problem is: how do you measure the effect of inflation's wealth transfer? There is a wide divergence of opinion as to the correct answer.

In concluding this chapter, I want to emphasize that no single method of accounting states profitability and financial condition with unerring accuracy. All systems of accounting are flawed, but all reveal some facet of fiscal truth. As you will see some accounting systems approximate truth much more closely than others do and are therefore more useful.

# Part 2

## How To Detect And Measure The Hidden Wealth Transfer of Inflation: Business Strategies For Minimizing Wealth Loss And Gaining The Wealth Transfer

**Introduction To Part 2**

Whether inflation will be benign or destructive to your economic health will depend upon your understanding of how inflation covertly invades your firm's capital and income; of how you can detect and measure its effects; and what measures you can take to mitigate its destructive force or turn it to your advantage.

It is the purpose of Part 2 to inform you of how inflation uses Historic Cost Accounting (HCA)—the accounting system we all use—as a screen to obstruct our view of inflation's covert transfer of income and capital. We tell of how the wealth transfer to and from your firm can be detected and measured.

You may have asked: How do you compute your true profits and capital in a period of inflation without a crystal ball and an advanced technology computer? As an answer, we give you a "quick and dirty" method for eliminating inflation's distortions from your financial statements. See Chapter 9.

We show you how inflation has invaded the financial arteries of your firm, and what you can do to neutralize its ill effects.

In summary, Part 2 pinpoints the seven reporting errors of Historic Cost Accounting.[1] These are:

1. Holding gains from debt are not reported — Chapter 4
2. Holding losses from monetary assets are not reported — Chapter 5
3. Cost of Goods Sold is understated — Chapter 6
4. Depreciation expenses are under-reported — Chapter 7
5. HCA P & L Statements lack comparability; thus, the amount of sales may erroneously appear to increase — Chapter 8
6. HCA understates the value of fixed assets — Chapter 9
7. The value of equity may be understated and the value of retained earnings overstated — Chapter 9

## NOTES

1. The seven reporting errors of Historic Cost Accounting were suggested by Chris Westwick's "Sandilands, PSSAP 7, But What Now?", *Accountancy* (London), December 1975, pp.38-39.

# 3

## What Is Historic Cost's Measurement Problem?

In a period of significant inflation, HCA, Historic Cost Accounting, generally overstates true profit or understates the true loss of an enterprise for a financial year. Enterprises which have a high ratio of inventory, depreciable assets and/or monetary assets to sales experience the greatest error in reporting profit or loss. What is not so well recognized is that profitable firms with a high ratio of long-term debt to sales may be underreporting income.

HCA's large error in reporting the operating results of capital intensive corporations is seen when HCA figures are compared with those produced by the inflationary accounting systems—Constant Dollar Accounting and Current Cost Accounting. Take the example of Pacific Gas and Electric Company's reporting of income from continuing operations under Historic Cost and Current Cost Accounting:

|  | Year ended 12/31/79 | |
| --- | --- | --- |
|  | Conventional Historic Cost | Current Cost |
| Income from continuing operation | $458 million | $10 million |

The large disparity in results reported by HCA and Current Cost stems from the fact that Historic Cost Accounting understated depreciation by $448 million. That is, when depreciation was computed on the current cost of fixed assets, it amounted to $699 million instead of the $251 million reported by HCA. This should give us something to think about, since we all compute our net profit under the Historic Cost method of accounting, and we pay income taxes on these invalid earnings.

The Pacific Gas and Electric's supplementary financial statement revealed another shortcoming of Historic Cost Accounting. HCA did not report a $634 million wealth transfer from PG&E's creditors. The value of money owed to bondholders, banks, and other creditors had declined by that amount. Thus, Historic Cost Accounting understated revenue by $634 million. But that is only part of the story. We do not know whose wealth increased by $634 million. We know the creditors lost that amount of ability to comsume, but we do not know who gained it. Accounting does not report, clearly, who the recipient of the wealth transfer of inflation is. But let's consider the problem later. For now, let's review why Historic Cost Accounting—the system of accounting we all use—does not report fiscal reality.

## WHY HISTORIC COST ACCOUNTING DOES NOT REPORT FISCAL REALITY

A basic reason for HCA's failure to state fiscal reality is that it violates a fundamental mathematical principle: You can't add, subtract, multiply or divide unlike terms. You can't add such diverse things as x and y, or frisbees and skateboards, or 1970 dollars and 1979 dollars. One could as well add German marks to American dollars, as add 1975 inventory acquisitions to those of 1978, as is shown in the inventory account below: German marks measure a different quantity of value than do American dollars. 1975 dollars measure a different quantity of goods, services and rights than do 1978 dollars.

Historic Cost Accounting would have us conclude that the inventory account, shown in Figure 3-1, has a cost of $539,159. Actually, what is shown is an irrational number. Yet HCA would compute the cost of goods

---

**Inventory Account (FIFO)**

| Year of Purchase | Cost of Goods Sold |
|---|---|
| 1978 | 388,688 – 1978 dollars |
| 1977 | 105,469 – 1977 dollars |
| 1976 | 33,002 – 1976 dollars |
| 1975 | 12,000 – 1975 dollars |
| Total | 539,159 – ? dollars |

**FIGURE 3-1**

sold on this figure, and would erroneously inform the readers of the balance sheet that the value of the ending inventory is $539,159.

## WHAT CAUSES THE REPORTING ERROR?

HCA would correctly report the financial results of a firm's operations, if it employed the cash convention of accounting. The cash convention of accounting correctly accounts for inflation because it measures both income and expense using only one standard of measurement—the current year's dollars. (See Chapter 13, *Cash Flow Accounting*).

However, Historic Cost Accounting uses several standards of measurement, several years' dollars, because it uses the accrual accounting convention to defer charging off costs over a period of years. It is the combination of the accrual convention—which defers expensing costs—with the Historic Cost Accounting method—which postulates that the value of the dollar is fixed—that causes the fiscal distortion in today's financial statements.

HCA measures income in current year's dollars. But it reports such deferred costs as inventory and depreciation in mixed year's dollars. As a consequence, HCA financial statements do not tell the fiscal truth.

### Example Of HCA Showing A Fiscal Distortion Of Profit And Loss

Two firms in the same business have identical profits of 100,000 1980 dollars before deduction for depreciation. They each operate with one identical asset, a building. However, Firm A purchased its building in 1970 at a cost of 100,000 1970 dollars, whereas Firm B purchased its building in 1980 at a cost of 200,000 1980 dollars. Useful life of the building is 10 years—for illustrative purposes.

|  | Firm A | Firm B | Difference |
|---|---|---|---|
| Profit for year 1980 | $100,000 | $100,000 |  |
| Deduction depreciation: |  |  |  |
|     Firm A = 10% × $100,000 | 10,000 |  |  |
|     Firm B = 10% × $200,000 |  | 20,000 | $10,000 |
| Net Profit before taxes | $ 90,000 | $ 80,000 | $10,000 |
| Federal income tax | 22,750 | 18,750 | 4,000 |
| Net Profit after taxes | $ 67,250 | $ 61,250 | $ 6,000 |

**FIGURE 3-2**

Firms A and B have identical economic incomes, as opposed to monetary incomes. Their 1980 income before depreciation is $100,000. Their real depreciation costs are the same. That is, each experienced one year's wear on identical buildings. But, as you can see, HCA computes Firm A's depreciation in terms of 1970 dollars, whereas Firm B's is computed in terms of 1980 dollars. As a consequence, Firm B has a charge of $10,000 more depreciation and $10,000 less profit before taxes than does Firm A.

Note that Firm A pays $4,000 more income tax than does Firm B, even though their real incomes are identical. This illustrates the heavy income tax charges businesses with older depreciable assets pay because taxable income is computed on the Historic Cost Accounting method. This fact is borne out in several studies which show that the relatively new computer industry, whose assets are of recent acquisition, pays less tax in real terms than does the steel industry, whose assets are substantially older.

Also, notice Firm A may distribute to its stockholders or owners $67,250 as profit, despite the fact there is short-fall in the depreciation reserve account of at least $100,000—the difference between HCA depreciable basis of $100,000 and $200,000 1980 replacement cost.

Let us now consider how each individual account in the profit and loss statement and balance sheet are affected by HCA's misrepresentation of fiscal reality. Let's also discuss strategies for gaining or mitigating inflation's wealth transfer.

# 4

## Historic Cost Accounting Does Not Report The Wealth Transfer Of Debt: Strategies For Maintaining The Wealth In The Firm

In this chapter, we will discuss the wealth transfer of debt and how you can profit from it, and how you must charge for it.

*Definition of profit:* Before describing the income measurement errors of HCA, it is necessary to define income, so we will know what we are trying to measure. Income is the amount of money (or purchasing power) over and above what is necessary to keep capital intact. Therefore, a profit and loss statement should measure the capacity to consume without invading capital.[1] It is against this criterion that we will now judge Historic Cost Accounting and, later, the inflation-accounting systems—Cash Flow Accounting, Constant Dollar Accounting, and Current Cost Accounting.

## HCA DOES NOT REPORT THE WEALTH TRANSFER OF DEBT: THEREFORE, INCOME IS UNDERSTATED OR OVERSTATED

The wealth transfer of debt is illustrated in the following example, which I have taken from Ralph Conghenour Jones' "Effects of Price Level Changes on Business Income, Capital and Taxes."[2]

The example involves two speculators in commodities. For convenience of identification, we shall call them Mr. Cash and Ms. Credit. Mr. Cash bought $100,000 worth of commodities. He used his own money to make the purchase. During the period Mr. Cash held his commodities, inflation caused prices to double, thus enabling Mr. Cash to sell out for $200,000. Mr. Cash made a monetary profit of $100,000. However, in real terms, he broke even. He made no profit—his ability to consume was not enhanced. At the end of the transaction, he could only purchase the same quantity of commodities as he had at the beginning of the transaction.

Ms. Credit, on the other hand, borrowed $100,000 from her friendly banker. She used the $100,000 to buy the same list of commodities as Mr. Cash did. Prices doubled, so Ms. Credit, like Mr. Cash, sold out for $200,000.

Ms. Credit returned $100,000 to her banker and pocketed the remaining $100,000. Unlike Mr. Cash, Ms. Credit gained in her ability to consume without invading her capital. She made a profit in real terms. At the end of the transaction, she had $100,000 more wealth than she had at the beginning of the transaction.

This curious disparity in experience between Ms. Credit and Mr. Cash is attributable to the fact that Ms. Credit made her profit by returning to her unsuspecting banker one half of the value she borrowed. She did not make her profit from selling commodities. She made her profit from the decline in the value of debt. She had a holding gain from debt.

When Ms. Credit repaid her bank $100,000, she returned one half the purchasing power she borrowed. She retained the other half for herself. Ms. Credit experienced the beneficence of inflation's redistribution of wealth.

The wealth transfer from debt, such as Ms. Credit experienced, is possible because it is a matter of decided law that all debts can be discharged, dollar for dollar, in whatever Congress has declared to be legal tender. The fact that the value of the dollar has declined during the term of the loan is of no legal consequence. No lender may inquire into the value of the money lent, as opposed to the value of the money returned. So long as the borrower returns the same number of dollars as were borrowed, the debt will be discharged. (*Norman v. Baltimore O.R. Co.,* 55 S Ct.)

## HOW TO PROFIT FROM DEBT

Inflation does not shower its bounty on us simply because we incur debt. There are conditions to be met. The first of these conditions is that the lender must not anticipate inflation and charge for it by raising his interest rates.

The second condition is that the debtor firm's profit, or the individual's net worth, must increase by the amount of the wealth transfer of debt. Let's examine these requirements.

**Lenders Must Not Anticipate Inflation
And Charge for It**

Holding gains from debt can be realized only if the lender does not anticipate the rate of inflation during the term of the debt and charge for it. How do you know whether the lender is charging for inflation in her interest rate?

The formula for computing the inflation cost of the lender is shown in Figure 4-1.

---

**The anticipated inflation over the term of the loan**
**1 − the combined Federal and State income tax rate**

*Example:* Assume a 10% rate of inflation and a 50% tax bracket. Term of the loan = one year.

Question: What is the inflation cost the lender must charge for?

Answer: 20%

$$\text{Inflation Cost} = \frac{.10 \text{ rate of inflation}}{1 - .50 \text{ tax rate}} = 20\%$$

**FIGURE 4-1**

---

Note that the lender in the above example must charge 20% interest just to break even. But a lender should earn a rent for her money. A normal return on the loan of money in a period of price stability is 3% after taxes. In addition, the lender should charge for risk. If we set the risk factor at 3%, then the lender should earn, in real terms, 6%.

The formula for determining the rate of interest that must be charged to anticipate inflation, plus a real return on money, is shown in Figure 4-2.

Please note that the graduated income tax causes each lender to have his or her own particular rate of loss from inflation that must be compensated for. A person in the 40% tax bracket would have a different holding loss for lending money than would a person in the 70% tax bracket.

The formula I have given is for a one-year, single payment loan. If the loan were for more than one year, an even greater rate of interest would be required because the inflation rate increases geometrically over several years.

*The Wealth Transfer of Inflation*

**Nominal rate of interest charged to anticipate inflation =**

$$\frac{\text{Real rate of interest + anticipated rate of inflation}}{1 - \text{income tax rate}}$$

*Example:* Assume: One year single payment loan
Tax rate of lender = 50%
Inflation rate = 10%
Real rate of interest lender wishes to charge = 6%

Question: What rate of interest must be charged to anticipate 10% inflation and to gain a real yield of 6%?

Answer: 32%

Nominal rate of interest = $\dfrac{.06 + .10}{1 - .50}$ = 32%

**FIGURE 4-2**

---

## How Lender Must Compute Interest On Loan Whose Term Is For A Period Of More Than One Year

What rate of interest must a lender charge to anticipate an average inflation of 10% over a future five-year period to gain a real yield of 6%?

Assume a tax rate of 50%. Loan principal $1,000. Interest to be paid annually, and principal to be returned after 5 years. Answer: 34.5%, but see demonstration.

*Computation of interest payments:* Consult table at Appendix B, which shows the number of future dollars required to maintain the present value of one dollar at various rates of future inflation. The interest payment in constant dollars is 6% per annum × $1,000 = $60. But over the five-year period of the loan, the value of the dollar is anticipated to decline by 10%. Therefore, we must multiply $60 by the factors shown under the 10% column, Appendix B: We find the debtor must pay a total interest of $402.94.

*Computation of the return of capital in constant dollars* The table at Appendix B informs us that it will take $1.6105 at the end of year 5 to equal the purchasing power of each dollar we loaned in year 1.

Therefore:

$1,000 × 1.6105 = $1,610.50, the number of year 5 dollars required to equal the purchasing power of $1,000 year 1 dollars loaned.

*Computation of the infla-tax the debtor must reimburse us for:* We have seen that, in order to receive an annual payment of $60 per year or $300

| Year | Interest Payment In Constant $s | × | 10% Inflation Factor | = | Interest Payment |
|---|---|---|---|---|---|
| 1 | $ 60 | | 1.100 | | $ 66.00 |
| 2 | $ 60 | | 1.2100 | | 72.60 |
| 3 | $ 60 | | 1.3310 | | 79.86 |
| 4 | $ 60 | | 1.4641 | | 87.85 |
| 5 | $ 60 | | 1.6105 | | 96.63 |
| | $300 | | | | $402.94 |

**FIGURE 4-3**

for 5 years in constant dollars, the borrower must pay us a total of $403. The government will tax us on the $103 difference, even though in real terms we have realized no more income. We will also be income taxed on the difference between the $1,000 loaned and the 1,611 year 5 dollars that will be repaid, or $611. Since our tax rate is 50%, we must require the debtor to reimburse us for the infla-tax we will have to pay. This added expense amounts to $714.

Excess interest paid to compensate for the decline in
the value of money ............................$103
Excess return of capital to compensate for the
decline in the value of money .................... 611
Total amount on which the infla-tax
must be paid ...............................$714

Computation of the income tax on the infla-income:

$$\frac{\$714}{1 - .50 \text{ tax rate}} = \$1428 - (50\% \text{ tax or } \$714) = \$714$$

*Total payments the debtor must be required to make:*

Return of capital .................... 1,611 year 5 dollars
Interest payments .................... 403 mixed years' $s
Infla-tax on illusory earnings .......... 714 year 5 dollars

Total payments ................ 2,728 mixed years' $s

*The Wealth Transfer of Inflation*

The lender of $1,000 for a term of 5 years at 6% interest in which it is anticipated that inflation will average 10% must require a total payment of interest and capital in the amount of $2,728, not $1,300. The rate of interest required is difficult to state because we are dealing in mixed years' dollars—dollars of different values.

For a further discussion of what the lender must charge, see Chapter 14, *Planning Cash Flow For Business And Investment Transactions.*

**Lenders Have Not Been Able To Anticipate Inflation
In Their Interest Charge**

A review of bond quotations in the newspapers reveals that lenders have not been able to charge for inflation. As a result, the cost of borrowing money has been one of the splendid bargains in the economy. Interest is the one expense that declines as the rate of inflation increases.

The best the lenders have been able to do in the past has been to require a rate of interest equal to the rate of inflation existing at the time of the loan. None of the lenders have been able to anticipate the future inflation rate, nor have they been able to charge for the income tax on the illusory infla-interest earnings.

I know of no instance where the lenders, either here or abroad, have been able to turn the wealth transfer of inflation from the debtors to themselves.

**Holding Gain From Debt Will Be Realized
If Revenue Is Increased By The Amount
Of The Wealth Transfer**

Seminar participant: "May I ask an embarrassing question?"
Seminar leader: "Please do."
Seminar participant: "If debt can be so profitable, as you say, why do heavily indebted firms go broke?"
Seminar leader: "Good question. Heavily indebted firms go broke because they cannot take advantage of the holding gain from debt. Inflation smiles only on those debtors who have a profitable operation. The wealth transfer, or holding gain from borrowed money, is realized only if it shows up in revenue—as a bulge in profits.

To be specific: A firm will realize the holding gain from monetary liabilities only if:

1. It is able to increase its revenue by all or a part of the gain, and

2. The Gain is realized in *CASH,* either immediately or sometime in the future. The holding gain must show up in the *CASH CYCLE* to have worth."[3]

The holding gain from debt results from a bargain purchase of the use of money. As in any bargain purchase, it should reduce cost—in this case, the cost of interest. The reduced expense, when set against revenue, should increase profit and cash revenue which should result in the firm experiencing an increased ability to consume without invading capital.

The reason heavily indebted firms file for Chapter XI—bankruptcy—is because they cannot sell their products for a profit. A debt-burdened auto company, which builds a product the public refuses to buy, cannot realize the holding gain from monetary liabilities because the company cannot convert the gain into cash. In the case of the Chrysler Company, they could not realize their enormous gain from the reduction in the real value of their monetary liabilities because they couldn't sell their products for a profit. A large part of the gain was locked in a stagnant inventory.

Generally, the holding gain from monetary liabilities can be converted to profit in real terms, only if the money borrowed is invested in a commodity that rises in price with inflation, or in a facility that produces a product whose price rises with the general price level.

For example: Consider the case of Aspen Company, which borrowed $10,000 for 5 years. During the term of the loan, Aspen could not find a suitable investment, so the borrowed money was held in the company's bank account. At the end of 5 years, Aspen repaid the lender $10,000. However, because prices rose an average of 10% per year during the term of the loan, Aspen, in real terms, repaid 3,791 year 1 dollars (see Appendix A-10%) less value than it received from the lender. Therefore, Aspen should have shown an increase in net worth of 3,791 year 1 dollars. But it didn't. It failed to profit from the holding gain, because the value of the money held in the company's checking account, also declined in purchasing power. Its value was subject to the full erosion of inflation. The lender lost 3,791 year 1 dollars, but Aspen gained nothing.

In contrast is the case of Ms. Credit. You will recall that Ms. Credit borrowed $100,000; employed the money to buy commodities; and latter sold out for $200,000. At the end of the transaction, Ms. Credit returned $100,000 to her lender and put the remaining $100,000 in her sock. She was able to profit from borrowing, because she invested her borrowed money in commodities that rose in price with the general price level.

## Holding Gain From Debt Is Taxable Income

The gain from holding debt will be realized if it is reflected in income. Since the gain shows up in the profit, it is taxable as ordinary income. Thus, the debtor realizes only a part of the wealth transfer. The Federal and State governments get the remainder.

There is one exception to what we have just said: If the holding gain from monetary liabilities is offset against holding losses from monetary assets, no gain or loss is recognized for income tax purposes. See "Strategy of Offsetting Holding Gains From Monetary Liabilities Against Holding Losses From Monetary Assets," page 48.

## How To Determine The Effective Rate Of Interest Paid On Debt

The borrower of money is considered to gain on debt if he pays less than 3% interest per annum in real terms, plus a charge for a risk factor. Historically, 3% interest after taxes has been considered the standard return on money lent to the most creditworthy borrower in a time of price stability. The borrower can determine his effective rate of interest on a one-year single payment loan, as follows:

---

**Effective Rate of Interest Charged** = Nominal interest rate charged, minus the inflation rate, minus the income tax deduction for interest paid.

*Example:* Assume an interest rate charge of 10%
Rate of inflation during the term of the loan = 10%
Income tax rate = 40%

$.10 - .10 - (.40 \times .10) = -.04$, or effective rate of interest of minus 4%.

**FIGURE 4-4**

---

In Figure 4-4, the borrower's rate of interest was subsidized by an income tax deduction for illusory infla-interest. In real terms, the borrower paid no interest. He paid 10% in nominal terms, but this was offset by the inflation rate of 10%, which decreased the cost of the loan to zero. But the tax law does not inquire into inflation's debt reduction. The borrower paid 10% interest in legal tender, so he gets a tax deduction in that amount. No questions asked.

The borrower reaped another benefit in the example given. He used the loan free of charge. The value of the rent of money is 3% in real terms, plus a risk factor, which I would set at 3%, for a total real rate of interest of 6%. Therefore, the borrower's total gain is 10%. Four percent is gained from the income tax deduction on the infla-interest, plus 6% from the use of money, 4% + 6% = 10%. If the loan was for $10,000, the borrower would gain $1,000.

The formula given applies only to a single payment loan for one year.

## HOW TO DETERMINE INTEREST COSTS ON LONG-TERM DEBT: ADVANTAGES

Continuous inflation over the term of a loan will cause a geometric acceleration in the decline of the real value of debt and in the real cost of interest. Inflation's increase is a geometric progression. Ten percent inflation does not cause the value of the dollar to decline steadily by 10%. Rather, it declines by 10% the first year, 11% the second year (1.10 × .10 = .11), 12.1% the third year (1.21 × .10 = .121), and so on. Thus, the value of the dollar declines by 46.4% (1.10 to the fourth power) over a four-year period of 10% inflation—not 40%.

Figure 4-5 demonstrates our point, that the geometric decline in the value of long-term debt confers a substantial benefit on the borrower. It also demonstrates that it is a disaster for the lender. Note discussion is in year 5 dollars.

### Facts of Figure 4-5

The Birch Company borrows $10,000 for 5-years. Terms of the loan are: single payment at the end of year 5. Interest rate 12% payable annually.

The value of the loan is not affected by inflation in the first year of the loan. But during years 2 through 5, inflation averages 10%. At the end of the 5-year term of the loan, Birch repays the lender 10,000 year 5 dollars. But since the value of the dollar has declined by 46.4%, Birch realizes a substantial holding gain from debt. In year 5 it requires $14,640 to repay the equivalent of the purchasing power of 10,000 year 1 dollars. Birch meets inflation in a beneficent mood and receives 4,640 year 5 dollars.

Note that in stating a holding gain or loss it is important to indicate the year's dollars you are using as your standard of measurement. In year

5 dollars, Birch gained $4,640, but in year 1 dollars, the firm gained $3,170.

Birch's holding gain, expressed in year 1 dollars, can be determined easily by referring to the Appendix A table, "Showing Future Worth of a Dollar at Various Rates of Inflation."

In Birch's case, we are concerned with the present worth of a 5-year loan of $10,000, after 4 years of 10% average inflation. The factor given in the 10% column is .6830. Therefore, the worth of a 5-year loan of $10,000 expressed in the dollars of the year the loan was made (year 1) is $6,830, assuming 10% average inflation during 4 years of the loan.

Birch gained more than just the wealth transfer from holding debt. It also gained from the decline in the value of the interest paid. Birch contracted to pay the lender an annual interest rate of 12%, or $1,200 per annum, for a 5-year period. However, while Birch paid $1,200 the first year of the loan, it paid decreasing amounts of value in the succeeding years, as is shown in the schedule below:

### INTEREST PAID IN CONSTANT YEAR 1 DOLLARS

| Year of Payment | Historic Cost Dollars | Divided by Inflation Factor | Constant Year 1 Dollars | Wealth Transfer to Birch |
|---|---|---|---|---|
| 1 | $1,200 | 1.00 | $1,200 | 0 |
| 2 | 1,200 | 1.10 | 1,090 | $110 |
| 3 | 1,200 | 1.20 | 1,000 | 200 |
| 4 | 1,200 | 1.33 | 909 | 291 |
| 5 | $1,200 | 1.464 | 819 | 381 |
| Total | $6,000 | | $5,018 | $982 |

**FIGURE 4-5**

If we want to express the worth of the loan in year 5 dollars, then we must multiply $10,000 by $1 + (.10)^4$. Or we can simply refer to the table in Appendix B, which shows the number of dollars required to express the present value of 1 dollar, at various rates of future inflation.

Column 10 − 4 years shows a factor of 1.464. Therefore, it will require $14,640 year 4 dollars to express the value of 10,000 year 1 dollars.

### COMPUTATION OF WEALTH TRANSFER OF DEBT TO BIRCH

|  | (1) Historic Cost Dollars | (2) Constant Year 1 Dollars | (1) − (2) Amount of Wealth Transfer |
|---|---|---|---|
| Interest paid | $ 6,000 | $ 5,018 | $ 982 |
| Less income tax @ 40% | 2,400 | 2,007 | 393 |
| Net interest cost | $ 3,600 | $ 3,011 | $ 589 |
| Loan repayment | 10,000 | 6,830 | 3,170 |
| Total interest and capital paid | $13,600 | $ 9,841 | $3,759 |
| Wealth Transfer |  | 3,759 | 3,759 |
|  | $13,600 | $13,600 |  |

**FIGURE 4-6**

The wealth transfer of $3,759 is stated in year 1 dollars. The wealth transfer stated in year 5 dollars is $5,503 ($3,759 × 1.464 year 5 inflation factor).

Note that the three factors causing inflation's redistribution of wealth from the lender to the debtor are: a reduction in interest, tax liability, and principal payment.

## THE ADVANTAGE OF FUNDING WITH DEBT INSTEAD OF EQUITY DURING A PERIOD OF MONETARY INFLATION

It is general knowledge that, even in a time of relative price stability, a profitable firm will gain by financing with debt instead of equity—at least in theory. The advantages of debt are realized when a firm earns revenue in excess of its variable and fixed expenses, including the interest charge for money borrowed. Under these conditions of profitable operation—of a firm's generating revenue in excess of its break-even point—borrowed capital will produce higher earnings per share than will equity capital of the same amount.

The advantage of funding with debt is derived from the bias of the income tax law, which favors those who finance with debt over those who fund with equity. The law gives a tax reduction for the cost of borrowed money, but gives no reduction in taxes for the use of equity capital—even though equity funds must have the same cost as borrowed funds. It is, one of the failings of accounting that it does not report the opportunity cost of the equity capital used by a firm.

The tax deduction for interest makes borrowed capital a cheaper source of funds than contributed funds. Inflation adds to the disparity in cost by providing a holding gain to the firm that funds with debt. Thus, inflation adds to the disparity in cost of funding with borrowed money as opposed to funding with equity. The following discussion demonstrates this depressing fact.
and 4-9.

## Comparison Of The Profit Earned By A Company Funded By Debt With One Funded By Equity Capital— Polonius Was Half Right

"Neither a borrower nor a lender be . . ." Is it good advice today? For an answer to our question, let's take a look at the experience of the two companies shown in Figures 4-8 and 4-9.

A perusal of the experience of the two companies will reveal that High Roller Inc., a firm financed wholly with borrowed money, made out scandalously well. It made 71% more profit than did the totally equity funded Neither A Borrower Nor A lender Be Inc.

The demonstration of the advantages of debt vs equity, shown in Figures 4-8 and 4-9, is difficult to follow, so permit me to summarize and explain why Neither A Borrower Nor A Lender Be Inc. made less profit than did High Roller Inc.

First, the facts of the case: Each company purchased an identical machine for $10,000, which had a useful life of five years with no salvage value. The operation of the machines produced an identical profit before taxes and interest for each of the companies. The inflation rate during the five years of operation averaged 10%. At the end of the useful life of the machines, the firms ceased to do business. They then repaid the capital used to purchase the machines. High-Roller paid the bank who lent it the money. The Neither Co. returned the equity capital to the stockholders. At this point, the firms had no liabilities, and their sole asset was cash. High Roller, had $13,936 more cash than did the equity funded, Neither Company. Here's why:

| Items | Neither Company | High Roller Company | Difference |
| --- | --- | --- | --- |
| 1. Dividends paid | $ 7,656 | | |
| vs. interest paid | | $ 6,000 | $ 1,656 |
| 2. Income taxes | 36,630 | 33,630 | 3,000 |
| 3. Return of stockholders' investment | | | |
| vs. payment of loan | 19,280 | $10,000 | 9,280 |
| Total | $63,566 | $49,630 | $13,936 |

**FIGURE 4-7**

**Comments on items:**

1. High Roller gained from the wealth transfer of inflation. The equity funded Neither Co. did not. High Roller paid interest in dollars of declining value. But the Neither Company had to pay dividends in constant value dollars, because you can't have a wealth transfer to and from yourself—to and from the owners of a corporation. The opportunity cost of money during the five years of operation was 12%. So the Neither Co. had to pay its stockholders 12% per year in real terms.

But High Roller did not operate under the requirement of paying interest in constant value dollars. It agreed to pay 12% of $10,000, or $1,200 per annum. That is all High Roller had to pay, regardless of the decline in the purchasing power of money. Thus, over a 5-year period, High Roller paid only $6,000 for the rent of borrowed capital, while the Neither Company paid $7,656 for the use of equity capital.

2. The $3,000 difference in income tax cost is attributable to the interest expense deduction of $6,000 permitted High Roller Inc. The Neither Company received no income tax deduction for the cost of equity capital because the opportunity cost of equity capital is not a tax deductible item.

3. At the termination of the business, before profit could be counted in cash, the Neither Company returned to its stockholders, 19,280 year 5 dollars, in payment for their contribution of 10,000 year 1 dollars. In contrast, High Roller was able to discharge its debt of 10,000 year 1 dollars, by a payment of only 10,000 year 5 dollars. Borrowed capital can be discharged dollar for dollar in the amount that was loaned. Equity capital

must be returned to the stockholders in dollars of constant purchasing power. Therefore, the Neither Company was compelled to pay $9,280 more to discharge its equity capital debt, than did High Roller in the discharge of its borrowed capital debt.

Neither Company's $19,280 return of capital appears to be an overpayment. Four years of 10% average inflation would cause the value of the dollar to decline by 46.4% stated in year 5 dollars. Therefore, only $14,640 ($10,000 × 1.464) appears to be required to return the year 5 equivalent of 10,000 year 1 dollars. But not to be forgotten is the fact that the stockholders contributed after-tax dollars. So they must be repaid $14,640 after-tax dollars. If they are paid $14,640, they will be taxed by the Federal and State governments as if they had a taxable gain of $4,640. So if the stockholders are to be returned the same wealth as they contributed, they must receive $19,280, assuming a 50% tax rate.

| | |
|---|---:|
| The original capital contribution | $10,000 |
| Plus the inflation rate<br>.4640 × $10,000 = $4640 / .50<br>(1 − 50% income tax rate) = | 9,280 |
| Return of capital | $19,280 |

Polonius was half right. Don't be a lender—unless you can charge for the inflation plus the tax on the infla-interest. To this must be added a modern word of caution: Don't be a stockholder in a 100% equity financed firm, unless the business earns a large profit.

### Inflation Will Increase Your Debt To Equity Ratio—How To Convince Your Banker Not To Worry About It

A long-sustained decline in the value of money will cause the debt-to-equity ratio of a firm to increase. As inflation decreases the purchasing power of the dollar, a firm has to incur greater debt in terms of money to finance its normal operations. Debt will appear to increase over equity because current liabilities, and possibly some long-term debt, will be stated in latter years' dollars than the equity invested in the firm.

## NEITHER A BORROWER NOR A LENDER BE, INC. (All Equity Capital)

### Assume 10% Inflation
#### Profit and Loss Statement

| | Year 1 | Year 2 | Year 3 | Year 4 | Year 5 | Total |
|---|---|---|---|---|---|---|
| 1. Profit before taxes | $12,000 | $13,200 | $14,520 | $15,972 | $17,568 | $73,260 |
| 2. Less: Income taxes | 6,000 | 6,600 | 7,260 | 7,986 | 8,784 | 36,630 |
| 3. Net earnings | $ 6,000 | $ 6,600 | $ 7,260 | $ 7,986 | $ 8,784 | $36,630 |
| 4. Dividends paid for use of equity capital | 1,200 | 1,332 | 1,493 | 1,692 | 1,939 | $ 7,656* |
| 5. Net earnings after payment of dividends | $ 4,800 | $ 5,268 | $ 5,767 | $ 6,284 | $ 6,845 | $28,974 |

### Cash Account

| | Neither Co. | High Roller | Difference |
|---|---|---|---|
| Cash from net earnings | $28,974 | $33,630 | $ 4,656 |
| Add charge for depreciation not requiring expenditure of cash | 10,000 | 10,000 | -- |
| Total | $38,974 | $43,630 | $ 4,656 |
| Return of stockholders' investment | 19,280** | | |
| Payment of note | | 10,000 | 9,280 |
| Cash on hand at termination of business | $19,694 | $33,630 | $13,936 |

**FIGURE 4-8**

\* Dividend increased to compensate for declining purchasing power of the dollar.
\*\* Stockholders' investment of $10,000 plus $9,280 for infla-tax factor of $4,640 / 1 − .50 income tax rate.

*The Wealth Transfer of Inflation* 37

## HIGH ROLLER INC. (All Borrowed Funds)

| Assume 10% Inflation<br>Profit and Loss Statement | Year 1 | Year 2 | Year 3 | Year 4 | Year 5 | Total |
|---|---|---|---|---|---|---|
| 1. Revenue from sales | $20,000 | $22,000 | $24,200 | $26,620 | $29,280 | $122,100 |
| 2. Less: Variable expenses | 6,000 | 6,800 | 7,680 | 8,648 | 9,712 | 38,840 |
| 3. Depreciation | 2,000 | 2,000 | 2,000 | 2,000 | 2,000 | 10,000 |
| 4. Total | $ 8,000 | $ 8,800 | $ 9,680 | $10,648 | $11,712 | $ 48,840 |
| 5. Profit before Int. & Tx. (1) minus (4) | $12,000 | $13,200 | $14,520 | $15,972 | $17,568 | $ 73,260 |
| 6. Less: Interest Expense | 1,200 | 1,200 | 1,200 | 1,200 | 1,200 | 6,000 |
| 7. Profit before taxes | $10,800 | $12,000 | $13,320 | $14,772 | $16,368 | $67,260 |
| 8. Income taxes 50% | 5,400 | 6,000 | 6,660 | 7,386 | 8,184 | 33,630 |
| 9. Net earnings | $ 5,400 | $ 6,000 | $ 6,660 | $ 7,386 | $ 8,184 | $ 33,630 |

**Cash Account**

| | |
|---|---|
| Cash from earnings | $33,630 |
| Depreciation charge | 10,000 |
| Net cash received | $43,630 |
| Less payment of note | 10,000 |
| Cash on hand at termination of project | $33,630 |

**FIGURE 4-9**

*Example:* Assume 10% inflation from year 2 to year 5. All earnings are paid out. At the end of 5 years, the value of the dollar has declined by 46.4%. Therefore, the firm must increase its debt to maintain normal operations by 1.464. This causes the firm's debt-to-equity ratio to rise from 60% in year 1 to 87.8% in year 5.

|  | Year 1 | Year 5 |
|---|---|---|
| Capital Stock | $100 | $100 |
| Monetary debt | 60 | 88 |
| Total | $160 | $188 |
| Debt-to-Equity ratio | 60% | 87.8% |

**FIGURE 4-10**

What one sees here is a repetition of the Historic Cost Accounting error of attempting to mathematically manipulate unlike terms. Capital stock is expressed in year 1 dollars, while ending debt is expressed in year 5 dollars. These quantities expressed in dollars of different years cannot be compared.

A person who would make a financial decision on a debt-to-equity ratio, as shown, would be basing his decision on irrational material. Your banker, a knowledgeable and agreeable person, will see the truth of this immediately.

## What Debt Yields The Highest Holding Gain?
## How To Shake The Money Tree

Interest-free debt yields the highest holding gain. It can be had by taking advantage of deferred taxes. A few examples:

1. The LIFO inventory convention permits the taxpayer to charge off inventory used at the latest, highest cost to the firm. Result: A higher cost of goods sold, a lower taxable income, and a decreased income tax liability. The decreased tax liability is a tax deferment, not a tax forgiveness. The tax must be paid someday, but, in the meantime, it is the loan of money without interest. (Chapter 11 discusses LIFO in detail.)

    A firm with a high ratio of inventory to revenue may generate a substantial interest-free loan from LIFO's deferral of taxes. And in addition, will gain the wealth transfer for inflation on the debt principal.

Business people have a reluctance to adopt the Last-in, First-out method of inventory. They find the accounting and tax implications difficult to understand. But the manager of a firm with a large inventory will find it very profitable to get a general understanding of the unnecessarily complicated Revenue rules and the preposterous accounting logic governing LIFO. The failure to take advantage of LIFO is probably the greatest single tax error managers of firms, with large inventories, make during a period of rapidly rising prices.

2. The use of the shortest asset lives permitted in computing depreciation for taxes also results in a deferral of taxes at no interest cost.
3. The accelerated methods of depreciation, such as the double declining balance method, provide a tax deferral of substantial value to a capital intensive firm.
4. Tax shelters offer a deferral of taxes.
5. Estate tax rules permit an election of a 10-year payout of estate tax attributable to an interest in a closely held business or farm. The interest charge on the deferred payment of estate taxes in this instance is currently 6%—a tremendous bargain. There is an understandable reluctance on the part of business people and farmers to avail themselves of this tax deferral bonanza, but death and taxes . . . .
6. There are instances when the taxpayer and the IRS are in deep disagreement over a proposed tax assessment. In this situation, the taxpayer must weigh the cost of litigation. A factor sometimes overlooked in making the decision is the inflationary wealth transfer received from the government during the three or four years hiatus before trial. A delay of four years, during a period of 10% average inflation, will reduce the tax assessment in real terms by about 43%. If the court sustains the government, or you make a settlement with Regional Counsel prior to trial, you will be assessed an interest charge on the amount owed. Currently, the interest rate charged is 12%. However, it is tax deductible.

## DEFERRAL OF PAYING ACCOUNTS PAYABLE—
## ANOTHER MUCH ABUSED, INTEREST-FREE
## OR PARTIALLY INTEREST-FREE, LOAN

An all too common practice during inflationary times is to delay payment of trade accounts past their due date. This practice creates an interest-free loan in many cases. However, it can be expensive for the debtor where the supplier offers a discount for prompt payment of 2%—10 days, net 30. The supplier is offering to pay 2% for the use of the customer's money for 20 days, or 36% per annum. Twenty days is 1/18th of a year. Therefore, 2% × 18 = 36%, assuming payment is made at the end of 30 days.[5]

However, if the debtor delays paying the supplier for 60 days, then it is the debtor who is paying 2% for the use of money for 50 days, or 15% per annum. But since the interest paid is tax deductible, the nominal effective rate of interest after taxes is 9%—assuming a 40% tax rate. If 9% is the approximate average inflation rate, the debtor would, in effect, pay nothing for the use of the creditor's money. Which hardly seems to support what I said at the beginning of this discussion about the evils of ripping off your suppliers.

Another noisome ploy for deferring payment of trade accounts is to write checks on a bank remote from the supplier. The debtor gains the use of the money during the time the check floats through the mails and through the banking system.

I think trade accounts should be indexed as they are in Brazil. It would take a good deal of the profit out of delaying payment of suppliers' bills.

## SMALL BUSINESS ADMINISTRATION LOAN—
## THE BEST, LOW-COST, 8¼% LOAN
## FOR SMALL- AND MEDIUM-SIZED BUSINESSES

It requires some effort to obtain a Small Business Administration Loan, but it is rewarding. If a bank lends the money, the top interest rate is 20½%. However, if the firm is turned down by the bank, it can apply directly to the Small Business Administration, which lends money at 8¼%. The required procedure is that the loan applicant first apply to a bank. If he or she is turned down there, the loan applicant can then apply directly to the Small Business Administration, either by visiting the SBA office or by corresponding with it.

A small business is defined by SBA regulations as a manufacturing firm that has up to 1,500 employees or a wholesaler who has maximum annual sales between $9.5 million and $22 million. A service company is eligible if it has maximum annual sales which do not exceed $2 million to $8 million. A retailer is qualified if it has top sales of $2 million to $7.5 million.

Working capital loans are usually limited to a maturity of 6 years. Loans to acquire property to construct facilities may have a 20-year maturity.

## PREFERRED STOCK—A LOAN FOREVER

Preferred stock is in some respects an ideal debt, particularly if it is the nonconvertible type. The sale of nonconvertible preferred stock is a loan forever. It has no termination date. I recently saw a news item which reported that the stockholders of a company consumed in a "takeover" were partially paid off in nonconvertible 7% preferred stock. What these poor unfortunates received was a fixed dollar debt, whose principal value will steadily decline as the dollar loses purchasing power. In addition, the 7% so-called dividend will also be subject to the erosion of inflation. How could you acquire a firm more cheaply?

Preferred stock has one serious defect. The dividends paid are not tax deductible, so the total cost of borrowing is increased. The cost, however, will decline as inflation erodes the principal and interest into insignificance.

## BONDS AND MORTGAGES HAVE THE INESTIMABLE ADVANTAGE OF BEING LONG-TERM DEBT

The wealth transfer of inflation has rewarded the long-term debtor handsomely in the past. There seems to be no reason to believe the holding gains from long-term liabilities will not continue.

The raising of money by the sale of bonds is pretty much a large company prerogative. However, some medium-sized firms have had some success in borrowing money by selling bonds.

Small firms can raise long-term money by mortgaging their real property. Real property loans run 20 to 30 years and bear a relatively low rate of interest.

## Conclusion

It is easy to demonstrate the realization of a holding gain from debt, in a simple transaction, where the money invested makes an easily detectable, complete cash cycle. Such was the case in the example of Ms. Credit: Cash was borrowed; cash was invested in commodities; commodities were sold for cash; loan was paid off in cash; remaining cash on hand is the holding gain from debt. All quite neat and clear.

It is also easy to demonstrate the holding gain from monetary liabilities in the slightly more complicated case of *High Roller Inc. v. Neither a Borrower Nor A Lender Be.* The holding gain experienced by High Roller is easily shown, because the financial transaction passed through the entire cash cycle and then terminated. The transaction was a reversible asset transaction. It went from cash to purchase of a machine, to cash again. The holding gain is tangible; it can be counted in cash at the end of the transaction.

But it is quite another thing to prove that a holding gain from debt can be identified in the reported profit of a complex continuing business. For example, did Pacific Gas and Electric realize a monetary liability holding gain in 1979 in the amount of $634 million as reported? Its Historic Cost Accounting P&L reported a profit of only $458 million. Are we to conclude that the entire $458 million profit was derived from the holding gain of $634 million? Or was the gain passed on to the customers in utility rates that did not fully compensate PG&E for its services, as some contend?

Cummins Corporation, a manufacturing firm, reported a $26.7 million holding gain from "the decline in the purchasing power of net amounts owed." Did the $26.7 million flow through the cash account? If it did, it was taxed as income. In that event, the firm would not have realized a holding gain of $26.7 million, less the income tax paid.

Neither Cummins nor PG&E assert that the holding gains contributed to their profits. We are of the opinion that they did not in the case of PG&E. But this is not to say that firms with substantial debt are not realizing holding gains from fixed dollar liabilites. Franco Modigliani, Professor of Economics and Finance at the Alfred P. Soan School of Management, and Richard Cohn, Associate Professor of Finance at the University of Illinois, are two financial experts who believe firms are profiting from monetary holding gains.[6] The professors argue that investors are grossly undervaluing stocks because they are not aware of the enormous holding gains from monetary liability large firms are realizing. Messrs. Modigliani and Cohn do not demonstrate that these gains from monetary liabilities have appeared as an added increment to profits in the past. Nor do they show that the gains are presently being realized in cash, nor that they will be realized in future cash inflow.

For all the writing on the subject, no one has prepared a study that would prove that American Telephone and Telegraph, a $60 billion debtor, or that Exxon, a $10 billion dollar debtor, have increased their cash flow by the holding gain from debt. Doubtless these firms are better off for having monetary liabilities—if for no other reason than that, in computing taxes, they are deducting interest expense which they are not incurring in real terms. It is possible that Exxon and AT&T have real cash gains from holding monetary liabilities but, to date, no one has shown the amount that has been retained by the companies.

My own view is that holding gains are potential income for any company that owes money. If the creditors lose wealth, then it follows that somebody must gain the amount lost. It is certain that the bondholders and the creditors are suffering frightful losses. But who profits from the losses? Is it the stockholders, the customers of the debtor firms, or the government? In most cases we can only guess.

I believe that each company, large or small, must demonstrate that cash revenue has been augmented by the amount of the wealth transfer before it can be counted as profit—before it can be said the firm has increased its ability to consume without invading capital. This implies that the owners of the business must receive the increment from holding debt as an increase in the value of their stock or as an increase in the amount of their dividends—in real terms.

## NOTES

1. Jeremy I. Bulow, "Inflation Accounting and Non-Financial Corporate Profits: Financial Assets," *Brookings Paper on Economic Activity 1976:* 1, p. 16.
2. Ralph Coughenour Jones, "Effects of Price Level Changes on Business Income, Capital and Taxes," *American Accounting Association* (1956), p. 26.
3. Professors A.J. Merrett and Allen Sykes, "What Sandilands Didn't Say," *Accountancy,* (London), November 1975, p. 42.
4. Ralph C. Jones, *Effects of Price Level Changes,* p. 24.
5. Leslie P. Anderson and John Heptonstall, "Planning Cash Flow," *American Management Associations Extension Institute,* pp. 14-15.
6. Franco Modigliani and Richard A Cohn, "Inflation, Rational Valuation and the Market," *Financial Analysts Journal,* March-April 1979, pp. 24-44.

# 5

## Historic Cost Accounting Does Not Report Losses From Holding Monetary Assets Of The Firm: How To Prevent And Compute The Loss

Inflation ineluctably drains value from monetary assets with the certainty of death and taxes. The longer the inflation period, the greater is the velocity of loss. A modest-sized firm may hold an average of $400,000 cash. In the first year of 10% inflation, the purchasing power of the cash will decline by $40,000; in the second year, it will lose value of $44,000, and so on.

If a firm is to continue to operate at its normal capacity, the losses of capital from holding monetary assets must be replaced. But this is difficult because the holding loss is not recognized by the income tax law—it is not a tax-deductible loss. However, while the holding loss is not deductible, the income that must be earned to replace the monetary loss is 100% taxable. Thus, a firm in the 50% tax bracket must earn $80,000 to replace a holding loss from monetary assets of $40,000.

How many firms include the monetary loss factor in computing their profit? We would guess—not many. Nevertheless, businesses continue to function despite holding losses on monetary assets. They must have found some way of coping with the problem—either unknowingly or by design. See Chapter 14 for a demonstration of how to include the monetary loss factor in setting prices.

One obvious measure for limiting monetary holding losses is to incur debt. Debt gives rise to holding gains which can be used to offset losses from holding dollar denominated assets. Let us now consider this inflation strategy and other measures that can be taken to limit monetary holding losses.

In this Chapter, we will show you how to compute the holding loss from cash and receivables.

## STRATEGY FOR OFFSETTING HOLDING GAINS FROM MONETARY LIABILITIES AGAINST HOLDING LOSSES FROM MONETARY ASSETS

The use of borrowed money to finance cash, accounts receivable, bonds, mortgages, etc. is a sure-fire way to limit losses from holding monetary assets. Holding gains from debt will offset, dollar for dollar, the holding losses from monetary assets because there are no tax consequences in the offset.

Historic Cost Accounting (HCA) does not report monetary holding losses for tax purposes, but does report monetary holding gains. The gains show up as an increase in HCA profits. However, when monetary holding gains offset monetary holding losses, there is no increase in HCA profits—there is no recognized holding gain for tax purposes. A taxable monetary holding gain is devoured by a nondeductible holding loss from monetary assets.

Perhaps you will recall the experience of Aspen Company, which we detailed in the last chapter. Aspen, you remember, borrowed $10,000 from their "go for it" banker. The term of the loan was for 5 years, during which period there was an average inflation of 10%. Aspen held the money in their bank account. At the expiration of the loan period, Aspen repaid the lender $10,000, as required. However, because the inflation had devalued the dollar 37.91% Aspen, in real terms, repaid only 6,209 year-1 dollars.

Aspen had a holding gain of 3,791 year 1 dollars. But, at the same time, the company had a holding loss in the same amount from storing $10,000 cash for 5 years. The holding gain canceled out the holding loss on a dollar-for-dollar basis. Furthermore, the holding gain, which is normally taxable, was not perceived. Historic Cost Accounting, which is used to compute taxable income, is fooled by the offset of monetary holding losses against monetary holding gains. The only way that gains from holding monetary liabilities can escape taxation is to offset them against losses from holding monetary assets.

Firms who employ borrowed money to finance cash on hand and in the bank and other fixed dollar monetary assets will have the same experience as the Aspen Company. The holding gain from debt will offset the holding loss from monetary assets on a dollar-for-dollar basis.

This discussion assumes that the firm does, indeed, have a monetary holding gain. That is, it is able to borrow funds at an interest rate that does not charge for inflation—for the decline in the value of the dollar, in whole or in part.

It is worth noting that, from the borrower's point of view, the holding gain represents a reduction in interest costs. However, if the interest cost is negative, then the negative interest represents a transfer of loan principal from the lender to the debtor.

## STRATEGY FOR REDUCING LOSS FROM HOLDING CASH

While firms are able to offset their monetary holding losses with monetary holding gains, they may be unable to offset their losses completely. So it is worthwhile to consider other strategies for reducing them. Let's review a common strategy for cash.

The first requirement for managing cash is to know why you hold it. Firms hold cash for three reasons:

1. to pay bills as they come due;
2. to meet unforeseen cash needs;
3. to speculate.

All of these motives for holding cash are legitimate, but they have a cost—an opportunity cost—such as the dividends and capital gains that would be earned if the money were invested in stocks. Furthermore, in times of inflation, there is the additional cost of monetary holding losses. When holding losses are added to the opportunity costs of keeping cash in reserve, the expense may be large, much larger than we would guess. Therefore, we will want to monitor the costs of holding money so that we can determine if the expense equals or exceeds the benefits derived.

We must estimate the yield the stockholders might get if their money were invested in Treasury bills or other types of investments. Or we must ask if the opportunity cost of money—what the firm might earn from holding raw materials, for example—would not produce a greater return than the benefits derived from holding currency.

The determination of opportunity costs is guesswork, but the determination of the holding loss from cash is a mathematical certainty.

*Example:* A firm has one asset. It is cash in the amount of $100.

Therefore, its balance sheet would show:

| Balance Sheet 1/1/X1 | |
|---|---|
| Cash | $100 |
| Stockholders' Equity | 100 |

But supposing the cash is held for 1 year, during which the purchasing power of money declines by 10%. The value of cash would decrease by $10, and so would the value of the stockholders' equity. Let us further suppose that the firm's management recognizes the holding loss and is able to charge for it in the price of products sold. In that event, the year-end balance sheet would show:

| Balance Sheet 12/31/X1 | |
|---|---|
| Cash | $110 |
| Stockholders' Equity | 110 |

The firm's purchasing power and the stockholders' purchasing power is no greater, nor no less, than it was at 1/1/X1.

But the government would tax the $10 earned to restore cash to its original value. Furthermore, when the firm is liquidated and the $110 is distributed to the stockholders, they will also be taxed on the $10 earned to maintain the original invested value of cash. Thus, in order to preserve cash and equity at their original 1/1/X1 value, the firm must not only charge for the $10 loss of purchasing power of cash, but also for the corporate and stockholders' income taxes that must be paid on the $10 restored to equity.

This leads us to the formula for determining the amount of the holding loss.

## How To Determine The Amount Of The Holding Loss

$$\frac{\text{Inflation rate}}{1 - \text{Corporate income tax rate}} \times \frac{1}{1 - \text{Stockholders' tax rate}} = \text{Holding Loss From Cash.}$$

*Example:* Assume: An inflation rate of 10%
Corporate and Stockholders' Tax Rate of 40%
Time period, 1 year.

$$\frac{.10 \text{ inflation rate}}{1 - .40 \text{ corporate tax rate}} \times \frac{1}{1 - .40 \text{ Stockholders' tax rate}}$$

$$= \frac{.1666}{.60} = 27.76, \text{ loss from holding cash.}$$

If the cash is held for more than one year, the cost escalates as the cumulative inflation rate increases.

## How To Compute The Combined Costs Of Holding Money

In addition to the wealth redistribution loss from holding money, which we computed above, there is the additional expense of opportunity costs. Assume that the firm or the stockholders could invest the cash held in an investment that would yield 3% in real terms. Using the formula shown above, we get a loss of 36.1%.

$$\frac{.03 + .10}{1 - .40} \times \frac{1}{1 - .40} = 36.1\% \text{ cost of holding cash.}$$

In our example, if we were to hold $100,000 cash, we would have to earn $36,100 from business operations to equal the opportunity cost of money, plus the holding loss.

It may seem incredible that the cost of holding cash—that is one's own money, not borrowed money—would be so high. But look at it this way. In our example, the actual cost of holding cash was only 13%—a 3% opportunity cost plus a 10% holding loss. But the income tax at the corporate and stockholders' level escalates the loss to 36.1%. The income tax law does not recognize the cost of holding currency as a deductible expense. But it does tax the illusory income generated to restore the holding loss—the loss from the decline in the purchasing power of cash—at both the corporate level and stockholder level.

The double taxation of illusory income makes the corporate form of business very expensive. Small- and medium-size firms, who are not reporting taxes under Subchapter S, should consider the infla-expense of doing business as a regular corporation during a period of high inflation.

## How To Determine The Monthly Loss From Holding Cash

Good cash management during a period of significant inflation requires a monthly computation of the firm's holding loss from currency. The Ralph Coughenour Jones procedure shown below can be used for determining the holding loss from all monetary assets.[1]

The objective of the mathematical operation of Figure 5-1 is to measure the holding loss by a constant dollar. In this case, we use the 1967 dollar because the Consumer Price Index, which we are using as our common denominator, is based on the 1967 dollar (1967 dollar = 100). The CPI is a mid-month index of prices.

What was our loss from holding an average balance of $400,000 cash in our bank account during the month of January 1979? Answer: $9,853.

*Procedure:* First, divide the $400,000 balance by the prior month's price index. Second, divide the $400,000 balance by the current month's price index. Subtract results of step 2 from step 1. Result: the loss stated in 1967 dollars. Multiply this figure by the current month's price index to get the loss stated in current month's dollars.

**COMPUTATION OF LOSS FROM HOLDING CASH, JANUARY 1979**

| Date of Price Factor | Average Number of Historical Dollars | Price Factor* | 1967 Dollars |
|---|---|---|---|
| December 1978 | $400,000 | 2.029 | $197,141 |
| January 1979 | $400,000 | 2.047 | 195,408 |
| | Loss from holding cash – 1967 dollars | | $ 1,733 |

**FIGURE 5-1**

*Consumer Price Index × 100

Convert the loss of $1,733 expressed in 1967 dollars into January 1979 dollars: $1,733 × January price index multiplied by 100 = $1,733 × 2.047 = $3,547. A firm in the 40% tax bracket would have to earn

$$\frac{\$3,547}{1 - .40} = \$5,912$$

to replace the $3,547 January 1979 holding loss from cash. However, the holding loss from cash is a reduction in the stockholders' equity, which is not recognized for tax purposes. Thus, in order to restore equity in real terms, we must provide not only for the corporate income tax on the restoration, but also for the stockholders' income tax. So we must make the additional computation. Assume the stockholders have a tax rate of 40%.

$$\frac{\$5,912}{1 - .40} = \$9,853, \text{ cost of holding } \$400,000 \text{ cash}$$

during month of January 1979.

**Proof:**

| | |
|---|---|
| Cost of holding cash | $9,853 |
| Less, corporate tax @40% | − 3,941 |
| Total | $5,912 |
| Less, Stockholders' tax @40% | 2,364 |
| Equity Restored to Stockholders | $3,548 |

**FIGURE 5-2**

For further discussion of how to restore capital taken by the wealth transfer of inflation, see Chapter 14, *Planning Cash Flow*.

The average cash balance for a month can be computed by adding end-of-the-week cash balances and dividing by the number of weeks in the month. A single month's loss of almost $10,000 in purchasing power from holding currency should give us pause. We should inquire as to whether our various motives for holding an average cash balance of $400,000 are necessary and can be justified in view of the cost.

The inexorable decline in the value of money in a period of significant inflation makes the knowledge of the holding cost of money a prime inflation strategy.

## HOW TO COMPUTE THE HOLDING LOSS ON ACCOUNTS RECEIVABLE

The holding loss on accounts receivable is computed in precisely the same manner as that in Figure 5-1 and 5-2.

Again, it is vital to know the extent of the holding loss. Accounts receivable represents a funding of the inventory of customers. This is not a small cost in doing business and it must be charged for. See Chapter 14.

In some instances, it is possible to increase prices sufficiently to offset the monetary holding loss. But it is difficult because the price increase must not only offset the loss from holding accounts receivable, but it also must fund the tax on the recoupment of the loss.

**Strategies For Reducing The Holding Loss From Accounts Receivable**

The principal strategy for reducing the holding loss from accounts receivable is to increase the velocity of collections. Some of the methods used to accomplish this objective are:

1. Require large amounts owed to be remitted by wire.
2. Use lock boxes as an effective means of shortening the time between the date the customer mails his remittance and the time the check is deposited in the bank. Lock boxes also improve the control over cash, but it should be noted that lock boxes can prove to be costly.
3. An efficient credit department may be the best strategy for obtaining timely collections of accounts.

There is a prevalent practice—especially profitable in a double-digit inflationary economy—to delay the payment of accounts by drawing a check on a bank remote from the supplier. The objective of this practice is to increase the float of the payer at the expense of the payee.

Another practice, costly to the creditor, is the delay of payment past due date. This prevalent practice enables the customer to use the supplier's money at no cost. These practices are too costly to be tolerated in an epoch of double-digit inflation.

It is time for trade associations to consider the problem of holding losses on accounts receivable. Brazil indexes accounts receivable. The amount due from the customer is increased by the amount the price index has risen during the hiatus between billing and payment.

In indexing accounts receivable, the income tax factor should not be forgotten. A 1% price rise should be compensated for by a charge of 1.666%, assuming a 40% tax rate. A 90-day delay in payment results in a monetary loss of 5% of the amount due, assuming an inflation rate of 1% per month and a tax rate of 40%.

$$\frac{.03 \text{ rate of inflation}}{1 - .40 \text{ tax rate}} = 5\%$$

Interest on delinquent payments should be added to the index assessment.

The example given at Figure 5-1 assumes a static sum of money held for one month. It would apply to the situation where a firm holds money for the precautionary motive as, for example, for a future contingency. It would also apply to money held for investment. "I think we can get a good buy if we just hold on to a little money," the purchasing agent says.

But does money that is constantly coming into the firm from accounts receivable decline in value, as we have shown in Figure 5-1? What about the money which came in on the last day of the month?

My opinion is that all money declines in value as general prices rise. If customers do not pay their accounts, the company would continue to hold accounts receivable, which are subject to the same holding loss as is any fixed dollar asset. The payment of the account merely transfers the holding loss from accounts receivable to the cash account. The loss cannot be avoided. It must be provided for in the sales price of goods sold.

## MONETARY HOLDING LOSSES CAN BE MATERIALLY REDUCED BY INSERTING GOLD OR FOREIGN MONEY CLAUSES INTO CONTRACTS

Holding losses from long-term contracts of savings and investments can be materially reduced by indexing the payment of principle to gold or to such stable foreign currencies as the Swiss franc. The objective of indexing the monetary consideration of a contract to gold or to a foreign currency, or to a basket of foreign currencies, is to give the contract a predictable value. It is an attempt to state the monetary consideration in terms of a quasi money (gold) or in currencies that are relatively constant and to avoid holding losses from fixed dollar monetary assets.

Almost all contracts written between the years 1880 to 1933 contained a gold clause which gave the obligee a right to demand payment in gold. Gold clauses were declared to be against public policy by the Congressional Joint Resolution of June 5, 1933.

However, in 1977 the Congress reversed itself and passed a bill which:

> Allows the inclusion of clauses which require payment in gold or any particular kind of coin or currency in contracts entered on or after the date of the enactment of this act.
> Senate bill, S. 79, 1/10/77. House Bill 6983, 5/6/77.

On October 27, 1977, the President signed the above provision into law. Public Law 94-147 gives the creditor the right to require:[2]

1. payment in gold bullion
2. payment in gold coin
3. payment in an amount of currency measured by gold
4. payment in a foreign currency
5. payment in a combination (basket) of several currencies, including gold.

The right to index monetary consideration by the price of gold or the exchange value of a foreign currency or basket of currencies is so new and generally unknown in the United States that very few creditors have availed themselves of this opportunity to limit holding losses from monetary assets.

There is, of course, nothing novel about gold clauses in contracts. As we have stated earlier, gold clauses were a part of the boiler plate in contracts during the period 1880 to 1933. Nor is there anything unusual about indexing contracts to a foreign currency. Trade contracts with merchants and manufacturers of foreign countries have long indexed consideration to Swiss francs, German marks, or a basket of currencies.

It seems certain that contracts will be written with clauses which give the obligee the right to demand payment in gold or in the equivalent of a foreign currency or a basket of foreign currencies.

## INDEXING LONG-TERM CONTRACTS TO COMMODITY AND LABOR INDEXES

It is a general practice in some industries to index long-term contracts of product sales to commodity and labor indexes.

The basis of the indexing is to state the percentage of cost each factor of production contributes to the total cost of the product.

*Example:* The component costs of producing widgets is:

| | |
|---|---|
| Labor | 20% |
| Material A | 25% |
| Other Costs, etc. | 55% |

If the labor index rises by 5%, the cost of the product would be increased by 5% × 20% = 1%.

# HOW TO COMPUTE YOUR NET HOLDING GAIN OR LOSS FROM MONETARY ITEMS

It is useful to determine the amount of your net monetary holding gain or loss. The method shown on the following page is the one suggested by the Financial Standard Board's Statement No. 33, paragraph 232.

If, indeed, a firm were to realize a net holding gain from monetary items, it would usually appear in income from trading. The holding gain would increase taxable income, and a tax would be paid on it. So it is appropriate to reduce the reputed gain by the amount of taxes that would be assessed against it.

Firms should not spend holding gains until they appear in the cash account. They will appear in the bank balance only if the firm is profitable and is able to charge for the wealth transfer of inflation in the selling prices of merchandise sold.

Obviously, if the monetary assets had exceeded the monetary liabilities in Figure 5-6, the computation would have resulted in a purchasing power loss. Whether the firm actually suffered a monetary holding loss would depend on whether the firm was able to charge for the amount of the loss in its sales prices. To offset the loss, the firm would have to increase its mark-up on merchandise sold to cover the holding loss, plus the corporate and stockholders' income tax on the increased revenue.

*Step 1:* Subtract total monetary liabilities from total monetary assets.

|  | Balance | |
|---|---|---|
|  | Dec. 1980 | Dec. 1979 |
| **Monetary Assets:** | | |
| Cash | $100 | $ 50 |
| Accounts Receivable | 200 | 100 |
| Total Monetary Assets | $300 | $150 |
| **Deduct Monetary Liabilities:** | | |
| Accounts Payable And Accrued Expenses | $100 | $ 50 |
| Income Taxes Payable | 100 | 0 |
| Short-term Bank Loan | 300 | 200 |
| Long-term Debt | 500 | 300 |
| Total Monetary Liabilities | $1000 | $550 |
| Net Monetary Liabilities | ($ 700) | ($400) |

*Step 2:* Restate the amount of net monetary items at the beginning of the year, changes in monetary items, and net monetary items at the end of the year into average 1980 dollars. Use the Consumer Price Index to convert these items into a common dollar.

|  | Nominal Dollars |  | G.P.I. Conversion Factor | Average 1980 $s |
|---|---|---|---|---|
| Balance 1/1/80 | $400 | × | 220.9 (Avg. 1980) / 243.5 (Dec. 1980) | $415 |
| Increase in net monetary liabilities | 300 |  |  | 300 |
| Balance 1/1/80 plus 1980 increase |  |  |  | $715 |
| Balance 12/31/80 | $700 | × | 220.9 (Avg. 1980) / 243.5 (Dec. 1980) | −635 |
| Purchasing Power Gain on Net Monetary Items |  |  |  | $ 80 |

*Step 3.* I would deduct from the holding gain of $80 the income tax that would be incurred if the wealth transfer were realized in profits:

Purchasing power gain on net monetary items ..... $80
Less income tax charge of 40% ..... −32
Net holding gain after taxes ..... $48

**FIGURE 5-6**

## NOTES
1. Ralph C. Jones, *Effects of Price Level Changes,* p. 25.
2. *Men and Money,* Vol. 2 No 6, Dec. 1977, Le Roy Sludder III, Editor.

# 6

# Historic Cost Accounting Will Transfer Your Wealth By Incorrectly Measuring Your Cost Of Goods Sold

In Chapter 6, we detail Historic Cost's third error—the understatement of the cost of goods sold. The error is derived from the HCA postulate that the price you paid for an item is its eternal cost.

Chapter 6 is also a tale of the tyranny of the taxation of illusory inventory profits. If in 1970 you had 1,000 units of inventory at a cost of 1,000 1970 dollars, and if that same inventory now costs $2,000, you will have paid an income tax on an illusory gain of $1,000. Each time you marked up the price of your goods, to provide for their increased replacement cost, you will have been income taxed on the mark-up for inflation.

Thus, to provide for future operations, you must increase the selling prices of your products, not only for the price increase of replacement inventory, but also for the corporate and individual income tax on the infla-mark-up.

## HCA UNDERSTATES THE COST OF GOODS SOLD, THUS CREATING AN ILLUSORY PROFIT ON WHICH TAXES MUST BE PAID

The value of an inventory to a going concern is its replacement cost.[1] A firm that does not generate enough income to replace the cost of goods sold will run out of money and out of business. It is that simple. Therefore, accounting records should report the replacement cost of goods sold in computing profit and loss, so that a reasonably accurate statement of the firm's operating experience can be communicated to the taxing authority, to management, and to creditors.

Historic Cost Accounting does not report the replacement cost of inventory sold. It reports an irrelevant historic cost, which causes the cost of goods sold to be understated. This error is derived from a misperception of money and its function in the economy.

Money is a symbol of goods. Its function in the economy is to communicate the value of goods. If a barrel of oil costs $15 on January 2, but $23 on June 30, then a barrel of oil purchased on January 1 will not be, and should not be, symbolized at $15 on June 30th. Only $23 can communicate the value of a barrel of oil on June 30.

But HCA would report the cost of the oil purchased on January 2 at $15, regardless of when it was sold. Even if it were sold to the owner of the last diesel auto in the year 3000, HCA would state the cost of the oil at $15. This dismal example of accounting pig-headedness is derived from the HCA postulate that the value of an item is determined by the number of dollars expended at the date of its purchase. If you paid $15 for an item, that—by George—is its eternal cost. That is its cost even if you were to sell the item to Saint Peter, as you pass through the pearly gates on your way to your great reward for having been a good business person.

HCA's fundamental error is that it attempts to separate money from goods, as if money had a value in its own right. But paper money and bookkeeping records of credit have no value except as a symbol of goods. For example: I have a worthless paper Chilean ten escudo bill which was in circulation in that beautiful country in 1970. At that time, it had purchasing power because it represented goods. Today it is utterly worthless. The Chilean Government has issued a different piece of paper to symbolize the goods and services of Chile. All the adherents of HCA, in concert, could not huff and puff value into my worthless ten escudo bill. It cannot be made to communicate the cost of anything, including something that was purchased in Chile in 1970.

Similarly, no one can give worth to last year's dollar. It is like my Chilean escudo. It is, in a sense, no longer in circulation. Therefore, we cannot express the cost of anything in dollars of past years. It is silly to pretend we can. But accounting attempts to measure the cost of goods sold and to communicate its value in past years' dollars—in goods symbols that have disappeared with the past years' snow. To attempt to communicate value in historic cost dollars is to give a false accounting message.

*The Communists agree: You must have an adequate return to finance the future:* Commerce has an unyielding and clear logic, which is limited neither by political persuasion, by boundaries, nor by time. The logic of commerce is that you must have an adequate return to finance the future. It doesn't matter whether the "Stars and Stripes," the "Swedish Cross," or the "Hammer and Sickle" flies over your factory, you must fund the replacement cost of whatever you are selling. If the replacement cost of inventory is rising, then income must be produced to provide for the rising prices.

"In fact," says John Hutton in his *The Mystery of Wealth*,[2] "practical businessmen in both capitalist and Marxist-inspired systems are increasingly demonstrating a remarkable convergency of opinion in emphasizing the importance of an adequate rate of return, however defined, to finance the future."

The failure to finance the future is severely punished. Plant, machinery, and equipment become obsolete. They produce at high cost. The firm with antiquated equipment cannot profitably compete with its competitors, who have provided for the future out of past profits, to purchase modern, more efficient productive facilities.

The unyielding logic of commerce has made successful business people forward looking. Their thinking is oriented towards future operations. They act on the knowledge that you must obtain an adequate return on today's sale of goods to finance the inventory and equipment that will be purchased tomorrow.

In contrast, conventional accounting is backward looking. It is blithely historically oriented. It is stranded in a by-gone time when Britannia ruled the waves and the pound sterling was backed by gold—when the value of money was stable.

So we have a divergence in point of view between management and accounting. While business managers are raising prices to provide cash to meet future higher inventory costs, laggard, illogical, backward looking HCA is depleting the firm's cash by reporting illusory inventory profits based on low, unreal historic costs. These phantom profits are eagerly taxed by the Federal and State governments as if they were real.

But this is not the only consequence of bad accounting. If management is deluded into believing that false inventory profits are an increase in the firm's wealth, they may distribute the after-tax portion of the infla-profits to the stockholders as dividends. This error occurred on a massive scale in American industry in 1975 and on a lesser scale since.

Thus, while management is earning cash to finance future inventory acquisition costs, accounting is causing the depletion of the firm's liquid resources by reporting that dividends can be paid, on the assumption that, if past costs are financed, the firm will continue in business.

The total cost of bad accounting for inventory costs are:

1. The replacement cost of the goods sold will not be funded.
2. An income tax will be paid on the illusory inventory profit at both the corporate and stockholders' levels.
3. Interest costs will be incurred on money borrowed to finance the replacement of the inventory sold.

It should be evident to government and to the private sector that enterprises must earn an adequate profit to finance future operations. It is ancient knowledge that the seed corn must be preserved at all cost. But the seed corn of industry cannot be preserved if accounting reports costs as profits, and if the government taxes these illusory profits at both the corporate and stockholders' levels.

## NOT ALL INVENTORY PROFITS ARE ILLUSORY

In the previous section, we argued that HCA understates the cost of goods sold because it does not price inventory consumed at its replacement value. But what about the inventory not consumed? Supposing you held one million barrels of oil on January 1 at a cost of $15 a barrel, and on June 30 you still held the same inventory of oil but its price had advanced to $23 per barrel. Would you realize a profit of 8 million dollars? The answer depends on how you define profit.

Earlier we defined profit as "an increase in the ability to consume without invading capital." The question to be asked of the definition is: The ability to consume what? Clearly, your ability to consume oil hasn't risen. If you sell your million barrels of oil for $23 a barrel, you will be able to buy only what you had in the first place—a million barrels of oil. But what about your ability to consume other items whose prices have not increased, or whose prices have risen more slowly than that of oil? Doubtless, your ability to consume has increased in relation to those items.

It would also seem that those companies who hold inventories of goods whose prices do not rise as rapidly as that of other items lose purchasing power in relationship to other goods. Small computers, poultry, and eggs were items whose prices declined, while the general price level rose by 14%. Those who held an inventory of one of these products lost, not only from the decline in the value of their inventory, but also from the decline in the purchasing power of the money they received when they sold their computers, chickens, or eggs. Historic Cost would report the decline in the value of the inventory due to the reduction of the cost of goods held (lower of cost or market), but it would not report the loss in purchasing power vis-a-vis other goods.

Which reminds us of the first principle of how to prosper from trading in commodities. Buy those commodities whose prices rise faster than those of other commodities. Or hold an inventory of goods whose prices are rising faster than prices in general. But it is not enough to outperform the market. An inventory holding gain will be realized only if the inventory increases in price in excess of the average inflation, plus the tax on the inflationary gain.

We can illustrate the point by recalling the case of Mr. Cash. Perhaps you remember that he invested $100,000 of his money in commodities; prices then doubled, and he sold out for $200,000. Figure 6-1 shows his actual transaction in one column, and in the other column we show what he should have done to break even. He should have sold his commodities for $266,000 instead of $200,000, because the Federal and State governments taxed his illusory gain of $100,000.

| Transactions | Actual | To Break Even |
|---|---|---|
| Mr. Cash sold his commodities for | $200,000 | $266,666 |
| He purchased his commodities for | 100,000 | 100,000 |
| Indicated gain | $100,000 | $166,000 |
| Income tax 40% | 40,000 | 66,000 |
| Cash remaining after tax payment | $ 60,000 | $100,000 |
| But prices doubled during the period Mr. Cash held his commodities; therefore, the real cost of commodities sold is $100,000 greater than shown | 100,000 | 100,000 |
| Loss on Transaction | ($ 40,000) | 00 |

**FIGURE 6-1**

The above example of Mr. Cash shows that just staying even with the average price rise, in holding an inventory, is not enough to realize a holding gain or to break even. Prices must be increased to cover inflation, plus the income tax on the illusory inventory profits.

**Conclusion On Holding Gains From Inventory**

A firm that holds an inventory whose prices do not rise as rapidly as that of other goods suffers a decline in the ability to consume those goods. The converse is also true. For example, a jewelry firm would experience a gain in its ability to consume other goods, if their inventory of gold increased in price by 100%, while that of other commodities increased by only 14%. The gain would be realized only if the jewelry firm chose to exchange its inventory for cash or for goods and services. Otherwise, it would have only a potential gain to be realized sometime in the future, if gold prices held up.

Usually a business cannot operate with the view of terminating its holding of inventory. Management must plan and operate a business as if it were to continue indefinitely. They must provide current income to finance future operations. For this reason, holding gains from inventory should be counted only when the trading is terminated. If holding gains on actively traded inventory were recorded as realized, it is a certainty they would be income taxed. In addition, dividends might be distributed from gains that were not realized in cash. If the unrealized holding gains were first taxed, and the remainder distributed as dividends, the firm would not have the cash to replace its inventory. It would be compelled to close its doors. Accountancy should be directed toward a system of accounting that insures the continuance of an enterprise.

To answer the question raised earlier: You may remember that I defined profit as an increase in the ability to consume. The question was asked: "The ability to consume what?" I would answer: The ability to consume all goods and services after future normal operations have been funded. An enterprise whose inventory prices advance at a greater rate than other goods should count its gain when trading in the inventory is terminated. If there is a gain, it will show up in cash.

A strategy for reducing the infla-tax on illusory inventory profits is discussed in the chapter on the LIFO Inventory convention.

## NOTES

1. Edgar O. Edwards, "The State of Current Value Accounting," *The Accounting Review,* New York, April 1975, pp. 235-245.
2. John Hutton, *The Mystery of Wealth,* Stanley Thornes (Publishers) Ltd., Cheltenham, England, p.211.

# 7

## Is Historic Cost Accounting's Understatement Of Depreciation Definancing Your Business?

This chapter is about HCA's fourth error in measuring income. It fails to state the true cost of depreciation. Depreciation is an account used in the accrual accounting convention. Its objective is to defer charging off a fixed asset until its cost can be offset against the income it is thought to produce. If a machine costs $1,000 and has a useful life of 1,000 hours, then the depreciation charge is computed at $1 per hour of machine operation. If the machine produces widgets at the rate of 10 per hour, then it follows that the depreciation charge to be added to the cost of producing one widget is 10¢ ($1 ÷ 10). Nothing complicated about that. All you have to do is to determine the cost of the asset and its useful life. Then divide the cost by the useful life of the asset, and you have the depreciation charge. The cost of depreciation can be ticked off against income with the certainty and regularity of time.

But this simple concept of charging off the cost of fixed assets used has been the source of endless debate. Like so many inventions, depreciation looks good on the drawing board, but doesn't work well on the street. It is an accounting invention that would operate perfectly in a business environment where there is no obsolescence and where money values remain constant. However, we conduct business in a world where there is obsolescence. This invalidates the most accurate prediction of the useful life of an asset. There is also inflation which invalidates the idea that you can assign the cost of a fixed asset to the income it produces, by dividing the number of dollars paid at its purchase, by its predicted useful life.

What follows is our contribution to the continuing debate over depreciation. It is not a frivolous argument. It is a discussion of how

American Industry is being definanced by a tax system, based on Historic Cost Accounting—a system that consumes the wealth of the private sector that is needed to finance present and future operations.

## HCA UNDERSTATES THE COST OF DEPRECIATION AND, THEREFORE, OVERSTATES PROFIT

Mr. John Armstrong, writing in the *Accountant,* August 8, 1903 issue, complained that: "The question of Depreciation is one upon which so many articles have been written and so many opinions expressed, that there would not appear to be much more which could profitably be said upon the subject."

Well, Mr. Armstrong, the question of Depreciation is still being hotly debated, even 78 years after you thought nothing more could be profitably said upon the subject. The reason for the long debate, the interminable discussion without resolution, is that depreciation, as conceived in your time and as perceived today, is a flawed concept. It just isn't true that machinery, equipment, and buildings are consumed in the operation of a business. Nor is it true, as a general proposition, that the rate of the loss of value of fixed assets can be accurately predicted, or that the computation of the loss of value should be based on historic cost.

If we will look about us, we will see that buildings are not usually consumed by wear and tear. Buildings are abandoned, not consumed. A building that is kept in good repair will last indefinitely. I occupied a beautiful 100-year-old granite stone building in the heart of San Francisco. That building, the Flood Building, will still be fit for occupancy 500 years from now, barring obsolescence or disaster. Jefferson's lovely wood frame home in Monticello stands in excellent repair, despite its daily trampling by hoards of admiring tourists. Old factory buildings are being remodeled into multiple-use manufacturing complexes or into very attractive offices and shopping centers.

It is obsolescence, neglect of upkeep, and the character of people living about the structure that have more to do with determining the life of a building than does wear and tear. So it is not true that buildings are consumed through use; rather their value is lost through obsolescence and neglect of repair.[1]

What we have said about buildings is true of machinery. Dr. David Rudd, BSC (Eng.), PhD C. Eng., in an *Accountancy* article entitled "The

Replacement Fallacy in Accounting," states that engineers were not responsible for the notion that fixed assets are consumed.[2]

"Engineering assets tend to have comparatively long useful lives, and the effects of inflation are cumulative, so engineers noticed before other people that HCA often resulted in a shortage of capital when such assets came to be 'replaced'—in the vague sense in which they and others use the term. But engineers were not responsible for the notion that fixed assets (or their value) are 'consumed.' Such a metaphor is not merely inept; it is positively misleading, because it gives the impression that the main cause of depreciation is to do with the use of the asset, whereas in most cases the main cause is external to such use."

It is obsolescence, the major "cause external to the use" of assets, that accounting has failed to adequately measure and to charge for. In addition to the conceptual error of what to measure, accounting has computed depreciation on a historic cost that has no reality.

The effect of these accounting errors has been to overstate profits. The overstated profits are income taxed, thus causing an infla-loss. The infla-loss may be further increased if management misperceives the illusory profit for a real gain in wealth and pays a dividend out of the phantom profit.

The consequence of bad accounting, combined with a ruinous income tax, has been to cause capital intensive firms to lose their ability to provide machinery and equipment for future profitable operations.

The steel industry is a case in point. Major sections of the American steel industry have been liquidated, or are in the process of liquidation because some steel firms have not been able to generate the capital needed to replace obsolete equipment. However, we need not look to big steel for an example of the deleterious results of bad accounting combined with a rapacious tax system. We can find ample examples in our own backyard. Older businesses, which are particularly penalized by the taxing of phantom profits, cannot generate the cash to replace obsolete depreciable assets.

Buildings used for housing, offices, and the retail trade, have generally not experienced the loss of value from obsolescence that industrial-type facilities have. The rental or use of housing-type buildings has no foreign competition as does manufacturing. They are not affected by cheap labor or subsidies, or the favorable depreciation deductions foreign competitors enjoy.

While housing-type buildings have not experienced great loss from obsolescence in the past, we anticipate they will experience substantial obsolescence in the future. The imminent era of high-cost energy will probably cause a substantial obsolescence of vacation-type facilities, such as hotels, motels, and shops. High-cost energy will also require a substantial remodeling of high-rise office buildings.

The principal losers from accounting's failure to adequately account for depreciation have been those firms which have a high ratio of investment in machinery and equipment to sales. These firms—particularly firms with older assets—have experienced a high rate of obsolescence which HCA has not reported. Furthermore, it seems likely that the rate of obsolescence will be greater in the future, if for no other reason than that governmental energy and environmental regulations will require the scrapping of a good deal of machinery.

The prospective obsolescence of industrial facilities must be recognized by accounting, and provisions must be made currently so that firms will have the cash to replace obsolete depreciable assets. The necessary funds can be accumulated only if the income tax laws are reformed, because it is the income tax on illusory profits that is impoverishing capital intensive companies.

## Conclusion

Depreciation is an accrual accounting concept. The objective of accrual accounting is to match income with the cost incurred in producing the income. It is accounting dogma that the matching of income and costs is possible, and that it will produce a correct statement of profit and loss and financial condition. One of the costs accrual accounting would measure and match with income is depreciation. But the matching process is flawed because Historic Cost Accounting has failed to state the correct cost of depreciation.

HCA fails to report the true expense of depreciation because it is based on three erroneous premises:

1. That machinery, equipment, and buildings are mostly consumed in the operation of the business.
2. That the rate of the consumption of the asset can be accurately predicted.
3. That the proper basis for the computation of depreciation is the asset's historic cost.

David Rudd, BSC (Eng.), PhD C. Eng., an expert on the technological obsolescence of engineering plants, informs us that the main cause of depreciation of engineering assets is not from use, as HCA accrual accounting postulates, but from factors external to use.

Accounting, having erred in postulating that the major cause of depreciation is from wear and tear, also erred in postulating that the rate of use or consumption can be predicted.

The final premise, the idea that depreciation should be computed on the historic cost of the asset, is indefensible, as we have previously shown in discussing the application of historic cost to the computation of the cost of goods sold.

Aside from producing financial statements that are unintelligible, the real damage that results from HCA's erroneous computation of depreciation is that it causes a firm to pay an income tax on a fallacious profit. This drains cash from the firm—cash that is needed to finance the replacement of obsolete depreciable assets.

## NOTES

1. Dan Palmon and Lee J. Seidler, "Current Value Reporting of Real Estate Companies and a Possible Example of Market Inefficiency," *The Accounting Review,* July 1978, pp. 77-78.
2. David Rudd, "The Replacement Falacy In Accounting," *Accountancy* (London), March 1979, p. 54-58.

# 8

## Historic Cost Accounting Profit And Loss Statements Lack Comparability: How To Determine Whether A Firm Is Increasing Sales In Real Terms

We use financial statements of past years to predict the future experience of a company. We look for trends, with the assumption that past experience will probably predict future experience. A trend which we are particularly interested in is whether the firm has been able to maintain or increase its sales volume. Historic Cost Profit and Loss Statements will not provide us with the information because the sales of one year are measured in dollars of different value than that of a subsequent year. Consequently, they are not comparable. In this chapter we discuss in detail HCA's fifth measurement error—HCA Profit and Loss Statements lack the element of comparability.

While it is general knowledge that the HCA P&L Statements lack comparability, it is rarely admitted by either the firm or their certified public accountants. It is standard accounting practice to publish comparative sales figures which purport to show a growth in sales dollars from one year to the next, and to explicitly assure the stockholders and other readers of the statement, that the firm has continued to enjoy an increase in customers' demand for the firm's products. A typical example of this kind of chicanery is as follows:

The Growth Company
Statement of Comparative Sales

| Sales 1978 | Sales 1977 | Sales Increase |
|---|---|---|
| $225,731,000 | $204,966,000 | $ 20,765,000 |

Obviously, the sales increase reported of $20,765,000 is a nonsense figure, because you can't subtract 1977 dollars from 1978 dollars. The above statement of comparative sales would be no less nonsensical if the 1978 figure were stated in Japanese yen and the 1977 figure were stated in Paraguayan guaranies.

The type of comparative statement we have shown is really a message from the management to all concerned, that management is earning every dollar they are being paid, and, if there were justice and gratitude in this world, the board of directors would grant, immediately, a hefty increase in salary and perquisites. Let's see if the management of Growth Company is entitled to a raise.

There are two common methods for measuring sales in constant terms. You can measure sales in constant dollars, or you can measure sales in constant product units sold. Let's analyze Growth Company by the first method—in constant dollars.

To measure Growth Company's sales in constant dollars, we need to convert the 1977 sales figure into 1978 dollars, so that when we compare 1977 sales to 1978 sales they will both be measured by a common dollar.

## HOW TO MEASURE SALES IN CONSTANT TERMS: CONVERSION PROCESS

Growth Company is a steel fabricator, so we want to know how much the price of steel increased from 1977 to 1978. The information is found in the Producer's Price Index, in the Survey of Current Business, a Department of Commerce publication. Under the heading "commodity prices," we find the index for iron and steel:

|  | Year | Index Number |
|---|---|---|
| Iron and steel price index | 1977 | 230.4 |
| Iron and steel price index | 1978 | 253.5 |

*Step 1:* Compute a restatement factor by dividing the 1978 index by the 1977 index:
253.5/230.4 = 1.100

*Step 2:* Convert 1977 dollars to 1978 dollars.
1977 sales $204,966 × 1.100 = $225,462,000 − 1978 dollars

*Step 3:* Make comparison of 1978 sales volume to 1977 sales volume:

| 1978 Sales | − | 1977 Sales Measured by 1978 Dollars | = | Decrease in Sales |
|---|---|---|---|---|
| $225,731,000 | | $225,462,000 | | −$269,000 |

So sales in real terms probably declined by approximately $269,000, rather than increasing by $20 million, as reported by the HCA P&L comparative statement.

Our figure of $269,000 sales decline is an approximation. It is inexact because it is derived from a comparison of price indexes which state the average price experience for the entire steel industry. Growth Company's prices may not have increased at the rate of the index average. But one thing is certain: Growth Company did not have a revenue increase of $20 million as management claims. So we don't owe them a raise.

## Alternative Method For Measuring Sales In Constant Terms

The alternative method for stating comparative sales in constant terms is to measure sales in terms of product units sold. The product unit sales method is useful in analyzing the revenue of a manufacturing firm. Units of goods sold are not often published, so the information must be requested from the comptroller.

I'll illustrate the method with an example:

> A company's profit and loss statement showed sales of $4,400,000 in year 2 vs. $4,100,000 in year 1.
>
> *Conclusion:* Sales increased by $300,000. But the number of units sold told a different story. Units sold declined from 556,555 in year 1 to 421,629 in year 2—a decrease of 134,000, or 25% in unit volume.

The firm had experienced a substantial price increase in the primary raw material used in the manufacture of its product. In reaction to the increased cost, the firm raised its price per unit by 40%. The sharp price increase caused a drop in sales volume of 25%. If management had relied solely on the dollar sales volume, it would not have detected its loss of customers. The firm could not continue to alienate consumers from its product, without paying an exhorbitant financial penalty.

*The Wealth Transfer of Inflation*

**Conclusion**

Creditors and lenders will find it worth their effort to analyze sales in terms of product units sold. The value of a product unit usually will have constancy in a time when the value of dollar sales units do not. If a firm has many lines of merchandise, the analysis—to save time—should identify which are the bread and butter lines. Our experience is that they are the "critical few" products that produce 80 to 90 percent of the total revenue. The unit sales trend in these lines will give a valuable indication of the firm's future ability to pay its bills and to repay its loans.

Obviously, one should also learn the profit per product unit sold. Many firms have gone bankrupt from selling too much too cheaply.

# 9

# Measurement Errors Appearing On The Historic Cost Accounting Balance Sheet

In this chapter, we show how HCA errors appearing on the balance sheet may provide a screen behind which poor management can hide as well as mislead creditors, lenders, and investors. We will also show you a simple method for determining the approximate profit and equity position of a firm in real terms.

## HCA WILL UNDERSTATE THE VALUE OF FIXED ASSETS

The value of a fixed asset on a HCA Balance Sheet is computed by adding the acquisition costs incurred during the life of the business. It is a meaningless value because it is the sum of dollars of different years. Nevertheless, investors and creditors rely on this information, and are thus misinformed. Assets such as timber, patents, land, good will, and plant may have radically greater dollar values than the balance sheet indicates. Many investors have recently learned, from a takeover fight, that the worth of the fixed assets of their firm is several times that shown on the company's balance sheet.

That is not all the stockholders have learned. The demonstration of the true worth of the firm's assets also revealed, for the first time, what a poor return on investment the management was producing. One of the harmful effects of sloppy accounting for the worth of the firm's assets is that it misstates the ratio of profits to capital.

A correct computation of this ratio, which informs of the percentage of return on net worth, is vital to the firm's owners. It gives them one of the best criteria for evaluating management's performance. It also provides a basis for deciding whether to continue the operation of the business. If net worth is understated and profits are overstated by HCA, a falsely high ratio of profits to capital is produced. This erroneous data will lead the stockholders to believe their management is generating a high return on net worth when, in fact, the reverse is true. Management may be performing badly. It may be that even the most competent management could not produce a better yield on investment. The mere possession of valuable assets does not guarantee a reasonable return on net worth. Capital intensive enterprises cannot make a profit, in real terms, in conditions of high inflation and ruinous taxes. But this does not excuse the failure to be candid with the stockholders. Financial statements are supposed to communicate the truth. The failure to inform the company's owners of the fiscal truth has been of great assistance to those who would transfer wealth through inflation. The wealth transfer of inflation is dependent upon the wealth losers not detecting the loss.

### The Understatement Of The Worth Of Fixed Assets May Misinform Bankers And Creditors

Bankers and creditors look to a firm's assets as the resource of last resort for satisfying loans and debts. If a firm understates the value of its assets, it presents a poorer basis for credit than would be the case if the assets were valued at their true worth.

One inexpensive method available, even to smaller firms, for determining the worth of their fixed assets is an insurance appraisal. The appraisal, if done by a recognized expert, will carry weight in the decision-making process of bankers and creditors. The appraisal will serve two purposes. It will reveal to creditors the true worth of the firm's fixed assets, and it will indicate if there is adequate insurance coverage.

## THE SECOND BALANCE SHEET ERROR OF HCA

Retained earnings reported on an HCA balance sheet may be erroneous because HCA overstates the income of those firms which have a substantial investment in inventory, plant, equipment, and machinery, and/or are in a net monetary asset position. The Grady method shown below gives a simple process for correcting the error.

# A "Quick And Dirty" Method For Computing The Infla-Income, Infla-Tax, And Approximate Inflation-Adjusted Earnings And Capital Of A Firm

Accountants, managers, and investors need to know the approximate true profit or loss and the equity position of their firm. This information can be obtained by eliminating the illusory infla-profits from the P&L Statement, and restating equity in constant dollars.

The academicians, in the field of accountancy, have proposed three methods for wringing inflation out of the accounts, Constant Dollar, Current Cost, and Cash Flow Accounting. These methods of infla-accounting have both virtues and debilitating faults, as we shall see in Part 3 of this book. Furthermore, Constant Dollar and Current Cost Accounting require an expenditure of more time than they are worth to closely held firms.

However, there is one practical, "quick and dirty" method for determining the approximate profit and equity position of a firm in real terms. It is based on the Constant Dollar system of accounting, but without its manifold complexities. Mr. Paul Grady is the author of the method.[1] Mr. Grady, Price Waterhouse Co. (Retired), is a practical accountant and a recognized authority in the field of accountancy. I have modified Mr. Grady's proposal somewhat, but basically the method shown is what he proposed.

Inflation adjusted, approximate profit and loss, and equity, can be arrived at by the following operation:

1. Multiply the capital equity base by the Consumer Price Index for the period under review. Capital equity base is defined as capital plus undistributed earnings, as of the beginning of the accounting year, less nondepreciable fixed assets (land, etc.) and LIFO inventory, if that is being used.

    The product resulting from multiplying the capital equity base by the Consumer Price Index is the "Loss of Equity From Inflation." It is the illusory infla-profit.

2. The loss of equity from inflation is deducted from net earnings to arrive at approximate earnings adjusted for inflation.

3. The loss of equity from inflation is entered in the equity section of the balance sheet with the following explanation:

"Purchasing-power losses of equity capital restored by charges against income for the periods since 1967, or from the date of the commencement of business, if later."

Earnings should be adjusted back to 1967 because it was in that year that the current epoch of inflation began to seriously distort Historic Cost Accounting. (See Appendix C for CPI index numbers.)

## EXAMPLE OF HOW TO REMOVE INFLATION'S DISTORTION FROM PROFIT AND EQUITY

The example of the Turbine Company Inc., that follows, illustrates how the profit and loss and the equity of an enterprise can be adjusted to reflect the loss from the wealth transfer of inflation. Schedule II shows that the value of equity in real terms declined by $45,675—it is the last item on the schedule. The loss of equity is carried over to the Profit and Loss Statement, item (4) Schedule III, where it is shown as a cost that reduces income. The $45,675 "wealth transfer cost" reduces Historic Cost profit from $73,250 to $27,575. Schedule IV shows how the loss of equity from inflation is restored, so that the value of the stockholders' investment is maintained in real terms. The Grady adjustments destroy inflation's illusion of phantom profits, and assures that capital will not be distributed in the guise of earnings.

Actually, the $45,675 wealth transfer cost is understated. It should be increased by the amount of tax the stockholders will have to pay when capital is returned to them. If we assume the stockholders' tax rate is 30%, then the wealth transfer cost that should be added to capital is $65,250 ($45,675/1 − .30). We have not made this adjustment because we wanted to keep the illustration simple.

## WHAT THE GRADY METHOD FOR COMPUTING THE INFLA-LOSS OF EQUITY DOES AND DOES NOT DO

The objective of the Grady infla-accounting method is to state the value of the equity of the enterprise in constant units of purchasing power, so that the stockholders' investment will not be dissipated by the surreptitious wealth transfer of inflation. The purchasing power of the equity investment in Turbine Inc. was $556,750 at year end 19X0. However, by the

**SCHEDULE I**

**Turbine Inc.**
**Balance Sheet**

|  | HCA $ 12/31/19X0 | HCA $ 12/31/19X1 |
|---|---:|---:|
| Current Assets: | | |
|   Monetary Assets | $ 220,000 | $ 200,000 |
|   Inventory (FIFO) | 80,000 | 90,000 |
| Nonmonetary Assets | — | — |
|   Depreciable Assets | 700,000 | 800,000 |
|   Land | 100,000 | 100,000 |
|     Total Assets | $1,100,000 | $1,190,000 |
| Current Liabilities | $ 50,000 | $ 90,000 |
| Long-Term Debt | 493,250 | 470,000 |
|     Total Monetary Liability | $ 543,250 | $ 560,000 |
| Equity: | | |
|   Undistributed Earnings: | | |
|   Year 12/31/19X0 | $ 56,750 | $ 56,750 |
|   Year 12/31/19X1 (Schedule III) | | 73,250 |
| Capital Stock | 500,000 | 500,000 |
|     Total | $1,100,000 | $1,190,000 |

**FIGURE 9-1**

---

end of 19X1, it required 45,675 additional year 19X1 dollars, or $602,425, to maintain the purchasing power of the stockholders' equity as measured in constant 19X0 dollars.

By purchasing power, we mean the command over the 382 items of goods and services measured by the Consumer Price Index. These items are goods and services the stockholders would personally consume: in short; food, shelter, clothing, and vital services.

The Grady method is an abbreviated version of the Constant Dollar Accounting system. It does not pretend to tell you what is required to maintain the productive capacity of your firm because it does not attempt to measure the replacement cost of your firm's assets. The replacement cost of your depreciable assets may have increased in price at a much more

**SCHEDULE II**
**Turbine Inc.**
**Computation of Loss of Equity from The Wealth Transfer of Inflation**

*Step 1:* Compute the loss of purchasing power of the dollar for the year 19X1.

| | |
|---|---:|
| Consumer Price Index, 12/31/19X1 | 110 |
| Consumer Price Index, 12/31/19X0 | 100 |
| Increase in Price Index | 10 |

10 divided by 100 = 10% decline in the purchasing power of the dollar.

*Step 2:* Compute the Capital-Equity base subject to the wealth transfer of inflation.

| | | |
|---|---:|---:|
| Undistributed earnings, 12/31/X0 | | $ 56,750* |
| Capital Stock | | 500,000* |
| Total | | $556,750 |
| Less: Land | $100,000 | |
|     LIFO Inventory | 0 | 100,000* |
| Equity Capital Subject to Inflation's Wealth Transfer | | $456,750 |

*Step 3:* Loss of Equity from Inflation:

| | |
|---|---:|
| Equity subject to wealth transfer | $456,750 |
| Decline in purchasing power of $ | × .10 |
| Wealth transfer of equity loss | $ 45,675** |

**FIGURE 9-2**

---

*From Balance Sheet, Schedule I
**Loss transferred to item (4), Schedule III, P&L Statement and to Schedule IV, "Equity Section of Balance Sheet."

**SCHEDULE III**

**Turbine Inc.**
**Profit and Loss Statement**

|  | Historic Cost | Inflation Adjusted | Difference |
|---|---|---|---|
| 1. Revenue | $300,000 | $300,000 | |
| 2. Less: Costs | 200,000 | 200,000 | |
| 3. Profit before taxes | $100,000 | $100,000 | |
| 4. Loss of Equity from inflation (Infla-Profit), Schedule I | | 45,675 | ($45,675) |
| 5. Adjusted Earnings before Taxes | $100,000 | $ 54,325 | ($45,675) |
| 6. Income Taxes | 26,750* | 26,750** | |
| 7. Historic Cost net earnings | $ 73,250 | | |
| 8. Net earnings in real terms | | $ 27,575 | ($45,675) |

**Computation of Infla-tax Paid**

| | |
|---|---|
| Income tax paid | $26,750 |
| Income tax due on adjusted earnings of $54,325 | 10,115 |
| INFLA-TAX | $16,635 |

**FIGURE 9-3**

---

\* Nominal rate of taxation = 26.75%
\*\* Real effective rate of taxation = 49%
    $54,325 adjusted earning / income tax paid $26,750 = 49%

*The Wealth Transfer of Inflation*

**SCHEDULE IV**

**Turbine Inc.**
**Equity Section of Balance Sheet**

CPI = Consumer Price Index
HCA$ = Historic Cost Dollar

**Schedule Showing Restoration of
Equity for Wealth Transfer of Inflation**

|  | HCA $ 12/31/19X1 | CPI $ 12/31/19X1 |
|---|---|---|
| Equity: |  |  |
| Undistributed Earnings |  |  |
| Year 12/31/19X0 | $ 56,750 | $ 56,750 |
| Year 12/31/19X1 | 73,250 | 27,575 |
| **Capital Restored 12/31/19X1** |  | 45,675* |
| Capital Stock | 500,000 | 500,000 |
| Total | $630,000 | $630,000 |

**FIGURE 9-4**

---

\* From Schedule II. Purchasing-power losses of equity capital restored by charge against income. See item 4, Schedule III, Profit and Loss Statement.

*Note:* Historic Cost computation of ratio of earnings to equity would be $73,250/556,750 = 13.16%. CPI's computation of the same ratio would be $27,575/$602,425 = 4.57%.

---

rapid rate than the Consumer Price Index. All that the Grady adjustment attempts to say is: "Look, the stockholders of Turbine Inc. could buy X quantity of the 382 goods and services measured by the Consumer Price Index at December 31, 19X0. If you want to maintain their ability to consume the same quantity of goods and services at 12/31/X1, you have to transfer from earnings $45,675 to their equity account." This is the financial concept of capital.

If this seems confusing, it illustrates the difficulty that accounting has in reporting the effects of the wealth transfer of inflation. If you want to know how much money is required to maintain the stockholders' command over household goods and services, you measure inflation's effect on the company by the Constant Dollar Accounting method. On the other hand, if you want to know the replacement cost of your assets and the ability of your firm to continue in business, you should employ the Current Cost Accounting method.

The Grady method is not perfect, but, as you will see, there are no perfect infla-accounting systems. All are flawed. But Mr. Grady's proposal has one great virtue that other infla-accounting systems do not have: it is simple, while being reasonably accurate. It should give small- to medium-sized firms enough information to keep them from paying out dividends from illusory profits. It should also give a clear indication of the real rate of income tax the firm is paying. It should make visible what has not been seen—the wealth transfer of inflation.

One of the criticisms that can be made of the Grady solution is that it does not report holding gains from monetary liabilities. I do not think the criticism is valid. If there are any monetary holding gains, they will appear as additional cash revenue and will be accounted for.

I believe that the two most practical, highly useful, easy-to-prepare financial statements that account for inflation are the Grady adjusted balance sheet and the Cash Flow Statement which we shall detail in Chapter 13.

**The Grady Infla-Accounting Method**
**Has An Important Application**
**To The Accumulated Earnings Penalty**
**Of Section 531, I.R.C.**

The Loss of Equity From Inflation adjustment to earnings shown above may be a potent defense against the accumulated earnings penalty often proposed by the Internal Revenue Service against closely held corporations (Section 531 of the Internal Revenue Code). If the adjustment show in Schedule II is made to profits for each year back to 1967, or to the year the business commenced earning profits, whichever is later, it will, in many cases, reduce the accumulated undistributed earnings below what would be considered necessary for the business. We do not know if the I.R.S. or the Tax Court would be persuaded by the evidence. We should think they would be.

## ARE THE SEVEN REPORTING ERRORS
## OF HCA IMPORTANT TO MANAGERS?

I think we are in agreement that inflation's redistribution of wealth affects every business. Some firms who are net debtors will experience a holding gain from debt—they will gain wealth. While others, who are net creditors, will experience a holding loss from monetary assets. They will lose wealth. The magnitude of the wealth transfer will be proportional to the amount of the monetary items held.

Historic Cost Accounting does not report these monetary holding gains and losses. But the wealth transfer both to and from a business is real—it is not an illusion, so the monetary accounting errors of HCA can vitally affect the interests of the owner-managers of a firm.

In contrast, the HCA errors of understating the cost of inventory and depreciation would not be of vital interest to managers if it were not for the income tax. The understatement of the cost of goods sold and depreciation do not transfer wealth. The number of units in an inventory are not changed by an accounting error. The useful life of a machine is not dependent upon the correct accounting for its useful life.

We do not mean to imply that managers cannot be misled by bad accounting. However, it is my experience that successful owner-managers of closely held firms do not put much faith in the information provided by HCA financial statements. Their accounting is essentially cash accounting. They equate profits with cash.

HCA accrual accounting statements have greater use outside the firm than within. The regulatory agencies, the taxing authority, and some creditors and bankers make decisions based on HCA statements. However, bankers and creditors are relying less and less on Historic Cost Profit and Loss Statements. The lenders of money and givers of credit are looking to the Statement of Cash Flow, similar to the one shown in Chapter 13, *Cash Flow Accounting,* which shows the amount of free cash a firm is generating. This makes sense because only cash will repay a loan or satisfy a bill.

HCA's reporting of depreciation and the cost of inventory sold has limited influence on the decisions management makes. If there is enough cash, managers will replace a machine that is uneconomic. The fact that the HCA depreciation account shows the machine has ten years of useful life remaining does not affect the decision to replace it. In fact, the managers or engineers who make the decisions as to when a machine should be scrapped may never consult the depreciation records. Similarly, the reporting of the cost of goods sold on an historic cost basis does not affect the decision to buy goods. For this reason, managers have little interest in accounting theory.

They listen with a glazed eye when I tell them that accrual accounting reports income, when no cash has been received—that a good part of the income reported is simply the recording of the expectation of receiving cash sometime in the future (accrued sales).

Their boredom is no less acute when I attempt to inform them that accrual accounting does not report costs, even though a large amount of cash has been expended for the purchase of merchandise and fixed assets. However, the "please get on with it, can't you see I'm busy" attitude dissipates immediately when management is given a P&L Statement which reports a large profit that is not accompanied by an equal increase in the cash account. Management shows an even greater interest when they are informed of the income tax that will have to be paid, in cash, on the alleged profit.

The point I am trying to make is that it is all very well to manage on a cash basis, but it is wrong not to know what Historic Cost Accounting is costing. The cash management is bringing in the front door may be going out the back door in tax payments on illusory profits and by the wealth transfer to debtors from holding monetary assets.

## NOTES

1. Paul Grady, Price Waterhouse Co. (Retired), in *Economic Calculation Under Inflation,* Liberty Press, pp.81-83, Helen E. Schultz, President.

# 10

## How To Determine How A Firm Is Funding The Cost Of Inflation's Wealth Transfer. Also, The Uses And Limitations Of HCA Financial Statements

Here we deal with factors that predict the future financial experience of an enterprise.

If you lend or invest money or if you give credit, you must spend some of your time in predicting the future. We daily attempt to forecast the future financial performance of our own firm and of those who owe us money—or would like to owe us money. It is our standard analysis procedure to review past years' financial statements, with the view that they will predict future financial performance.

This practice of looking backwards is derived from the assumption that the future will resemble the past. A large part of our future financial experience appears to be a random walk. Our next step may not at all resemble the one that preceded it.

Nevertheless, the past does repeat itself in many ways.

Business is a game of many variables. These variables can be classified as financial and nonfinancial. It is the heretical position of this chapter that it is the nonfinancial variables—like the batting average of the business person—that are the better predictors of the future financial success of an enterprise than are the financial factors.

It is naive to believe that HCA financial statements will accurately predict the future financial performance of a company. But HCA data can be made to yield useful information. One item of HCA information we can obtain from the balance sheet is the source of funds the firm is using to finance the loss of equity from inflation's wealth transfer. Are the funds derived from Capital, from loans, or are they derived from profit? There is a demonstration of how you can obtain this vital information through common size and index trend analysis. A firm has a terminal illness if it does not finance inflation's drain on equity with profits. This chapter, the chapter on *Cash Flow Accounting,* and the one on *Cash Flow Planning,* all deal with the problem of forecasting the future performance of an enterprise.

## CAN YOU PREDICT FUTURE FINANCIAL PERFORMANCE BY ANALYZING PRIOR YEARS' HISTORIC COST FINANCIAL STATEMENTS?

*Looking backwards while going forwards may be unsafe:* We attempt to predict future financial performance by analyzing past financial performance.

Mr. James R. Vertın, a distinguished and witty financial manager, likens this practice to "driving into the future with both eyes firmly fixed on the rear view mirror." Mr. Vertin counsels that this is not only unsafe, but it is also silly.

Mr. Vertin advises: "My experience has taught me that there is little value in looking backward. The past is not where the action is. It is necessary to look forward, to think in expectational probabilistic terms, and to make investment decisions accordingly."[1]

In contrast to Mr. Vertin's distrust of the predictive value of past years' financial statements is the unquestioning faith of financial analysts in yesteryear's data. They will assure us that Historic Cost financial statements will tell all and will reveal all about the future financial prospects of a company. The most ludicrous form of this gullible attitude is seen and heard, on a weekly stock analyst's television program.

Example: Television moderator, Smoothtalker, to panelist Chuzzlewitz, manager of a mutual fund:

> Chuzzlewitz, we have a letter from a viewer, Widow Brown. She writes that at the time of her husband's death, her broker advised that she should invest her widow's dowry in bonds. The broker said the bonds would give Ms. Brown a steady secure income. Widow Brown says the broker was right about the income being steady—it bought steadily less and less.
>
> She says she thought she had security in bonds, but now finds that the only security against the ravages of inflation is to

be employed. So Widow Brown has cashed in her bonds to raise the cash to purchase the tools of her new trade: a bucket, a brush, and a bar of soap. But she has money left over. She wants to know how it should be invested.

Panelist Chuzzlewitz: "I would recommend that Widow Brown buy a good growth stock like Excelsior Company. It sells for five times earnings and pays a good dividend of 6%. (In a year of 14% inflation?)

Here we have a stock analyst's expression of blind and undying faith in HC earnings. He quotes the price-earnings ratio, of five times earnings, as if it were cash in the bank. He does this while the Chairman of the S.E.C., members of the Federal Reserve Board, various presidents of financial institutions, editors of financial journals, and the Financial Accounting Standards Board assure us that reported corporate earnings are bogus.

Furthermore, Chuzzlewitz believes—as do many financial analysts—that corporate reported earnings of the past are predictive of corporate earnings of the future. There is no evidence that this is true. There is some evidence that it is not true—that earnings follow a random walk, and are, therefore, generally unpredictable.

Past years' financial statements are poor predictors of future net cash inflows. Even if the financial statements were inflation adjusted, they would still not serve as an accurate forecaster of profits to come. However, it is a truism that a rich and healthy firm is a better prospect for survival than one that is sick and poor, all other things being equal.

The source one consults to learn if a firm is rich or poor is the balance sheet. The indicators of health or sickness are found in the P&L Statement and in the unpublished nonfinancial factors of the enterprise. Of the two sources of information, it is the nonfinancial factors that are the better predictors of a firm's ability to pay its bills, reward its investors, and replace its worn assets. The nonfinancial factors I refer to are: the character and ability of management, the demand for the firm's products, the firm's ability to produce new products, the type of industry—is it a high profit or low profit industry? Is it in lumber, a low profit industry; or is it in broadcasting and telecasting, a very high profit industry? The political and economic prospects of the firm's markets are other nonfinancial factors that will substantially influence the firm's future profitablility. These are the expectational and probabilistic features that must be weighed in making the forecast of future financial health.

*Conclusion:* Financial statements are only one of the predictive factors to be used in analyzing a firm's future ability to reward its investors, to pay its debts, and to replace its used assets. But financial statements are a very weak reed with which to support a prediction of future net cash earnings. It is the nonfinancial factors that must provide the foundation for financial forecasting.

However, while HC financial statements may not be the best indicators of future cash inflow, they are one of them. Furthermore, financial statements are often the only source of information we have. So we must use them, like it or not. This being the case, let's turn to considering how inflation distorted HC financial reports can be made to yield information that will assist us in forecasting the future free cash of an enterprise. By free cash, we mean money generated through trading that is not needed to continue the enterprise in its normal operating condition.

This subject is also discussed in Chapter 13, *Cash Flow Accounting.*

**Historic Cost Statements**
**Accurately Predict Short-Term Liquidity**

If someone were to ask: "What's right about HC financial statements?" I would reply that HCA reports the monetary items shown on the balance sheet correctly. The cash reported is the exact amount of cash on hand, as of the date of the balance sheet. Similarly, the accounts receivable is the precise amount of cash due from customers. The accounts payable informs us of the amount of cash that will be paid to suppliers. The long-term debt account states the number of dollars required to pay off the lenders.

Since the dollar denominated current assets and liabilities are reported correctly by HCA, it follows that the conventional tools of financial analysis of short-term liquidity, the acid test ratio and the current ratio, are reliable indicators of an enterprise's short-term cash flow potential.

Acid test ratio:
$$\frac{\text{Cash + Cash Equivalents, and Receivables}}{\text{Current liabilities}}$$

Current ratio:
$$\frac{\text{Current Assets}}{\text{Current liabilities}}$$

The current ratio will be reliable only if the cost of inventory, included in the computation of current assets, has not increased over historic cost. However, if the inventory is stated at LIFO cost, the current asset ratio will be of no use whatsoever, because the value of the inventory will probably be grossly understated.

**The Long-Term Predictive Ability Of HC Financial Statements Is Notoriously Inaccurate—But Useful**

The long-term prediction of net cash inflow of an enterprise falls into the category of an event which has a large number of variables. By a long term prediction, we mean a forecast of a period in excess of six months.

The problem of treating a future event can be simplified by decomposing the problem into the vital few variables and the trivial many. That is, we should identify the variables, and then classify them as vital or trivial. We should concern ourselves only with the vital few.

The vital variable we shall discuss here is the inflation factor.

## WHY THE INFLATION FACTOR IS IMPORTANT TO FINANCIAL ANALYSIS

The inflation factor is important in forecasting future financial trends because the wealth transfer of inflation can make a heavy demand on cash. If we can demonstrate that the company has successfully funded inflation's demand on cash from earnings, then we can conclude the firm is probably well managed and that its prospects are worth further study. On the other hand, if the firm has not met the challenge of the wealth transfer of inflation, then we can tentatively conclude that the enterprise is not effectively managed. It must either change its perception of fiscal reality or run out of cash and out of business.

It would be ideal if we could discuss with management our analysis of the firm's ability to finance inflation from earnings. It would also be extremely desirable if we could study the various nonfinancial factors affecting the future net cash inflow of the firm, such as the future demand for the firm's products, the prospective economic conditions of its markets, the history of profits in the industry, etc. We would combine the analysis of financial statements with the appriasal of the nonfinancial factors.

## HOW THE WEALTH TRANSFER OF INFLATION WILL AFFECT FUTURE NET CASH INFLOW

The inflation factor is of primary importance in financial forecasting because it will make an irresistible demand on future cash inflow. The decline in the future purchasing power of the dollar, and the attendent rise in prices, will require the enterprise to continuously invest more and more money in inventory, monetary assets, and in fixed assets, just to maintain current normal operations.

The investment of additional money, just to keep the business operating at its present normal capacity, seems to contradict our financial expectations of what cash investment should do. Even after more than a decade of inflation, we still tend to think that the investment of additional money will result only in increased production, sales, and free cash flow. If such is our expectation, we reckon without taking into account the cash demands of the wealth transfer of inflation.

Of course, there will be offsetting cash inflows. The tide of inflation will also flow to the firm's advantage. Suppliers will be compelled to increase their dollar investment in the inventory and accounts receivable of the firm. We may also derive additional cash from holding gains from long-term debt. Loans can be increased without agumenting debt in real terms. But no matter how we finance inflation, we shall have to account for it. Otherwise our long-term forecasts will be erroneous at the start.

Let us now consider two methods for determining the source of funds a firm has used, in the past, to finance inflation's demand on cash—common size analysis and index trend analysis.

## HOW TO DETERMINE THE SOURCE OF FUNDS A FIRM HAS USED TO FINANCE INFLATION'S DEMAND ON CASH

A part of the procedure of financial analysis is to look at past P&Ls and Balance Sheets. We conclude from our review that if this is how the firm has financed inflation's cash demands in the past, this is how it will probably respond in the future. Ideally, our scrutiny of financial statements will go back ten years, to a time when inflation was moderate—when it did not significantly distort income or asset values. From this base period, we will be able to observe how the enterprise responded to the wealth transfer of inflation over the subsequent ten years of monetary instability—when the value of the dollar steadily declined.

To illustrate how we might analyze the firm's response to the inflation factor, I have chosen a computer-assisted study of Mr. O.F. Roach, F.I.A., a partner in the Australian firm of consulting actuaries, E. S. Knight and Company. Mr. Roach reported his finding in an article entitled, "Accounting for Changing Money Values," published in the *Chartered Accountant* in Australia, December 1975.[2] Mr. Roach's study demonstrates what will happen to the financial condition of an enterprise, during a 10-year period of constant inflation if it relies on historic accounts to set prices, to determine the amount of dividends that can be paid, and to determine profits on which income taxes are paid.

What Mr. Roach did was to develop a computer model of a company, operating at a constant rate of production over a 10-year period. During the that decade, the company fixed the selling prices of its products on the basis of historic cost, and declared as dividends the whole historic cost profit remaining after taxes. The FIFO inventory convention was used in computing cost of goods sold.

During the first 5 years under study—that is, the years 1X00 to 1X05—the rate of inflation averaged 6.2%. In the second 5-year period, 1X06 to 1X10, the rate of inflation averaged 12.7%. Perhaps this is better illustrated in a table:

| Period | Average Annual Rate of Inflation | Consumer's Price Index at End of Period |
|---|---|---|
| To end of year 1X00 | 0% | 100 |
| From end of year 1X00 to end of year 1X05 | 6.2% | 134.9 |
| From end of year 1X05 to end of year 1X10 | 12.7% | 245.0 |

**How To Make A Common Size Analysis**[3]

The financial results of Model Company's operations can be seen in Figures 10-1 and 10-2. The Historic Cost P&L Statement reports a steady profit—a net inflow of free cash, which presumably was available for distribution as dividends. The P&L Statement would also lead us to believe that the business was generating the funds to finance the yearly increased costs of inventory and fixed assets. However, we learn that this is not true when we apply "common size analysis" and "index trend analysis" to the Model Company Balance Sheet. From these two types of analysis, we learn that the firm failed to fund inflation's cash requirements from earnings.

## Model Company
### PROFIT AND LOSS STATEMENT

|  | Year 1X00 |  | Year 1X05 |  | Year 1X10 |  |
|---|---|---|---|---|---|---|
| Gross Sales |  | $1,185,502 |  | $1,548,202 |  | $2,714,083 |
| Less: |  |  |  |  |  |  |
| Cost of Sales | $1,069,597 |  | $1,374,477 |  | $2,380,252 |  |
| Depreciation | 68,565 |  | 74,387 |  | 104,172 |  |
| Interest and expenses | 12,330 | 1,150,492 | 39,820 | 1,488,684 | 153,164 | 2,637,583 |
| Income tax |  | $ 14,879 |  | $ 25,295 |  | $ 32,510 |
| Accounting Profit |  | $ 35,010 |  | $ 59,518 |  | $ 76,495 |
| Dividends |  | $ 20,131 |  | $ 34,223 |  | $ 43,985 |
| Profit carried forward |  | 0 |  | 0 |  | 0 |

**FIGURE 10-1**

## MODEL COMPANY BALANCE SHEET

|  | Year 1X00 | Year 1X05 | Year 1X10 |
|---|---|---|---|
| **Assets** | | | |
| Plant | $308,761 | $ 354,858 | $ 547,695 |
| Inventory | 378,817 | 506,380 | 911,771 |
| Accounts Receivable | 109,769 | 147,162 | 264,885 |
| Total Assets | $797,347 | $1,008,400 | $1,724,351 |
| **Liabilities and Equity** | | | |
| Accounts Payable | $ 49,520 | $ 66,758 | $ 121,213 |
| Bank Loan | 212,817 | 382,124 | 1,026,643 |
| Capital | 500,000 | 500,000 | 500,000 |
| Provisions for tax | 14,879 | 25,295 | 32,510 |
| Provisions for dividend | 20,131 | 34,223 | 43,985 |
| Total liabilities and equity | $797,347 | $1,008,400 | $1,724,351 |

**FIGURE 10-2**

### Model Company
### EQUITY TO ASSETS—DEBT TO ASSETS
### COMMON SIZE ANALYSIS STATEMENT

|  | Year 1X00 | Year 1X05 | Year 1X10 |
|---|---|---|---|
| Total Assets | 100% | 100% | 100% |
| Stockholders' Equity | 62% | 50% | 29% |
| Bank Loan | 27% | 37% | 59% |

**FIGURE 10-3**

---

Figure 10-3, the Common Size Analysis Statement, shows us that the percentage ratio of equity to assets fell from 62% in year 1X00 to 29% in year 1X10, ten years later. The analysis shows that the increase in the dollar value of assets was partially financed by equity. The ratio of debt to assets rose from 27% in year 1X00 to 59% in year 1X10. This tells us that the firm also funded inflation's wealth transfer by borrowing. Debt was increased in real terms to fund the company's loss of wealth from the decline in the value of the dollar. This precisely mirrors the debt condition of a large part of American manufacturing firms.

Common size analysis is simply the computation of the ratio of items on a balance sheet or profit and loss statement to a base item. You have made a common size analysis when you have computed the percentage of cost of goods sold to sales. In our example, we have confined our analysis to the balance sheet. We have established "total assets" as our base item (100) and computed the percentage ratio of other items on the balance sheet to it.

Example of the computation of equity to total assets:

Year 1X00 $\dfrac{\text{Total Equity per Balance Sheet}}{\text{Total Assets per Balance Sheet}}=$

$\dfrac{\$500,000}{\$797,347} = 62\%$, as shown in Figure 10-3

### How To Make An Index Trend Analysis[4]

The index trend analysis is even more revealing of the company's failure to provide, from earnings, the necessary cash to fund inflation's transfer of wealth. The Index Trend Analysis Statement, Figure 10-4, shows that by the end of the year 1X10 the Consumer Price Index stood at 245. In sharp contrast, the bank loan index of Model Company stood at 482. It had doubled the rate at which the cost of living had increased over the 10-year period 1X00 to 1X10. The value of debt had increased in real terms.

**Model Company**
**INDEX TREND ANALYSIS**

|  | Year 1X00 | Year 1X05 | Year 1X10 |
|---|---|---|---|
| Price Index | 100 | 134.9 | 245 |
| Total Assets | 100 | 126 | 216 |
| Capital | 100 | 100 | 100 |
| Bank Loan | 100 | 179 | 482 |

**FIGURE 10-4**

Please also notice that the stockholder's equity index, which should have kept pace with the Consumer's Price Index, remained frozen at 100, the index for the year 1X00. This tells us that the stockholders lost 60% of the purchasing power of their equity over the 10-year period under study (100 ÷ 245 CPI 1 × 10 = 40%).

The HC P&L Statements would deceive us into thinking that the firm had free cash to distribute as dividends. But the balance sheet tells the truth. The firm had little profit in real terms; little, if any, net cash inflow.

The computation of an index trend analysis is made by choosing a base year and giving it an index value of 100. In our example, we have chosen the year 1X00 as our base year. We determined our index trend by dividing each subsequent year's dollar total by the base year's dollar total.

Example of computation of index trend of asset:

$$\text{Year 1X05} = \frac{\text{Asset total for year 1X05}}{\text{Asset total for year 1X00}} - \text{the base year}$$

$$= \frac{\$1,008,400}{\$797,347} = 126 = \text{Year 1X05 Asset index.}$$

We can conclude, from the above demonstration, that although financial statements err in their reporting of income and financial conditions, they can be made to divulge information as to whether the firm has, in the past, financed inflation's wealth transfer from operating profits, or whether the firm has financed the wealth transfer from capital and borrowed money. Index trend and Common-size analysis inform us of this vital predictive fact.

We bring this discussion to an end by reporting one of Mr. Roach's important conclusions, arrived at by applying his computer model to a wide variety of model companies, operating under various conditions of inflation. He found that, for companies which regularly purchase new plant, the shareholders' equity ratio to assets will be halved:

1. If inflation is constant, up to and during a period in which all prices double.
2. If the firm uses historic cost to determine both income tax payable and dividend distribution.

Does this describe your company's experience? An index trend and common size analysis for the period 1970 thru 1979 will show you whether you are maintaining the equity of your firm in real terms. If you are not, it will show you how you are financing the wealth transfer.

## Conclusion

The analysis of historic cost financial statements may yield valuable information. However, we should not assume that past financial experience is predictive of future financial experience. There are too many variables in the future equation for them to be solved so easily.

Nonfinancial factors largely determine the future net cash inflow of a firm. The competence and integrity of management is the nonfinancial factor that will most influence the future financial experience of the company. The future demand for the firm's products, the firm's ability to develop new profitable products, and the condition of the firm's markets will all have their effect on future cash inflow. But, in the long run, the trend of these factors will be largely controlled by management. In the final analysis, we bet on people.

This is not to say that the analysis of financial statements is unproductive. Historic Cost balance sheets correctly report and predict short-term liquidity. The analysis of the balance sheet through index trend analysis and common size analysis, as shown in the Model Company example, will inform us as to whether the enterprise is financing the wealth transfer of inflation by earnings retention, or whether it is financing it by depleting capital or by borrowing. Whatever our findings, we will gain an insight into the firm's ability to meet the costs of inflation. However, this will not tell us of the firm's future ability to meet the cost of the wealth transfer of inflation. Our financial analysis of prior year's P&Ls and Balance Sheets will only yield information of the dead past. If we combine our financial analysis with our nonfinancial analysis, we will be able to think in "expectational probabilistic terms" about future net cash inflow.

For further discussion of how Historic Cost financial statements can be made to yield useful information, see Chapter 13 on *Cash Flow Accounting*.

## NOTES

1. James R. Vertin, "What Can The Future Tell Us About The Past?" *The Journal Of Portfolio Management,* New York, Fall 1979, p. 63.
2. O.F. Roach, F.I.A. "Accounting For Changing Money Values," *The Chartered Accountant in Australia,* December 1975.
3. Leopold A. Bernstein, *Financial Statement Analysis Theory, Application, and Interpretation, Revised Edition,* Richard D. Irwin, Inc. Homewood, Ill. 60430, pp. 465, 468-69.
4. Leopold A. Bernstein, *Financial Statement Analysis,* Richard D. Irwin Inc., Homewood, Ill., p. 606.

# 11

## The LIFO Convention Of Inventory: Zany, But It May Save You Money. It May Also Be An Accounting "Shuck And A Sham"

You may have seen, as I have, in business and accounting periodicals, the assertion that the LIFO method of inventory reports the cost of goods sold at their current market price. These articles also assure us that a firm using LIFO will avoid the income tax on illusory inventory profits. These assertions are incorrect. However, if the units of your inventory are increasing or are remaining constant while prices are rising, the LIFO convention of inventory can save you a bundle of money. Let's see why.

### WILL THE LIFO (Last-in, First-out) INVENTORY METHOD SAVE YOU MONEY?

The LIFO inventory method is an attempt to match current inventory costs with current revenues, while at the same time observing the Historic Cost maxim that the value of an item in inventory is determined by the number of dollars paid at its purchase. LIFO does not succeed in consistently matching current costs with current revenues but, under the right conditions, it will substantially reduce the income taxes assessed against illusory inventory profits. The tax savings can be huge, as can be seen in Figure 11-7. Those not interested in accounting theory may want to go directly to page 117 "LIFO May Reduce Your Income Taxes."

**LIFO Is An Attempt To Correct
Problem "A" While Creating Problems "B" And "C"**

Have you ever bungled a job of repair, as I have, and found that the more you attempted to correct it, the worse it got? You attempt to correct problem "A," but this creates new problems "B" and "C." You correct problem "B," and this creates problems "D," "E," "F," and "G." Well, this is the case with LIFO, the Last-in, First-out method of inventory accounting.

It was seen in industry that during a protracted period of inflation the Historic Cost system of accounting grossly overstated the profits of firms with large inventories. While the profits were a source of great satisfaction to managers, who are often judged on the magnitude of income reported, the illusion was frightfully expensive to maintain. An income tax had to be paid on what were imaginary inventory profits. While the Certified Public Accountants employed by the large firms were quite willing to assure the public that the phantom profits were real, there were some managers, directors, and accountants who thought the government should not be allowed to impoverish their employers—the stockholders.

The solution arrived at was to retrieve the LIFO convention of inventory from accounting's dustbin. Until its unexpected retrieval from oblivion, LIFO had languished in ill repute among the discarded ideas of accountancy. The Privy Council of England had banned it from English soil because it could not tell the fiscal truth (Anaconda American Brass). All the other industrialized nations, except the United States, confirmed the Privy Council in its adverse decision. LIFO was universally declared to be persona non grata. But the lords of U.S. accounting policy decided that LIFO was the cure for illusory inventory profits, and LIFO was therefore, accorded the honorable title of "Generally Accepted Accounting Principle." It is possible the Treasury forced the decision. Let's hope so.

**LIFO Is Premised On A Zany Idea**

LIFO is based on the zany idea that the value of an item in inventory is determined by the order it is withdrawn from stock. If an item is withdrawn from inventory in the order in which it was received—First-in, First-out, or FIFO—it is believed to have a different value than if it were withdrawn in reverse order; that is, Last-in, First-out, or LIFO.

An example of this remarkable LIFO thinking can be seen in Figure 11-1. The example contrasts how the LIFO and FIFO conventions of inventory would report the cost of a chair sold. The firm has two identical chairs in inventory. One was purchased on April 1 for $5. The other was purchased 20 days later, on April 20, for $10. One chair is sold on May 3. Which chair was sold? What is the cost of the chair sold? What is the cost of the chair left in inventory?

As can be seen, at LIFO costs, the chair sold at $10, the last-in April 20th cost, whereas at FIFO costs, the chair sold at $5, the first-in cost. If we assume that the value of the chair sold is determined by the inventory method we use, this makes perfect sense. But I think we would reject this assumption. We would insist that the value of any item in an inventory, to a going concern, is its replacement cost. In our example, that would be $12. However, if we were discontinuing the item—we would say its worth is its net realizable value—what we could sell it for minus sales costs.

---

*Example:* You have two identical chairs in your inventory:

| | |
|---|---|
| The first one received—April 1 cost | $ 5 |
| The second one received—April 20 cost | $10 |
| Replacement cost of chair—May 3 | $12 |
| A customer buys a chair May 3 for | $15 |

Under the LIFO method of Inventory, you would compute profit as follows:

| | |
|---|---|
| Sold chair for | $15 |
| Cost of chair, 4/20, last-in | $10 |
| Profit | $ 5 |
| Value of chair left in inventory April 1 cost (first-in) | $ 5 |

Under the First-in, First-out, (FIFO) method of inventory valuation, you would compute profit as follows:

| | |
|---|---|
| Sold chair for | $15 |
| Cost of chair 4/1 (first-in) | 5 |
| Profit | $10 |
| Value of chair left in inventory April 20 cost (last-in) | $10 |

**FIGURE 11-1**

## A LIFO Inventory May Report Goods On Hand That Were Sold

We have just discussed the LIFO premise that requires us to assume that the value of an item sold is determined by the order it is withdrawn from stock. This illogical premise requires us to make another assumption of equal merit. It requires that we pretend that units of inventory are withdrawn on a last-in, first-out (LIFO) basis, even though they are actually withdrawn FIFO, or first-in, first-out. The "let's pretend everything is sold LIFO" is necessary because shelf and rack inventories are withdrawn from stock in FIFO order, whereas bin and pile inventories are drawn down LIFO. Shelf and rack inventories are sold FIFO because they are perishable, like canned goods, or they go out of style, like women's apparel.

Bin and pile inventories are sold LIFO because they are not perishable and because it is impractical to draw them down on a first-in, first-out basis. If we have 1000 tons of coal piled in the yard, and we sell a ton of the fuel, we wouldn't remove all the last-in coal from the top of the pile, to get the first-in coal at the bottom, just to validate an inventory method.

The "let's pretend" fantasy that rack and shelf inventories are sold LIFO, when they are actually sold in FIFO order, produces a statement of inventory that is also fantasy—goods that have been sold, will be shown as still on hand.

Take the example of the electrical motor supply house. It has 1000 type A motors on hand on January 1. The motor manufacturer has greatly improved its product, which it designates as its type B motor. The supply house receives 1000 of these type B improved motors on January 5. The supply company sells the unimproved type A motors first. See how LIFO will reflect these facts in Figure 11.2.

Here we have the LIFO inventory telling us that we have 500 type A motors on hand, as of December 31, at a cost of $50,000, while actually we have 500 type B motors in stock at a cost of $62,500. The specific goods method I have shown in the example is rarely used now. Practically all firms have adopted the dollar-value LIFO method. They account only for the dollar value of goods, not for the specific items in inventory. In our example, the dollar value of the inventory would be shown as $50,000. Of course this is erroneous because the dollar totals of inventory are supposed to measure the value of goods on hand. We know that $50,000 does not measure the historic cost of 500 type B motors, and LIFO is an historic

| | | | |
|---|---|---|---|
| Inventory January 1 | 1000 type A motors | @$100 ea. | $100,000 |
| Add motors received January 5 | 1000 type B motors | @$125 ea. | 125,000 |
| Total motors available for sale | 2000 | | $225,000 cost |
| Sold during year: | 1000 type A motors | | $100,000 cost |
| | 500 type B motors | | $ 62,500 cost |
| Total motors sold | 1500 | | $162,500 cost |
| Actual motors on hand December 31 | 500 type B motors | | $ 62,500 cost |
| But LIFO, which pretends last-in type B motors were sold first, would report an inventory of | 500 type A motors | | $ 50,000 cost |

**FIGURE 11-2**

cost method of inventory. The historic cost of 500 type B motors is $62,500. However, we do know that the $50,000 figure measures the historic cost of 500 type A motors which were sold. So we cannot escape the illogic of LIFO's measurement of inventory by abandoning the specific goods LIFO method. It is silly to say that I can't tell you what the dollar total of the inventory measures. By definition, an inventory is a measurement of goods in stock, not of goods that were sold.

This is problem B, created while solving problem A.

**LIFO Errs In Stating The Value Of Inventory On The Balance Sheet**

Perhaps the most illogical aspect of LIFO is that it misstates the value of the inventory on the balance sheet. In our example, LIFO would report the inventory at $50,000, when actually its historic cost is $62,500. The error is corrected in a footnote to the balance sheet to the effect that the inventory figure shown is incorrect, that the real value of the inventory is something else. This is problem C created by attempting to solve problems A and B.

## The Accounting Justification For LIFO—
## When Does LIFO Report Inventory Costs
## At Current Prices?

Theoretically, LIFO provides a better matching of the current cost of goods sold to revenue than does FIFO. The last-in cost is presumed to be the current cost of goods sold. This is a large assumption. But even if we accept it as correct, we find that LIFO's correct measurement of current cost is dependent upon the movement of two variables against each other. The two variables are the prices of items, and the quantities of items in inventory. Are prices rising or falling? Are inventory units increasing or decreasing? LIFO's correct statement of current costs depends on how prices and inventory quantities move against each other.

If inventory quantities remain constant or are increasing, LIFO will correctly measure the current cost of inventory sold. This is true whether prices are rising or falling. See Figures 11-3 and 11-4. These figures compare the results obtained by using LIFO inventory costs with current inventory cost—the most recently paid price for goods purchased. You will see that LIFO states the cost of goods sold in the same amount as does Current Cost and reports the same profit. The reason for the agreement is that the prior years' inventory was not invaded. Quantities of inventory were increased so all goods taken from inventory were reported at the current price of $8 per unit.

Had the prior years' inventory been invaded, whose unit cost was $6, LIFO would have reported the unit cost at $6, not at the current cost, $8. The invasion of prior years' inventory levels is referred to as a "LIFO layer liquidation." "LIFO layer liquidation" occurs when we reduce the number of units in inventory below what it was at the close of the prior year. In other words, we haven't replaced inventory as quickly as we sold it.

Example of LIFO layers:

| | |
|---|---|
| Base year inventory | $1,000,000 (year of conversion to LIFO) |
| 19X1 layer | 241,000 |
| 19X2 layer | 303,000 |
| 19X3 layer | 167,000 |
| Inventory 12/23/19X3 | $1,711,000 |

This is an example of a company that has increased its inventory quantities in each of three years. If, by the end of 19X4, we have sold

## SCHEDULE SHOWING THAT LIFO STATES CURRENT COST WHEN INVENTORY UNITS INCREASE[1]
### *WHILE PRICES RISE*

| | \multicolumn{5}{c}{Prices Rise While Inventory Increases} | | | | |
| --- | --- | --- | --- | --- | --- |
| | Units | Price | LIFO | Units | Price | Current Cost |
| Sales | 100 | $20 | $2,000 | 100 | $20 | $2,000 |
| Beginning Inventory | 50 | $ 6 | $ 300 | 50 | $ 8* | $ 400 |
| Inventory Purchased | 120 | $ 8 | 960 | 120 | $ 8 | 960 |
| Inventory for Sale | 170 | | $1,260 | 170 | | $1,360 |
| Ending Inventory | 20 | $ 8 | | | | |
| | 50 | 6 | 460 | 70 | $ 8 | 560 |
| Cost of Goods Sold | 100 | | $ 800 | 100 | | $ 800 |
| Profit | | | $1,200 | | | $1,200 |

**FIGURE 11-3**

---

*Stated at current cost.

---

## SCHEDULE SHOWING THAT LIFO STATES CURRENT COST WHEN INVENTORY UNITS INCREASE
### *WHILE PRICES FALL*

| | Prices Fall While Inventory Increases | | | | | |
| --- | --- | --- | --- | --- | --- | --- |
| | Units | Price | LIFO | Units | Price | Current Cost |
| Sales | 100 | $18 | $1,800 | $100 | $18 | $1,800 |
| Beginning Inventory | 50 | $ 6 | $ 300 | 50 | $ 5* | $ 250 |
| Inventory Purchased | 120 | $ 5 | 600 | 120 | $ 5 | 600 |
| Inventory for Sale | 170 | | $ 900 | 170 | | $ 850 |
| Ending Inventory | 50 | $ 6 | | | | |
| | 20 | $ 5 | 400 | 70 | $ 5 | 350 |
| Cost of Goods Sold | 100 | | $ 500 | 100 | | $ 500 |
| Profit | | | $1,300 | | | $1,300 |

**FIGURE 11-4**

---

*Current cost is $5.

more merchandise than we manufactured in that year, we will have made a LIFO layer liquidation. We will have been forced to take merchandise first from the 19X3 layer, and proceed backwards into the LIFO inventory until we have accounted for the units of merchandise sold.

If LIFO layer liquidation happens while prices are either rising or falling, LIFO will not report the current cost of inventory sold, as can be seen in Figure 11-5.

## LIFO May Reduce Your Income Taxes

There isn't a competent manager or accountant in all business who would bother his or her head about the vagaries of LIFO, if it weren't for

### SCHEDULE SHOWING EFFECT OF LIFO LAYER LIQUIDATION

|  | Inventory Units Decrease Prices Increase | | | | Inventory Units Decrease Prices Decrease | | | |
| --- | --- | --- | --- | --- | --- | --- | --- | --- |
|  | Units | Cost | LIFO | C. Cost* | Units | Cost | LIFO | C. Cost* |
| Sales | 100 | $20 | $2,000 | $2,000 | 100 | $18 | $1,800 | $1,800 |
| Beginning Inventory | 50 | 6 | 300 |  | 50 | 6 | 300 | 300 |
|  | 50 | 8 |  | 400 | 50 | 5 |  | 250 |
| Inventory Purchased | 80 | 8 | 640 | 640 | 60 | 5 | 300 | 300 |
| Inventory Available | 130 |  | $ 940 | $1,040 | 110 |  | $ 600 | $ 550 |
| Ending | 30 | 6 | 180 |  | 10 | 6 | 60 |  |
| Inventory | 30 | 8 |  | 240 | 10 | 5 |  | 50 |
| Cost of Goods Sold |  |  | $ 760 | $ 800 |  |  | $ 540 | $ 500 |
| Profit |  |  | $1,240 | $1,200 |  |  | $1,260 | $1,300 |

FIGURE 11-5

*Current Cost

the fact that LIFO does reduce the infla-tax on illusory inventory profits. It will report a lesser income than FIFO, and thereby reduce income taxes; provided prices are rising, and the quantity of inventory remains constant or is increasing. Under these conditions, LIFO's effect is to defer taxes. The taxes deferred are the equivalent of an interest free loan of money from the government. In addition, since the government does not make an interest charge for inflation, the taxpayer realizes a holding gain from the declines in the value of the tax debt owed.

The almost unbelievable financial savings of LIFO—which managers have such difficulty in perceiving—can be seen when we compare the infla-tax a firm would pay under the FIFO and LIFO methods of inventory. Figure 11-6 vs 11-7. The medium sized firms in our example, save $1,778,445 by using LIFO instead of FIFO to compute its cost of goods sold over a 10 year period. See column (6), Figure 11-7, item (F).

The illustration assumes:

> An average of 7% inflation per annum for 10 years. The inventory in year 10 is identical to the inventory in year 0. That is, the inventory remains constant during the entire 10 years under study. The inventory turns over at least once each year.

A review of Figure 11-6 shows that when FIFO is used, the firm is required to report for tax purposes an illusory profit of $2,578,664, in order to fund a $967,000 increase in the dollar cost of inventory. (Figure 11-6, Columns (3) and (6).)

The 7% annual rise in prices, over a 10 year period, causes the dollar cost of the inventory to advance from 1 million year 0 dollars to 1,967,000 year 10 dollars. The taxing authority sees the $967,000 rise in the dollar value of the inventory as profit. They therefore tax it at both the corporate and individual levels.

The insane tax laws that govern the computation of the cost of goods sold under the FIFO convention of inventory, is premised on the wacky notion that the cost of items sold is determined by the number of dollars paid for their purchase. It is also assumed that items are sold first-in first-out. Thus, under FIFO, the company reports the cost of inventory vended in year 1 at prior year 0 costs, or 1 million dollars. But $1,070,000 are required in year 1, to express the value of the merchandise sold. Thus, the cost of goods vended is understated by $70,000, and taxable income is overstated by an equal amount.

*How Illusory FIFO Profits Are Taxed.*

| | |
|---|---|
| Illusory FIFO Inventory Profit | $70,000 |
| Corporate Income Tax Paid At Rate of 50% | 35,000 |
| After Tax FIFO Profit Is Credited to Equity As Undistributed Earnings | $35,000 |
| These infla-earnings are distributed to the stockholders in the guise of dividends, however the distribution is really a return of capital. The stockholders are taxed at 25% | 8,750 |
| Capital retained by stockholders after tax | $26,250 |

The point of the illustration is that a FIFO firm that raises its prices in an amount which will only fund the increased dollar cost of inventory, will lose substantial capital. In a period of price rises, a corporation must increase its revenue by the amount of the increase in dollar cost of inventory, plus the infla-tax that will be paid at the corporate and stockholders levels on the illusory inventory profits.

Formula for Computing the infla-revenue Required to Fund the Replacement Cost of Inventory, Figure 11-6, Column 3.

$$\frac{\$70{,}000 \text{ price increase to be funded.}}{\dfrac{1-25\% \text{ stockholder tax rate}}{1-50\% \text{ corporate tax rate}}} = \frac{\$93{,}333}{.50} = \$186{,}666 \text{ per year 1.}$$

Figure 11-6 was deliberately overdrawn to provide ease of mental computation. Most firms do not have a marginal tax rate of 50%. But even if the infla-tax were halved, the cost would still be appalling. Some would argue that it is unrealistic to assume that all retained earnings will be paid out to the stockholders. My reply is that neither firms nor stockholders are immortal. Therefore, at some time the stockholders or their estates or heirs will liquidate their holdings. When that happens, the illusory inventory profits, which have been added to equity will be taxed, either as dividends or as capital gains.

I have also heard it stated that a FIFO firm will not report illusory inventory profits if the inventory has a high turnover velocity. I think this is wrong, because each turnover of inventory will yield an added revenue, required to provide for the increased dollar cost of its replacement. This infla-increment will show up on the tax return as profit, and will be taxed.

Two-thirds of American manufacturing firms still use the FIFO inventory convention. It is my prayer that our demonstration will show them the error of their ways. But you don't have to take my word for it. The highly successful chairman of the General Electric Company, Reginald H. Jones states that: "The most damning thing is that nearly two-thirds of the inventory of U.S. industry is still accounted for on FIFO . . ." Interview with the New York Times, January 27, 1981, p 26.

Talk to any accountant and he will tell you how very difficult it is to get business managers to switch to LIFO. Once the accountant begins to explain the tax complications of the last-in first-out method of inventory, the manager loses interest. It is true that the tax regulations governing LIFO are unnecessarily complicated. It is rare that you find a person in the I.R.S. who understands them. Nevertheless, the switch to LIFO can be the difference between surviving or failing in business. LIFO saves cash.

Let's now look at the LIFO inventory savings portrayed in Figure 11-7. LIFO contrasted With FIFO.

Figure 11-6 shows that FIFO causes a firm to annually report a phantom inventory profit, which is taxed. In contrast, LIFO defers the reporting of the infla-profit until there is a LIFO layer liquidation—until prior year's low cost levels of inventory are invaded. In our example LIFO will carry the goods on hand at their 19X0 cost of $1 million, until such time as more goods are sold than are received in a year.

If the inventory were completely liquidated—the firm ceased to do business at the end of year 10—then LIFO would report the cost of goods sold at its year 0 cost of $1 million dollars, not at its year 10 investment of $1,967,000. Therefore, the cost of goods vended would be understated by $967,000, and earnings from trade would be overstated by an equal amount, or losses from trade would be understated by a like sum.

Let us assume that there was a profit of exactly $967,000, which would be a completely illusory inventory profit. In that case the firm would be assessed an infla-tax of 50% or $483,500 ($967,000 × .50), and the stockholders would be levied a 25% tax on the corporate after tax profit of $483,500 or $120,875. Total individual and corporate infla-tax would be $604,375. This illustrates that LIFO does not forgive taxes completely, it just defers them until a LIFO layer liquidation is made.

However, as Figure 11-7 demonstrates the infla-cost of LIFO is sub-

## SCHEDULE SHOWING THE INFLA-TAX COST OF FIFO

| (1) End of Year | (2) (000) Dollar Cost of FIFO Inventory | (3) (4)+(5)+(6) $s Required To Fund Increased Cost | (4) 50% Corp I.T. On Col. (3) | (5) 25% Indv. I.T. On (3)−(4) | (6) Increased Dollar Cost Of Inv. |
|---|---|---|---|---|---|
| 0  | $1,000 | 0           | 0           | 0         | 0         |
| 1  | 1,070  | $186,666    | $ 93,333    | $23,333   | $ 70,000  |
| 2  | 1,145  | 200,000     | 100,000     | 25,000    | 75,000    |
| 3  | 1,225  | 213,333     | 106,666     | 26,667    | 80,000    |
| 4  | 1,311  | 229,333     | 114,666     | 28,667    | 86,000    |
| 5  | 1,403  | 245,333     | 122,666     | 30,667    | 92,000    |
| 6  | 1,501  | 261,333     | 130,666     | 32,667    | 98,000    |
| 7  | 1,606  | 280,000     | 140,000     | 35,000    | 105,000   |
| 8  | 1,718  | 298,666     | 149,333     | 37,333    | 112,000   |
| 9  | 1,838  | 320,000     | 160,000     | 40,000    | 120,000   |
| 10 | 1,967  | 344,000     | 172,000     | 43,000    | 129,000   |
|    |        | $2,578,664  | $1,289,330  | $322,334  | $967,000  |

**FIGURE 11-6**

---

stantially less than that of FIFO. The bottom of column (6) tells us that LIFO saved the firm, 1,232,229 year 10 dollars in infla-taxes. In addition the deferral of infla-tax payments until the end of year 10, allowed the company to retain the use of the money that FIFO would cause the firm to pay out to the government. The value of the use of the money at 7%, yielded a benefit of 546,216 year 10 dollars. Total LIFO savings equaled $1,778,445.

The example illustrates that any firm with a high ratio of inventory to sales should investigate how switching to LIFO would affect their firm.

***Explanation of Column (3), (Figure B), "7% interest factor":*** The 7% interest factor was derived from subtracting the numeral "1" from the factors shown in the interest table, "The Future Worth of $1 Per Period With Interest at 7%, Annual Compounding.

## SCHEDULE SHOWING LIFO SAVINGS (CORPORATE ONLY) OF INTEREST AND VALUE OF TAXES DUE

| | | | | Convert (2) to Yr. 0 $s | |
|---|---|---|---|---|---|
| (1) Year | (2) Infla-Tax* Paid On FIFO | (3) 7% Interest Factor to Year 10 | (4) (2) × (3) LIFO Interest Savings | (5) Col. (2) Conversion Factor To Yr. 0 $s | (6) (2) × (5) Year 0 $s Value of Taxes Paid |
| 0 | 0 | | 0 | | 0 |
| 2 | $ 93,333 | .9671 | $ 90,262 | .9346 | $ 87,229 |
| 2 | 100,000 | .8384 | 83,840 | .8734 | 87,340 |
| 3 | 106,666 | .7181 | 76,597 | .8163 | 87,071 |
| 4 | 114,666 | .6057 | 69,453 | .7629 | 87,479 |
| 5 | 122,666 | .500 | 61,333 | .7130 | 87,460 |
| 6 | 130,666 | .4025 | 52,593 | .6633 | 87,062 |
| 7 | 140,000 | .3107 | 43,498 | .6227 | 87,178 |
| 8 | 149,333 | .225 | 33,560 | .5820 | 86,912 |
| 9 | 160,000 | .144 | 23,040 | .5439 | 87,024 |
| 10 | 172,000 | .0700 | 12,040 | .5083 | 87,427 |
| | | | $546,216 | | $872,182 |

(a) FIFO Tax Cost in Year 0 Dollars from Col. (6) — $872,182

(b) LIFO Tax Cost assuming liquidation in year 10:
$967,000 × .50 IT × .5083, present value
of $1 at 7% for 10 years — −245,763

(c) LIFO Savings in Infla-tax cost, year 0 $s — $626,419

(d) Convert Year 0 dollars to Year 10 dollars:
$626,419 × 1.9671, future value of $1 − 7% −10 year — $1,232,229

(e) Add LIFO interest savings, from Col. (4) — 546,216

(f) Total LIFO Savings in Year 10 dollars — $1,778,445

To retain $1,778,445 a firm in the 50% marginal tax
bracket would have to earn — $3,556,890

**FIGURE 11-7**

*FIFO Infla-tax from Figure 11-6

*The Wealth Transfer of Inflation*

*Explanation of Conversion Factor, (Figure A), shown in column (5):* The inflation rate averaged 7% per year. Therefore, the conversion factors shown in column (5) are taken from the interest table, "The Present Worth of One Dollar At 7%, Annual Compounding."

To summarize: Ideally, a firm that adopts LIFO should be immortal, never have a LIFO layer liquidation, and have inventory prices rise continuously. An enterprise that could meet these exacting standards would fully realize LIFO's purported tax benefits, because it would never be taxed on phantom inventory profits.

Some firms—usually very large ones—give the appearance of enjoying the Jovian attribute of immortality, but smaller firms do not. However, no firm, large or small, can assure itself that it will not invade prior years' inventory levels. In 1977, U.S. Steel had a LIFO layer liquidation which caused the firm to report an $88.2 million "LIFO Profit." This does not mean that it experienced a profit. It was not better off by $88.2 million. Rather U.S. Steel was worse off by the amount of income tax it had to pay on the $88.2 million illusory "LIFO Profit." "LIFO Profit" is TAXSPEAK for describing a loss from the taxation of illusory inventory profits.

### LIFO Will Report A Greater Profit Than FIFO When Prices Are Falling

Figure 11-8 shows that, when prices are falling, LIFO will report a greater income and cause a greater tax to be paid than will FIFO. It will do this whether the inventory units are rising or falling. Also note that the LIFO firm retains less cash than does the FIFO firm.

## HOW THE LIFO TAIL MAY WAG THE BUSINESS DOG—LIFO IS COSTLY TO MAINTAIN IN BOTH TIME AND MONEY

The accounting cost of converting to LIFO and maintaining it is significant, but the managerial costs may be even greater. LIFO may influence how much inventory will be purchased and, also, when it will be purchased. The longer a firm is on LIFO in a period of rising prices, the greater will be the potential tax liability if a deep LIFO layer liquidation is made. As in the case of U.S. Steel, which we just cited, a penetration of old low historic cost layers of inventory will trigger an illusory LIFO Profit to be reported, on which an income tax will be assessed.

## SCHEDULE SHOWING THAT
## WHEN PRICES DECREASE LIFO DOES NOT SAVE TAXES

|  | Inventory Increases Prices Decrease | | | | Inventory Decreases Prices Decrease | | | |
|---|---|---|---|---|---|---|---|---|
|  | Units | Cost | LIFO | FIFO | Units | Cost | LIFO | FIFO |
| Sales |  |  | $1,800 | $1,800 |  |  | $1,800 | $1,800 |
| Beginning Inventory | 100 | $18 | 300 | 300 | 100 | $18 | 300 | 300 |
| Inventory Purchase | 50 | $6 |  |  | 50 | $6 |  |  |
|  | 120 | $5 | 600 | 600 | 60 | $5 | 300 | 300 |
| Inventory Available | 170 |  | $900 | $900 | 110 |  | $600 | $600 |
| Ending Inventory | 50 | $6 |  |  | 10 | $6 |  |  |
|  | 20 | $5 | 400 |  | 10 | $5 | 60 | 50 |
|  | 70 | $5 |  | 350 |  |  |  |  |
| Cost of Goods Sold |  |  | $500 | $550 |  |  | 540 | 550 |
| Profit |  |  | $1,300 | $1,250 |  |  | $1,260 | $1,250 |
| Income Tax |  |  | 650 | 625 |  |  | 630 | 625 |
| Profit after Taxes |  |  | $650 | $625 |  |  | $630 | $625 |
| Change in Cash* |  |  | $550 | $575 |  |  | $870 | $875 |

**FIGURE 11-8**

*Sales – inventory purchase – income tax.

The Wealth Transfer of Inflation   119

Many factors can cause a firm to make a liquidation of prior years' layers of inventory. Strikes in the supplier's plant, demand in excess of what the supplier can produce, and acts of God can all cause a scarcity of supply, and result in an invasion of old low cost levels of inventory, which cannot be replaced by year end.

Poor demand for the firm's products can force management to consider reducing inventory quantities below prior years' levels. In this circumstance, management must weigh not only the business advantages and disadvantages of replacing inventory, but also the tax cost of a LIFO layer liquidation as well. This is the case where the LIFO tail may wag the business dog. It is the ultimate in accounting madness.

## HOW LIFO OFFERS THE UNSCRUPULOUS AN OPPORTUNITY TO MANIPULATE EARNINGS

A firm, with an intent to deceive investors and lenders, can fictitiously increase reported earnings through the simple expedient of letting the inventory run down below the point at which prior years' low cost levels are invaded. The effect of the liquidation in a period of rising prices is to report a fictitiously low cost of goods sold and an imaginary "LIFO Profit."

A "LIFO Profit" can also be reported if a firm reduces inventory quantities because of adverse business conditions or because it does not have the cash to maintain its normal levels of inventory. Under these conditions of LIFO layer liquidation, the enterprise's P&L Statement will report a fictitiously low cost of goods sold and, probably, a handsome profit. The P&L Statement may give a message of robust earnings when, in fact, the company is losing money in real terms.

Needless to say, the Profit and Loss Statements of firms employing the LIFO convention should be viewed with skepticism. Every LIFO balance sheet should also be viewed with doubt because it will not report the potential tax liability that will come due when there is a LIFO layer liquidation. This off-balance sheet liability may be substantial and awkward for a cash-short firm.

### Conclusion

The LIFO convention of inventory is an accounting grotesquery. It asks us to contort our thinking so that we assume that we draw our products down from inventory in the last-in, first-out order, even though we do not, and would not—if we have an inventory of perishable goods—because it would ruin us.

LIFO also asks us to pretend that the value of an inventory is determined by the order in which it is sold. It isn't. In addition, it requests that we inform the readers of our balance sheets, that the LIFO statement of our ending inventory is incorrect; that the historic cost is decidedly different.

If we perform these mental contortions, we are assured that LIFO will match the current cost of inventory sold with current revenues. As we have seen, this is true if inventory quantities are stable or rising. It is not true if the number of units in inventory has decreased below the prior years' level. Finally, we are informed that LIFO will reduce our income taxes because it eliminates the reporting of phantom inventory profits. This is false.

What LIFO may do is to defer the payment of an income tax on imaginary inventory profits. It will not forgive them completely. The best that can be said for LIFO is that it may confer an interest-free loan of deferred taxes and a wealth transfer of part of the taxes deferred. This may be a substantial benefit, particularly for firms that are growing rapidly and have a significant amount of inventory. It is worth the time of all managers of companies who have inventories to investigate the possible benefits of borrowing money through LIFO's tax deferral and wealth transfer.

*How to increase the odds in your favor:*

The odds are one hundred to one that, sooner or later, a firm that has adopted LIFO will experience a LIFO layer liquidation and be compelled to pay the consequent, often ruinous, infla-income tax. Given the certain operation of Murphy's law, it is a thousand to one chance that the inventory layer invasion will occur at the worst possible time—when the firm is cash-short. This is borrowed trouble, created by those in government and accounting who can't think straight.

Those who make accounting and tax accounting policy could greatly increase the odds, not only in our favor, but theirs, if they would cease to pretend that LIFO is a solution to the infla-inventory accounting problem. It isn't. I submit that the better practice would be to adopt the inventory accounting solution used by practically all the industrialized countries of the world: that is, to price index the cost of inventory. Indexing is not the perfect solution, but it is a sensible solution. Furthermore, it is honest.

The objective of price indexing of inventories for tax purposes is to measure costs and revenue by the same year's money. This is an inventory accounting convention that is light-years ahead of LIFO.

## NOTES

1. Pro-Forma suggested by Walter A. Varvel, "LIFO Inventory Accounting, Effects on Corporate Profits etc.," *Economic Review,* Federal Reserve Bank of Richmond, July/Aug. 1978.

# 12

## The Accountant's Duty To Clients, To The Public And To The Government

### ARE THERE TWO DIFFERENT DEFINITIONS OF INCOME?

The Federal government is essentially a service organization. Like the telephone company or an accounting firm, the government performs services and is paid for it. The income tax return is the bill for services rendered. Like any other bill, it should be correctly computed. Whether it is correct depends, in large part, on accounting's ability to accurately define income.

The accounting and economic definitions of income are identical. Income is the amount that can be consumed without invading capital. Or, if you prefer the modern tone-deaf economist's "nail on the slate" definition: "Income is—God help us—better offness." The AICPA Study Group on the Objectives of Financial Statements adopted, as their description of income, this accurate, but ear-offending, definition.

The legal definition of income differs little from that used by the economists and accountants. The Supreme Court, in deciding what constituted taxable income, said, in the leading case of *Doyle v. Mitchell Brothers:*

> In order to determine whether there has been gain or loss, we must withdraw from the proceeds an amount sufficient to restore the capital value that existed at the commencement of the period under consideration.
>
> (247 US at 184-188)

All of us are aware that taxable income is no longer arrived at by "withdrawing from the proceeds an amount sufficient to restore the capital value that existed at the commencement of the period under consideration." Nor is income defined, for tax purposes, as the ability to consume without invading capital. Nor is it characterized as "better offness."

Instead, we find that accounting reports taxable income in terms antithetical to its legal, accounting, and economic definition. Unconsciously, accounting has come to use two different languages to describe the same set of fiscal facts. One language is the true lexicon of accountancy. The other is the corrupted official tax-accounting language, which has its basis neither in economics nor in law.

The official tax accounting language was insinuated into the vocabulary of accounting by inflation.

While accountancy had its head in the sand, waiting for inflation to go away, someone inserted an official tax-accounting language into its vocabulary, called TAXSPEAK. Those of you who have read George Orwell's *1984,* will recognize that the term TAXSPEAK is derived from Orwell's Newspeak.

Both TAXSPEAK and Newspeak are antithetical languages whose use is enforced by the courts. The effect of an antithetical language is to cause the mind to confuse semblances with fact. How insidious it is! Do we not all speak and write TAXSPEAK without being conscious of it? How often have you seen the excellent and fiscally wise *Wall Street Journal, Barrons, or The New York Times,* use the antithetical TAXSPEAK term, "capital gains," in the sense of the following example?

### Examples of TAXSPEAK

*Taxable capital gains:* The proceeds from the sale of an asset, not held for sale, which exceeds the number of dollars paid at its purchase. For instance: Jane sells the stock of her closley held business for 200,000 1980 dollars. Her tax basis, determined at the date she commenced business, is 100,000 1967 dollars. TAXSPEAK causes our mind to report that Jane had a taxable gain of $100,000 when, in fact, she had an economic loss. The Consumer Price Index was 100 in 1967 when Jane started her business, but 230 in 1980 when she sold her stock. The value of the dollar declined by over 50%, so 200,000 1980 dollars are of less worth than 100,000 1968 dollars. Figure 12-1 shows that Jane had a loss of 30,000 1980 dollars. The illustration holds true for all sales of long-held capital assets.

*Taxable interest income:* A sum received from a borrower designated in the lending contract or imputed by the Internal Revenue Service as interest. Example: A payment of $350, designated as interest from a $10,000 bond, bearing 3½% interest, in a year of 10% inflation. The payment received is a return of capital. It can be nothing else because the lender is not better off. She is worse off by 6½% or $650, the amount by which inflation exceeded the rate of interest. (10% − 3½%).

*LIFO profit:* A taxable gain made by invading the lower historic cost levels of a LIFO inventory. The invasion of an inventory cannot produce an increase in the ability to consume unless you define income in terms opposite to its true meaning.

These are but a few examples of TAXSPEAK's antithetical definitions. What is truly remarkable is that the application of the definitions of TAXSPEAK to the computation of taxable income has elicited so little dissent from the accounting societies or from the keeper of the accounting conscience, the Financial Accounting Standards Board.

I doubt that there is any other profession that would permit the state to corrupt its technical language. Certainly the American Medical Association would not permit the government to require a diagnosis of cancer to be described as a state of well-being, or a headache to be defined as a condition of euphoria. Nor should the accounting profession permit the state to corrupt its language—to define income in terms antithetical to its true meaning.

## The Cost Of TAXSPEAK

The economic loss from defining income as what the government says it is, is obvious and calculable. But there is another loss that is not perceived, which cannot be measured. The loss I refer to is the right to hold property by rule of law—the right to hold property against the government. It is the liberty that distinguishes capitalist from collectivist governments. It is the liberty fundamental to capitalism. The legal right to hold property is one of our most precious liberties. No other right exerts so great a restraint on the tyranny of the state.

Accounting has a role to play in preserving our ancient right to hold property under law. It is the role of accounting to compute what is income and what is capital. The income tax law permits the taxation of income. It does not permit the taxation of capital. Therefore, accounting must define income and compute income as an increase in ability to consume, or as "better offness." In playing its role of reporting what the state may tax, accounting should be as neutral as truth. It should not prepare tax bills that are false. But, above all, accounting should not permit the government to use accountancy as a tool to wrongfully invade a client's property. It is as much to the advantage of the state, as it is to the advantage of the citizen, that the right to hold property under law be preserved.

Accountants should inform their clients when income for tax purposes does not meet the legal, accounting, and economic definitions of income. They should also inform their clients of the tax consequences of the government's invasion of property. The notice should accompany the income tax return on which the error appears.

Example of such notice is applicable to the case of Jane, who purchased stock in 1967, when the Consumer Price Index was 100, and sold out in 1980 when the CPI stood at 230:

"Dear Jane, please be informed that, while your sale of stock is reported as a $100,000 capital gain for tax purposes, you actually suffered a $100,000 economic loss as shown in Figure 12-1:"

Accounting organizations have an even greater responsibility to inform taxpayers when the official tax accounting rules permit the government to invade private property without the right of law: For instance, where the government is clearly in error in defining as taxable income the 7½% interest paid small savers in a year of 14% inflation. It is the duty of accounting societies to inform the public that the government's accounting is in error.

Finally, after due notice, accountants should refuse to characterize as income, on a tax return, what is not income. If the state insists on taxing what does not meet the economic and legal definition of income, accountants should require that the amounts be clearly labeled as something other than a wealth gain.

The surest cure for the stealth of inflation is to account for it—to honestly report its cost—to report who gained and who lost. Inflation cannot contend with truth. It exists only when we prefer to believe in semblance rather than fact.

## Conclusion

The only sure way to figure out how we are coping with inflation is with a brand new set of accounting tools that accurately measure its effect, in real terms. The first move in the right direction came in the form of the

|  | Price Index Divided by 100 | 1967 Dollars |
|---|---|---|
| Cost of stock in 1967 |  | $100,000 |
| Less: 1981 sales price of $200,000, divided by | 2.30 | 86,956 |
| Loss on sales of stock stated in 1967 dollars |  | $ 13,044 |

|  |  | 1981 Dollars |
|---|---|---|
| **Convert loss to 1981 dollars** |  |  |
| Restate loss in 1981 dollars $13,044 × 2.30 |  | $ 30,000 |
| Add income taxes paid on illusory capital gain of $100,000 .............. |  | 20,000 |
| Total loss of sale of stock ............. |  | $ 50,000 |
| But since you are in the marginal 50% tax bracket, you will have to earn $100,000 to replace your loss of capital of $50,000. |  |  |
| Tax that will be paid on $100,000 earned to replace loss of capital ............ |  | 50,000 |
| Therefore, your total loss from the sale of your stock is ...................... |  | $100,000 |

**FIGURE 12-1**

Financial Accounting Standards Board's (FASB) Statement No. 33, "Financial Reporting and Changing Prices." It requires about 1,000 of the largest publicly owned firms, starting with 1980 annual reports, to issue supplemental statements which show the effect of changing prices on the financial experience of these enterprises. The firms must account for inflation's impact on capital and earnings by the two inflationary accounting systems, Constant Dollar Accounting and Current Cost Accounting. We shall discuss both of these accounting systems in the third part of this book. It is the hope of the FASB that the inflation-adjusted financial statements will inform the lawmakers of the real income of enterprises and whether income taxes are being derived from income or capital. All accountants and business persons should give moral, economic, and political support to the FASB. No other organization can bring realism to tax accounting.

# Part 3

## Step-By-Step Illustrations For Adjusting Financial Statements For Price Level Changes

"... we must plant a guard
    Of thoughts to watch, and ward
At th'eye and eare (the ports unto the minde)
    That no strange, or unkinde
Object arrive there ..."

Ben Jonson—Epode

Accountancy's attempt to "plant a guard of thoughts to watch and ward" at the eye and ear is detailed in the chapters that follow. Our minds have been, and are now, beguiled by inflation's illusions, that trick the eye into perceiving and reporting phantom profits, but blinds it to losses that are real.

The watchers and warders that academic accountancy would plant at the door of our mind, are Cash-Flow Accounting, Constant Dollar Accounting, and Current Cost Accounting. These infla-accounting systems propose that we use a dollar which accurately gauges the value of revenue and acquisition costs. They would measure both income and expense by the same dollar unit of value.

However, each system of infla-accounting has a different objective. Constant Dollar Accounting insists that no profits should be struck before provisions have been made for the maintainance of the purchasing power of the stockholder's investment. Investors look to their equity account to provide future household goods and services. Constant Dollar Accounting would assure the stockholders that their future purchasing power has been maintained, by measuring income and acquisition costs by a Consumer Price Index dollar.

On the other hand, Current Cost Accounting postulates that the objective is to provide for the continuance of the firm. To realize this goal, the future higher dollar costs of operations must be provided for out of current revenue. Therefore, the current cost of operations must be measured by Current Cost or replacement cost dollars.

Cash-Flow Accounting also assumes that the objective of a firm is to survive and to continue in business. However, its proponents believe, that a firms longevity is best indicated by its ability to produce cash flows. Therefore, accounts should inform of whether the enterprise can meet its costs, repay its loans, and reward its investors. Cash-Flow Accounting would discover the information by measuring with an Historic Cost Cash Accounting dollar.

Also reviewed in this section is how to plan future cash flows during a period of inflation. This includes a discussion of the infla-charges that must be included in marking up goods.

# 13

## Cash-Flow Accounting: How It Works And How To Use It

**BUSINESS MANAGERS ARE CASH-FLOW ACCOUNTANTS**

Accountants frequently hear a client cry out in outrage and disbelief at the large profit, and the resulting income tax payable shown on the HCA Profit and Loss Statement. The sequence of events is as follows: The accountant hands the client the year-end P&L Statement. As the eyes of the client move from "Sales" down to "Net Earnings," an ominous silence seeps into the room. The client's blood pressure visibly rises and then comes the explosion!

"If," cries the client, "we made so much blankety blank PROFIT, where in Henry Hogan's Hades is all the dashedy dash MONEY?"

The client's query: ". . . where is all the money?" reveals that he or she defines PROFITS to mean CASH. Successful business people know that accounting profits will buy nothing. They know that only cash will enable the company to survive—to continue in business. Only cash will meet the costs of operations, repay loans, and pay dividends. A firm can continue to operate in the red for years if it has money. But the day the enterprise runs out of cash is the day it runs out of business—unless it is an industrial giant. In that event, it is the day it runs to Congress for a loan guarantee.

For these reasons, those responsible for the management of businesses expect profit to represent money. It is also their expectation that financial statements will communicate the cash inflow and outflow of their firm, so that the net income reported will represent a measure of the firm's liquidity. Successful managers are Cash-Flow accountants, though they may not know it.

# WHY MANAGERS SHOULD BE JUDGED ON THEIR ABILITY TO PRODUCE CASH PROFITS

Managers are correct in their belief that profits should be a measure of the firm's liquidity. It is also reasonable to say that managers should be judged on their ability to produce cash profits, rather than bookkeeping profits, because the production of cash is the primary objective of practically all businesses. All investments, whether in projects, machines, or in an entire business, are made with the expectation that the funds invested will be returned along with a reasonable cash profit.[1]

If managers are to be judged on their ability to produce cash profits, the accountng system used should show if the objective is being met.[2] Cash-Flow Accounting (CFA) is uniquely able to report the data. It states, clearly, the net cash flow—money that has been generated by the business, project, or machine, after operating costs have been paid for. It enables managers to track the return of capital and the production of cash profits. No other system of accounting provides this information so clearly and with so little distortion from inflation.

**Cash-Flow Analysis Provides Very Useful Information To Investors, Creditors, And Lenders**

CFA postulates that the value of the equity in a firm is dependent upon the present value of future cash flows to investors.[3] That agrees precisely with the investor's concept of equity.

At the time of this writing, most stocks on the exchanges are selling for considerably less than their inflation-adjusted book values. I think investors are correct in their low opinion of the value of stocks. They appraise the equity of an enterprise at its present value of future cash flows. A firm that cannot produce a cash flow that will return the value of money invested, plus a rent for the use of the investor's cash, as adjusted for inflation, is of limited worth.

If you want to determine if an investment in a firm is justified, run a three-year Cash-Flow Analysis (see Figure 13-2) on the enterprise. It will show you what the present value of future cash flows might be.

If you are a creditor or a lender, you, too, will want to determine the liquidity of the debtor firm on the basis of the present value of future cash flows. The computation will inform you as to whether the enterprise is generating enough money to pay its bills on time. It will also demonstrate the company's ability to generate enough cash in the future to pay off a prospective loan.

## WHAT IS CASH-FLOW ACCOUNTING?

If you define profits to mean free cash, and if you link profitability with liquidity, you will be interested in Cash-Flow Accounting (CFA) because it also defines profits to mean free, unencumbered cash. It is a system of accounting uniquely able to accurately measure income and acquisition costs in a period of inflation. It measures the cash inflows and outflows of a business by the current year's dollar. As a result, the Cash-Flow Analysis Statement does not report illusory infla-profits. (See Figure 13-2.)

## CASH-FLOW ACCOUNTING IS ACCOMPLISHED BY THE PREPARATION OF A CASH-FLOW ANALYSIS STATEMENT

CFA uses Historic Cost data. All that is required to convert Historic Cost Accrual data into Cash-Flow data is to prepare a Cash-Flow Analysis Statement, also known as "Source and Application of Cash Statement." The source of information used in preparing a Cash-Flow Analysis Statement is the Historic Cost Balance Sheet and related P&L Statement. (See Figures 13-1 and 13-2.)

Cash-Flow Accounting is simplicity itself. You can convert an Historic Cost P&L Statement and Balance Sheet into a Cash-Flow Analysis Statement in a few hours time.

## HOW TO CONVERT AN HCA PROFIT AND LOSS STATEMENT INTO A CASH-FLOW ANALYSIS STATEMENT

Before discussing the mechanics of preparing a Cash-Flow Analysis Statement, let's take a look at one, shown in Figure 13-2. Figure 13-2 shows how differently Historic Cost Accounting and Cash-Flow Accounting (CFA) report the same set of accounting facts. HCA, which uses accrual accounting and is divorced from cash, informs us that the B-1 Company had net earnings of $266,000. But CFA, which is cash accounting, sharply disagrees. It insists that B-1's profits were only $12,000—see line

(9) of the CFA column. CFA arrives at this conclusion because it defines profits to mean cash.

The HCA Profit and Loss Column leaves us wondering where the net earnings were expended. In contrast, the CFA column tells us precisely where the firm's cash inflow was disbursed. It also informs us about the source of funds received. For instance, it says that, if we had not received additional credit from suppliers in the amount of $301,000 (line 10), B-1 Company would have had a negative net cash inflow of $289,000, despite the $266,000 profit reported by HCA ($301,000 − $12,000).

I think you will find that the contrasting HCA and CFA data shown at Figure 13-2, is very useful financial information. The uses of the CFA information will be detailed under the heading "Explanation of Adjustments," which will immediately follow Figure 13-3, "Reconciliation of Cash, etc." Accountants will recognize that the CFA column is a rearrangement of the "Source and Application of Funds Statement." It is believed that the rearrangement presents information concerning cash flow in a more useful form than does the traditional "Funds" statement. I would suggest to accountants who know the mechanics of preparing the CFA column that they skip over to the discussion of the adjustments.

For those who are uncertain about how the CFA figures were arrived at, let me explain the procedure: Our objective is to determine from the Historic Cost Balance Sheet and the Profit and Loss Statement the cash income and the cash outlays of B-1 Company for the year 19X1. The information can be arrived at by removing the accrued income and expense from the accounts in the Balance Sheet and the P&L Statement. Specifically, we must:

1. Remove from income amounts of revenue for which no cash has been received. These amounts were derived from unpaid credit sales.
2. Increase costs reported, like Cost of Goods Sold, by the amount of cash expended for their acquisition but suspensed in asset accounts in the balance sheet.
3. Decrease the amount of expenses reported for which no cash has been expended, as, for instance, depreciation.

Examples of these adjustments:

1. Accrual accounting records sales when merchandise has been sold on credit. The bookkeeping entry to record the extension of credit to customers is: debit Accounts Receivable, credit Sales. The entry

does not represent the receipt of cash; it is only the recording of the expectation of receiving cash sometime in the future. So, to arrive at our objective of stating the firm's actual cash inflow from trading, we must reduce sales by the amount of credit extended to customers for which no cash has been received. This amount is indicated by the increase in the Accounts Receivable balance. See adjustment (A) in the Balance Sheet, Figure 13-1.

The Balance Sheet, Figure 13-1, shows that Accounts Receivable increased by $337,000 in the year 19X1. We know that this amount is included in the HCA Sales Figure on the P&L Statement, Figure 13-2. So we reduce HCA sales of $8,490,000 by $337,000 to arrive at the cash actually received: that is, $8,153,000, as shown in the CFA column.

2. We must increase costs by the amount of cash disbursed but suspensed in such accrual accounts such as Inventory. For example: The Cost of Goods Sold is increased in Figure 13-2 by $253,000, because that is the amount of money expended for goods and services, but suspended in the Balance Sheet accrual account "Inventory." See adjustment (B), Figure 13-1 and 13-2.

3. Accrual accounting reports expenses for which no cash was disbursed in the current year. Depreciation is one of those accounts. So the amount reported for such accounts is returned to cash income. See adjustment (C).

## Explanation Of Adjustments Made To Arrive At Cash Flow (See Figure 13-2)

*Adjustment (A) explanation:* The accrued Sales total $8,490,000 is reduced by $337,000, the amount of credit sales for which no cash was received in the year 19X1. Cash receipts from trading were, therefore, $8,153,000, as shown in the CFA column, line (1). If the firm had received nontrading income, the amount would be shown immediately after "Net Operating Cash Flow," line (9).

*Comment on adjustment (A): Cash Flow Analysis will discover fraud.* Accrual accounting offers the dishonest a golden opportunity to inflate profits and net worth by the simple expedient of an accounting entry. I

### B-1 COMPANY
(000)
**Balance Sheet To Figure 13-2**

|  | 12/31/X1 | 12/31/X0 | CFA | P&L State. |
|---|---|---|---|---|
| **Current Assets** | | | | |
| Cash in Bank & on Hand | $ 102 | $ 26 | $ 76 (16)* | |
| Accounts Receivable | 936 | 599 | | $337 (A) |
| Inventory | 725 | 472 | | 253 (B) |
| Prepaid Expense | 72 | 30 | 42 (17) | |
| Total Current Assets | $1,835 | $1,127 | | |
| **Fixed Assets** | $ 434 | $ 317 | 117 (15) | |
| Less Depreciation | 118 | 72 | | 46 (C) |
| Total Fixed Assets | $ 316 | $ 245 | | |
| **Other Assets** | | | | |
| Cash Surrender Value of Insurance Policy | $ 26 | $ 13 | 13 (18) | |
| Total Assets | $2,177 | $1,385 | | |
| **Liabilities and Equity** | | | | |
| Accounts Payable | $ 655 | $ 354 | 301 (10) | |
| Loan Payable to Bank | 300 | 360 | (60) (19) | |
| Accrued Profit Sharing | 117 | 74 | | 43 (D) |
| Federal and State Tax | 249 | 2 | | 247 (E) |
| Total Liabilities | $1,321 | $ 790 | | |
| Stockholders' Equity | 861 | 595 | | |
| Less Dividend | 5 | | 5 (20) | |
| Total Liab. & Equity | $2,177 | $1,385 | | |

**FIGURE 13-1**

---

*Refers to line number on CFA column.

**B-1 COMPANY**

### Profit And Loss Statement And Cash-Flow Analysis Statement
### For Period Ended December 31, 19X1

HCA = Historic Cost Accounting P&L  
CFA = Cash-Flow Analysis Statement

|  | (000) HCA | Adjustments + Cash Flow | Adjustments − Cash Flow | (000) CFA |
|---|---|---|---|---|
| Sales | $8,490 |  | $337 (A) | $8,153 ( 1) |
| Less Cost of Goods Sold | 5,454 |  | 253 (B) | 5,717 ( 2) |
| Total | $3,026 |  | $590 | $2,436 ( 3) |
| Less Expenses | 2,193 | $ 46 (C) |  | 2,147 |
| Total | $ 833 |  |  | $ 289 ( 5) |
| Less Profit Share Cont. | 117 | 43 (D) |  | 74 ( 6) |
| Earnings before Taxes | $ 716 |  |  | $ 215 ( 7) |
| Less Tax on Income | 450 | 247 (E) |  | 203 ( 8) |
| Net Earnings | $ 266 |  |  |  |

|  |  |
|---|---|
| NET OPERATING CASH FLOW | $ 12 ( 9) |
| Add: *External Financing* |  |
| Increase in Accounts Payable | 301 (10) |
| Bank Loan | 0 (11) |
| Stockholders' Contributions | 0 (12) |
| TOTAL CASH INFLOW FROM ALL SOURCES | $ 313 (13) |
| **APPLICATION OF CASH TO PURCHASE FIXED ASSETS:** |  |
| Replacement of Plant and Equipment That Did Not Increase Productive Capacity | $ 0 (14) |
| Improvements Made to Increase Productive Capacity | 117 (15) |
| **APPLICATION OF CASH TO OTHER PURPOSES:** |  |
| Increase in Cash Balance | 76 (16) |
| Increase in Prepaid Expense | 42 (17) |
| Increase in Cash Surrender Value of Insurance | 13 (18) |
| Reduction in Bank Loan Balance | 60 (19) |
| Dividend | 5 (20) |
| TOTAL | $ 313 (21) |

**FIGURE 13-2**

**B-1 COMPANY**

**Reconciliation of Cash on Hand And in Bank**

| | | |
|---|---:|---:|
| Cash on Hand and in Bank, 1/1/19X1 | | $ 26 |
| Add: Total Net Cash Inflow (Item 13, Fig. 13-2) | $313 | |
| Less: Total Cash Expenditures | 237* | |
| Equals Increase in Cash Balance (Item 16) | | 76 |
| Cash On Hand and in Bank, 12/31/19X1 per Balance Sheet | | $102 |

*Schedule of Cash Expenditures From Figure 13-2.

| | |
|---|---:|
| Increase in Shipping Capacity | $117 |
| Increase in Prepaid Expense | 42 |
| Increase in Surrender Value of Insurance | 13 |
| Reduction in Bank Loan | 60 |
| Dividend | 5 |
| Total | $237 |

**FIGURE 13-3**

---

have a thick file of newspaper clippings that tell the sad and often-told story of investors, creditors, lenders, and accountants who were duped by false financial data. All of the fraud reported in my file lacked one vital element—CASH!

How often were investors and lenders defrauded by financial statements that overreported income. The imaginary revenue was most often created by inflating accounts receivable on the balance sheet and sales on the P&L Statement. Accrual accounting, which disassociates profits from cash, makes possible this type of fraud. Airy income can be created by doing nothing more than debting accounts receivable and crediting sales. This act of accounting legerdemain creates accrued income, a deceptive thing void of cash, but full of promise for the gullible—the promise of a rich reward in the future.

The management of Equity Funding is said to have used this accounting device to create $77 million in profits. CPAs, investment analysts, creditors, and investors were all taken in by these gaseous earnings. But they need not have been. A cash-flow analysis would have revealed that the profits reported were not confirmed by cash.

Cash-Flow Accounting makes the fraudulent practice of overstating sales self defeating. The greater the puffing of revenue, the smaller the cash inflow reported. For example: If the B-1 Company had attempted to puff its sales in the amount of $100,000, its cash inflow, as reported in the CFA column, would decrease by an equal amount. Cash inflow would decrease because adjustment (A), whose purpose is to subtract credit sales, would cause CFA cash inflow to decrease by $100,000. Net Operating Cash Flow, item 9, would also decline from $12,000 to a negative $88,000 ($100,000 − $12,000).

The firm's management would be hard put to explain how B-1 could report $226,000 historic cost profit, but a negative $88,000 Net Operating Cash Flow. It would cause us to inquire into the validity of the value of accounts receivable. This demonstrates what bankers and creditors have learned: Cash flow analysis reveals fraud in financial statements. All inflated earnings lack one vital element—CASH!

*Cash-Flow Analysis lacks comparability:* While CFA will give an accurate statement of cash income, it may, at the same time, give an erroneous impression of business growth. In a period of inflation, when an ever increasing number of dollars are required to measure the same quantity of goods and services, income can appear to increase from one year to the next. The nominal dollar increase in income can give the illusion that the firm is experiencing vigorous growth while, in reality, it may be in decline. The solution to the problem is to convert all amounts being compared to a constant value dollar. Or one can compare product units sold. (See Chapter 8.)

*Adjustment (B) explanation:* The accrual accounting convention does not report the cost of inventory at the time it is paid for. It suspends the cost until it can be associated with the income it is thought to produce. The B-1 Company paid $253,000 for merchandise that was suspensed in the inventory account. Adjustment (B) causes the Cash-Flow Accounting column to record the actual amount of money paid out for inventory in the year 19X1.

*Comment on Adjustment (B): Inventory is a fixed asset.* CFA theory holds that inventory is a fixed asset, similar to land, because its value will not be realized in cash until the firm ceases to do business. Since CFA equates profits with unencumbered cash, it does not recognize revenue that is tied up in inventory.

*Example:* A supermarket opens in a shopping mall. The day it opens its doors it will have on hand merchandise valued at approximately $300,000. It will maintain that investment in constant dollars so long as it in business. The value of the inventory cannot be withdrawn from the firm until it ceases to do business. Therefore, the inventory is not unlike the building it is housed in. It cannot be disposed of until the enterprise closes its doors. That is, so long as it is a going business, it must always replace goods sold with an equal amount of goods, unless, of course, its business falls of drastically.

*Adjustment (C) explanation:* Depreciation deduction of $46,000 required no cash expenditure. So it is added to cash flow.

CFA charges off all fixed assets as they are paid for. Therefore, there are no deferred expenses for plant and equipment that need be charged off over a period of years in units of money whose value is constantly declining.

*Adjustment (D) explanation:* Adjustment (D) is made to reflect the actual cash payment made to the profit sharing fund in the year 19X1 in the amount of $74,000.

*Adjustment (E) explanation:* To report cash disbursed to pay income taxes in the Year 19X1, in the amount of $203,000.

*Comment on Adjustment (E): Where did all the money go?* When outraged clients ask: "If we made so much profit, where is all the money?" The answer is: "Sir or madam, the government has taken your money, but has generously left you with the profit." The truth of this statement is shown in lines (7) and (8) of the CFA column, Figure 13-2. B-1 Corporation had $215,000 CFA earnings before taxes. But cash expenditure for income taxes took $203,000, or 95% of the free cash the firm generated. So the government took the firm's cash but left the profit which, according to the Historic Cost Accounting column, was $266,000. What could be fairer?

*Explanation of Adjustment (10) increase in Accounts Payable:* The increase in Accounts Payable of $301,000 represents additional credit suppliers provided B-1 Company in the year 19X1.

*Comment on adjustment (10): Accounts Payable is a loan for an indefinite term:* Please note that adjustment (10) is carried from the Balance Sheet to the CFA column, line 10, where it is shown as "External Financing." While no cash was actually transferred to B-1, the creditor's extension of $301,000 additional credit has the effect of a loan of money. These are revolving funds that usually must be repaid each 30 to 60 days. The funds are invested in inventory and accounts receivable, possibly cash. The location of the funds depends on the velocity of the firm's cash cycle. It should be our inquiry to determine whether these accounts will liquidate the debt.

*Adjustment (15) improvements to increase productive capacity. Explanation and comment:* Cash Flow Accounting states separately the cash expended for improvements which will increase unit output, and should, therefore, increase free cash flow in the future. Investors and lenders will find the information to be of value. Greater capacity for output will promise investors an increase in dividends and lenders a larger security for their loans.

CFA also reports, separately, the amount of cash invested to maintain current normal operating facilities. Line (14) of the CFA column informs us that no cash was expended for the replacement of plant and equipment to maintain present operating capacity. The Historic Cost P&L Statement reports that a charge of $46,000 (Adjustment (C)) was made for depreciation. But the CFA column tells us that none of the $46,000 was expended for the replacement of plant and equipment. However, we know that this practice cannot continue without injury to the operating efficiency of the business.

Managers have paid dividends for a protracted period of time from funds that should have been expended for repairs and replacements. It is done to placate the demands of investors. It is frequently alleged that this practice has wide currency in American firms, and that this debilitating practice has caused us to lose our ability to compete with foreign industry.

A cash-flow analysis will demonstrate the source of funds used to pay dividends. In the case of the B-1 Company, it is obvious that the dividend payment of $5,000 came from funds that should have been husbanded for the replacement of assets. CFA will also inform us of whether the replacement and repairs are being funded from borrowed capital—a frequent practice of utilities.

A useful ratio for determining whether a firm is making repairs and replacements on a timely basis is to compare the cash expended for these items to the current cost of depreciable assets in use. The result of the computation will reveal the number of years required to liquidate the investment. At least three consecutive years should be used in the study.

*Example:* Replacement cost of depreciable assets year 19X3.

$$\frac{\$800{,}000}{\$ \ 20{,}000} = 40 \text{ years.}$$

Average 3-year/annual cash expenditure

Few firms have a life of 40 years or even 30 years.

## CASH-FLOW ANALYSIS REQUIRES THAT WE MAKE A STUDY OF THE CURRENT YEAR AND THE TWO PRIOR YEARS. IN ADDITION, WE SHOULD MAKE A CASH-FLOW FORECAST FOR THE ENSUING YEAR

The objective of financial analysis is to provide one of the factual bases for predicting whether a firm will be able to pay off its loans, pay dividends, and satisfy the suppliers' bills. A Cash-Flow Analysis of the current and the two prior years' operations will provide a good indication of the financial health of the firm. The cash-flow analysis should also include a cash-flow forecast for the succeeding year. See Chapter 14.

## WHAT'S WRONG WITH CASH-FLOW ACCOUNTING?

The primary fault of Cash-Flow Accounting is that it doesn't produce a balance sheet because it expenses all items purchased. As a consequence, it retains no record of inventory on hand, or fixed assets, etc. Those who lend, extend credit, or invest need to be informed about the value of these assets. Lenders look to the firm's inventory, accounts receivable, and fixed assets as their ultimate source of funds for liquidating a loan.

Furthermore, only a balance sheet will show the liabilities that must be paid. A review of the B-1 Company's Balance Sheet shows the company had to meet liabilities in the approximate amount of $1 million within 2 to 90 days, after December 31, 19X1. This information is indispensible to creditors, investors, and managers.

There is no need to belabor an obvious point. Balance Sheets are indispensible. Fortunately, CFA's lack of a balance sheet is easily remedied. We can use the Historic Cost Balance Sheet, as adjusted for inflation by the Grady method explained in Schedules I-IV, Chapter 9.

However, while the Historic Cost Balance Sheet will inform us of the value of monetary items and equity as adjusted for inflation, it will not prevent cash accounting from reporting extremes in income and loss from year to year.

It is the function of the balance sheet to smooth out the reporting of net income from operations. The balance sheet is an accrual accounting invention whose purpose is to store the value of acquisitions until they can be associated with goods sold. In contrast, cash accounting does not attempt to associate costs with revenues produced. It charges off all acquisitions when paid for. This can cause net income to lurch from gain to loss and from loss to gain when, in fact, common sense would tell us that the earnings of the enterprise are stable.

**Conclusion**

Cash-Flow Accounting is a system of inflationary accounting you can use now, at little cost of time or money. CFA reports fiscal reality in large measure.

Cash-Flow Accounting assumes that the primary objective of a company is to survive and to continue in operation. This means that the firm must have the ability to meet its costs, repay its loans, and pay dividends. The proponents of Cash-Flow Accounting believe that the accounting system should show to what extent these objectives are being achieved.

Cash-Flow Accounting also assumes that the value of the equity in a firm is dependent upon the present value of future cash flows to the investors. Investors expect the return of their capital plus a reward for the use of their money in cash. The accounting system should, therefore, show the source and the amount of cash distributed or available for the payment of dividends and return of capital. This information should be presented in a clear, concise manner.[4]

The advantages of Cash-Flow Accounting are:

- It accounts for inflation. It measures revenue and acquisitions costs by the same standard of measurement: that is, the current year's dollar. It eliminates the troublesome and inaccurate accrual accounts: inventory, depreciation, and all other suspense accounts. As a consequence CFA does not report illusory profits as does Historic Cost Accrual Accounting.[5]
2. CFA is objective because it reports acquisitions at their historic cost. This is possible because CFA is the cash convention of Historic Cost Accounting. Since CFA reports items at the price paid, its accounts are easily verified.[6]

3. It avoids the problem of accounting for monetary gains and losses by reporting these items of income and loss when they are reflected in cash. However, it should be said that not reporting monetary gains and losses until they are confirmed by the cash account is not the total accounting solution. One objection to the CFA treatment of monetary gains and losses is that it reports these items of income and loss as being derived from operations. They are not.[2]
4. CFA reveals fraud in Historic Cost Accrual financial statements. Accrual accounting offers the dishonest the opportunity to overstate income by puffing the asset accounts, inventory, and receivables. A cash-flow analysis will reveal that the false income reported is not confirmed by the receipt of cash.

The principal fault of Cash-Flow Accounting is that it does not produce a balance sheet. But this fault can be remedied easily by using an Historic Cost Balance Sheet, as adjusted for inflation, as shown in Chapter 9, Figure 1-4.

All systems of accounting are flawed, but Cash-Flow Accounting approaches verity much more closely than do the other systems of accounting. Cash is real.

## NOTES

1. In writing Chapter 13 on *Cash Flow Accounting,* I have drawn heavily on Professor G.H. Lawson's monographs entitled:
   (a) "Cash Flow Accounting," Working Paper Series 16, Manchester Business School and Center for Business Research, 1975, Copyright Gerald H. Lawson, 1975.
   (b) "Memorandum Submitted to the Inflation Accounting Committee in July 1974," Copyright Gerald H. Lawson, 1975.
   (c) "The Rationale of Cash Flow Accounting," May 1976.
2. Yuji Ijiri, "Cash Flow Accounting and It's Structure," *Journal of Accounting, Auditing and Finance,* pp. 331-347 (1979).
3. *Inflation Accounting,* Report of the Inflation Accounting Committee, E.P. Sandilands, Esq, CBE., Her Majesty's Stationery Office, London, pp. 156-158.
4. Yuji Ijiri, "Cash Flow Accounting and It's Structure," *Journal of Accounting, Auditing and Finance,* pp. 331-347 (1979).
5. *Inflation Accounting.* Report of the Inflation Accounting Committee, E.P. Sandilands, Esq, CBE., Her Majesty's Stationery Office, London, pp. 156-158.
6. Yuji Ijiri, "Cash Flow Accounting and It's Structure," *Journal of Accounting, Auditing and Finance,* pp. 331-347 (1979).

# 14

## Planning Cash Flow For Business And Investment Transactions

"Where," asks my neighbor, Fred Jason, "am I going to buy a bond that will yield 31.4% interest?" Fred's question is made in response to Figure 14-3, which illustrates why Fred must plan a cash flow of 31.4% on a proposed bond investment to realize an after-tax yield of 5%, over a 5-year period in which inflation averages 8%.

Business managers join Fred in expressing consternation when they see the "weighted inflation factor" that I propose they add to their mark-up on sales.

"The competition would murder us if we marked up our prices that much," they say. See Figure 14-11.

It is an idle and useless thing to suggest solutions that no one can use. But what is suggested here is not useless. My neighbor, Fred, is more likely to make a sound investment if he knows that he must plan a cash flow of 31.4%, instead of 10%, on a proposed bond investment. Knowledge bestows the rich gift of options.

The fixed dollar investors—the Fred Jasons of this world—believe that AAA bonds are risk free, and that they will provide a certain and invariable income. Their belief in the chimera of fixed and certain income forecloses the possibility of considering other investments that are erroneously perceived to carry a greater risk. But if these conservative investors acquire the knowledge that bonds and money funds are a high-risk investment in a period of inflation, they gain the option of comparing the almost certain loss from fixed dollar paper, with the possible gain, or at least a lesser loss, from other types of investments.

For example: Fred Jason learned from Figure 14-3 that, if inflation averages 8% during the term of his proposed 5-year investment in bonds, he would have to plan a cash flow of $193,800 just to obtain the return of his $100,000 capital expenditure. This information gave to Fred the opportunity to weigh the advantages of many alternative types of investments whose yield might exceed the loss from the decline in the value of money and carry no more risk than AAA bonds.

Similarly, the knowledge of how to compute the inflation factor—an expense of doing business in an epoch of inflation—which must be added to the cost of goods sold confers options on the business person. The profitability of some items is wiped out by the wealth transfer of inflation. A cash flow forecast will uncover this fact, if it includes the inflation factor in its computation. The knowledge will offer the option of directing the firm's future efforts toward producing products whose selling price will allow a normal profit and, at the same time, cover all costs, including the wealth transfer of inflation.

## HOW DO WE ASSIMILATE THE INCREDIBILE FACTORS OF INFLATION IN FORECASTING CASH FLOW?

Earlier I said that one of the faults of this chapter is that is seems to lack credibility. Its message is difficult to assimilate. It requires that we suspend our functional way of thinking about fiscal matters. For instance, on three different occasions, I have gone over the case of Fred Jason with a client. He understands perfectly that his investment in fixed dollar securities is a losing proposition. Nevertheless, when I last saw him he was still buying bonds with the expectation of a secure return on his money. While he seems to understand the mathematical demonstration of the case of Fred Jason, his inner man rejects it. He cannot act on the knowledge because it requires that he put his money in areas of perceived financial risk. He has a functional fixation that does not permit him to assimilate the facts of inflation.

A good portion of the business community appears to suffer from the same emotional disability. They cannot bear the frightening gaze of inflation. A cash-flow forecast, which uses the guidelines of this chapter, will compel us to stand eyeball to eyeball with inflation. It will tell us if the firm has the ability to recover the wealth transfer of inflation from the selling price of its goods, and whether the enterprise has the future ability to pay off its creditors and reward its investors, not from capital, but from profits.

## HOW INFLATION DISTORTS CASH-FLOW PLANNING

In this chapter, we demonstrate how the two costs of inflation can be computed and funded in cash-flow planning. That is, inflation distorts cash-flow planning in two ways: One, it causes a decline in the purchasing power of cash inflow, and two, it causes an illusory income to be reported from the return of capital. The illusory income is taxed, thus substantially reducing net cash retained in the business.

Let's start our consideration of how inflation affects the planning of cash flow, with the simplest type of business transaction, an individual's investment in fixed dollar assets, e.g., bonds, money funds, notes, mortgages, C.D.s, and savings accounts. From this discussion, we will proceed to review the more complex problems of cash-flow forecasting for corporate businesses. We will consider how inflation affects the forecasting of the inflow and outflow of cash from the purchase of a machine. Then we will detail the method for computing the inflation factor that must be added to the mark-up of a product, so that we can plan a cash inflow that will defray all costs, including the wealth transfer of inflation.

I have chosen to discuss the cash-flow planning of a fixed dollar investment first, because it is the simplest and least complicated way to demonstrate the basic problems that inflation injects into both investment and business cash-flow planning.

## HOW TO PROVIDE FOR THE INFLATION FACTOR IN PLANNING THE CASH FLOW FROM A FIXED DOLLAR INVESTMENT

Every day millions of people and tens of thousands of trusts make fixed dollar investments in savings accounts, bonds, mortgages, etc. These investments are made with the expectation of receiving a contractually stated income and, at the termination of the investment, the return of capital. An investment in fixed money obligations is believed to be a prudent, safe, conservative investment. Let's see what an inflation adjusted cash-flow analysis reveals.

## The Case Of My Neighbor And Yours, Mr. Fred Jason

Figure 14-1 shows what happened to the fixed dollar, bond investment, of our middle-class neighbor, Mr. Fred Jason. Fred confidently expected that his $100,000 investment in the triple A bonds of Computer Age Incorporated, would yield an income of $50,000 over a period of five years. Fred also thought that his investment of $100,000 would be returned when the bonds matured.

Figure 14-1 shows that Fred's expectations were not realized. In real terms, he did not receive income, nor the total return of capital. Instead, Fred Jason suffered a loss of capital in the amount of 9,008 constant value 19X0 dollars, or 13,232 year 19X5 dollars. See item (j), column (4), Figure 14-1.

To state the facts another way, Fred made a wealth transfer to the debtor, Computer Age Inc., and to the State and Federal governments, in the amount of $62,955.

Facts concerning Figure 14-1, the case of Fred Jason:
 Purchase price of bonds at 12/31/19X0, $100,000
 Annual interest rate, 10%
 Term of bonds, 5 years
 5 year average rate of inflation, 8%

The inflation factor, column (3) = 1 + the inflation rate. The average inflation rate is computed as follows:
 Year 1 = .08
 Year 2 = .166
 Year 3 = .259, etc.

The progression of the inflation factor can be obtained from the table at Appendix B.

Computation of Wealth Transfer:
 The debtor underpaid interest in real terms by ............$10,063
 The debtor paid interest of 50,000 nominal dollars, column (2), item (h), but only 39,937 Constant Value 19X0 $s, items (b) through (f), column (4).

The debtor underpaid principal by......................31,927
($100,000 − $68,073, item (g), column (2), minus item (g), column (4)).

Wealth transferred to the State and Federal gov'ts..........20,955
Infla-tax = $25,000 − $4,005 (50% × $8,010, item (h), column (4)).

Total Wealth Transferred from Fred ................$70,955

What happened to Mr. Jason's net cash flow from an investment in a $100,000 bond? He forgot to provide for 8% inflation.

### EXAMPLE OF CASH FLOW, IN REAL TERMS, WHERE INFLATION FACTOR IS NOT PROVIDED FOR

| Item | (1) Year | (2) Apparent Nominal Cash Flow | (3) Divide (2) by Inflation Factor | (4) Cash Flow In Constant 19X0 $s |
|---|---|---|---|---|
| (a) | 0 Investment | −$100,000 | 0 | −$100,000 |
| (b) | 1 Interest | + 10,000 | 1.08 | + 9,259 |
| (c) | 2 Interest | + 10,000 | 1.166 | + 8,576 |
| (d) | 3 Interest | + 10,000 | 1.259 | + 7,942 |
| (e) | 4 Interest | + 10,000 | 1.360 | + 7,353 |
| (f) | 5 Interest | + 10,000 | 1.469 | + 6,807 |
| (g) | Return of Capital | + 100,000 | 1.469 | + 68,073 |
| (h) | Income | +$ 50,000 | | +$ 8,010 |
| (i) | Income Tax on Apparent Income | − 25,000 | 1.469 | − 17,018 |
| (j) | Apparent Gain | +$ 25,000 | Real Loss | −$ 9,008* |

*9,008 19X0 dollar loss = 13,232 year 19X5 dollars (9,008 × 1.469 = 13,232)

**FIGURE 14-1**

## The State And Federal Government's Cash Flow From The Wealth Transfer Of The Infla-Tax

It is instructive to trace the cash flow of the wealth transfer of inflation to its final disposition. For this purpose, let's review the true experience of Mr. Jason, shown in Figure 14-1, who failed to anticipate, and charge for, an average inflation rate of 8% which persisted during the five year term of his loan to Computer Age Inc.

|  | Wealth Transfer to Debtor | State & Federal Infla-Tax |
|---|---|---|
| 1. Debtor under paid interest $50,000 − $39,937. Col. (2)(g) − Col (4)(b) thru (f) | $10,063 | |
| 2. Debtor underpaid principal $100,000 − $68,073, Col (2)(g) − (4)(g) | + 31,927 | |
| 3. Total Wealth Transfer to Debtor | $41,960 | |
| 4. Wealth transfer will appear in income of debtor and be taxed at 50% | − 20,995 | $20,995 |
| 5. After tax wealth transfer is distributed to debtor's stockholders | $20,995 | |
| 6. Assume debtor's stockholders are taxed at 50% | − 10,498 | $10,498 |
| 7. After tax wealth transfer retained by stockholders of debtor | $10,497 | |
| 8. Jason paid tax on illusory income of $41,990 ($50,000 − $8,010, Col. (2)(h) − (4)(h) × .50 tax rate | | 20,955 |
| 9. Total infla-tax paid to gov'ts. | | $52,488 |

**FIGURE 14-2**

**152** *The Wealth Transfer of Inflation*

Figure 14-2 informs us that, while Fred did a poor job of planning his cash flow, the State and Federal governments planned theirs with consumate skill. It was the iron maw of taxation that consumed most of the wealth transferred from Fred.

## An Example Of How Fred Should Have Planned The Cash Inflow From His Fixed Dollar Investment

Figure 14-3 shows how Fred Jason should have planned the cash inflow from his fixed dollar investment in bonds. He should have provided a cash inflow from interest in the amount of $63,340, instead of $50,000. He should have also projected a return of capital in the amount of $193,800, instead of $100,000. Fred's great fault was that he didn't understand the wealth transfer of inflation.

Jason should have required the debtors to increase their yearly interest payments by the amount of the inflation factor, as shown in Column (4). Most investors understand this. But what is not generally comprehended is the requirement that the number of dollars of capital that will be repaid to the investor when the loan matures should also be increased, not just to offset the dollar's loss of value, but also to pay the infla-tax on the illusory income from the return of capital.

Since the return of capital in excess of the number of dollars originally invested is taxed, Fred and all other investors in fixed dollar securities must require the debtor to not only return capital in constant value dollars, but also to pay the infla-tax on the illusory gain from capital repayment in constant value terms.

In our example, if there were no income tax, Fred Jason would be satisfied with a return of investment of 146,900 year 19X5 dollars:

$$\frac{146{,}900 \text{ year 5 dollars}}{1.469 \text{ year 5 inflation factor}} = 100{,}000 \text{ year 19X0 dollars}$$

which is the value of the purchasing power Fred invested.

But the State and Federal governments would say: "Wait a minute, Mr. Fred Jason, you made a profit of $46,900."

| | |
|---|---|
| Computer Age paid you | $146,900 |
| You lent them | $100,000 |
| Therefore, you made a profit of | $ 46,900" |

Since there is no appeal from the government's faulty accounting, Fred must require the debtor to pay double the illusory profit from return of capital—$46,900 × 2 = $93,800 for a total capital payment of 193,800 year 19X5 dollars. Remember, Fred is in the 50% tax bracket.

| | | |
|---|---|---|
| Correct return of capital | $193,800 | year 5 dollars |
| Less 50% income tax on $93,800 | $ 46,900 | year 5 dollars |
| Net return of capital | $ 146,900 | year 5 dollars |

*Explanation of the computation of the inflation factor used to compute return of capital, column 3:* The inflation rate—that is, the decimal portion of the inflation factor (see Appendix B)—was increased by a factor of 2, from .469 to .938, to provide the cash flow to pay the 50% tax on the infla-gain. The double inflation rate of .938 is Fred's true rate of inflation with regard to the return of capital. The infla-tax is a part of the inflation rate. This illustrates that the expected general average price rise over the term of a loan is only the starting point in computing the anticipated inflation factor. The forecasted inflation rate must be increased by the rate of the infla-tax.

If Fred's effective tax rate were 30% instead of 50%, the decimal portion of the inflation factor would be .67. This figure would be arrived at by dividing the predicted average inflation rate of .469 by .70 (1.00 − .30) to arrive at .67. The inflation factor for year 19X5 would then be 1.67.

*Explanation of Computation of Tax Payment of $78,570 Column (4)(i):* The tax payment of $78,570 shown at the bottom of column (4), item (i) is composed of the following items:

| | |
|---|---|
| 50% income tax on interest income in the amount of $63,340 (4)(b) thru (f) | 31,670 |
| 50% income tax on return of capital in the amount of $93,800, (4)(g) − (2)(g) | 46,900 |
| Total tax that would be paid | 78,570 mixed dollars |

*What part of the tax paid is infla-tax?* Sixty-eight percent of the $78,570 of the income tax that would be paid, or $53,570, is an infla-tax on illusory gains.

Tax to be paid, assuming 8% average inflation
is charged for during the 5-year term
of the bond                                         $78,570

Tax that would be paid if there were
no inflation. 50% × $50,000                          25,000

Remainder is the infla-tax on illusory gains        $53,570

Eighty-seven percent of the infla-tax (87% × $53,570 = $46,900) is derived from taxing capital. The remaining $6,670 ($53,570 − $46,900) is the infla-tax on illusory income from interest.

How Mr. Jason should have planned his cash-flow.

**CASH FLOW—HOW TO CHARGE FOR INFLATION'S WEALTH TRANSFER**

| Item | Year | (1) | (2) Apparent Nominal Cash Flow | (3) (2) times Inflation Factor | (4) Cash Flow Required to Charge for Inflation | (5) Divide (4) by (3) Constant 19X0 $s |
|---|---|---|---|---|---|---|
| (a) | 0 | | −$100,000 | | −$100,000 | −$100,000 |
| (b) | 1 | interest | + 10,000 | 1.08 | + 10,800 | + 10,000 |
| (c) | 2 | interest | + 10,000 | 1.166 | + 11,660 | + 10,000 |
| (d) | 3 | interest | + 10,000 | 1.259 | + 12,590 | + 10,000 |
| (e) | 4 | interest | + 10,000 | 1.360 | + 13,600 | + 10,000 |
| (f) | 5 | interest | + 10,000 | 1.469 | + 14,690 | + 10,000 |
| (g) | | Return of Capital | + 100,000 | 1.938* | + 193,800* | + 100,000 |
| (h) | | Income | $ 50,000 | | $157,140 | $ 50,000 |
| (i) | | Income Tax on Apparent Gain | 25,000 | | 78,570 | |
| (j) | | Apparent Gain in Mixed $s | $ 25,000 | | $ 78,570 | |

*The income tax is assessed on the return of capital if it exceeds the number of dollars originally invested. Here it required 146,900 19X5 dollars to measure the same value as the 100,000 19X0 dollars invested. But the income tax will be assessed on the $46,900 difference. So twice $46,900 is paid the investor, or $93,800—$46,900 to pay the tax and $46,900 to restore the value of money lent.

**FIGURE 14-3**

### Conclusions Concerning Planning Cash Flow
### From Fixed Dollar Investments

Would a reliable borrower pay Fred Jason $157,140, item (h), Column (4), or 31.4% interest per annum, for the rent of his $100,000 for a five-year period? I think not. Not when money can be had for half the price. But this does not detract from the value of making the kind of cash flow analysis suggested in Figures 14-1 and 14-3. One should know where fiscal reality lies. The analysis provides a rational basis for judging the value of fixed dollar investments. It reminds us again that inflation is a tax on savers.

Figures 14-1 and 14-3 very clearly demonstrate that an investment in high-grade bonds, or other supposedly safe-fixed dollar investments, are neither safe, prudent, nor conservative, as is generally believed. You can lose your fortune holding Grade AAA Bonds.

Figure 14-1 tells us that bondholders must cause the State and Federal governments to cease taxing what is clearly not income. Furthermore, they must find some means for requiring the debtors to pay interest and capital in constant value dollars.

The wealth transfer of inflation from the savers to the debtors and to the governments is morally and economically indefensible. What I have said about bonds applies to all fixed dollar investments.

The same type of analysis should be made in evaluating an investment in stocks, as is shown in Figure 14-3.

## HOW THE INFLATION FACTOR AFFECTS
## THE NET CASH FLOW FROM THE OPERATION
## OF A MACHINE. A CORPORATE CASE

*Facts in the case of Fashions Incorporated:* Ziva, the president and general manager of Fashions Incorporated, in one year's time, divorced her husband, quit her job at the Gunny Chic Garment Company, found a financial backer, and started to manufacture dresses in a loft building. Now, five years later, she has a very respectable and prosperous garment firm.

Ziva is fond of informing the professionals she employs that: "If it weren't for us high school dropouts, there wouldn't be anyone around to hire you PhDs, CPAs, and BSers."

Today Ziva wants our advice. What she wants to know is how much cash inflow a new cutting machine must produce to pay dividends of 10%

of equity capital invested ($100,000) on a declining balance and, in addition, to return capital at the rate of $20,000 per year for five years. Both dividend and capital payments are to be made in constant value dollars. Assume an average inflation rate of 8%.

In answer to Ziva's question, the cash flow requirements can be summarized as follows:

|  | To Pay in Constant Value 19X0 Dollars | You Must Have A Cash Flow of Mixed $s of |
|---|---|---|
| Dividends (Figure 14-5 Schedule I, Columns (2) and (4),(f)) | $ 30,000 | $ 72,138 |
| Return of capital (Figure 14-5 Schedule II Columns (2) and (4),(1)) | 100,000 | 206,836 |
| Total | $130,000 | $278,974 |

**FIGURE 14-4**

Ziva, on seeing the cash flow requirement of $278,974, shouts: "Holy Toledo!"—her favorite expression of surprise and dismay. She informs us that she is accepting suggestions.

We have three:

1. That Ziva marry the extremely rich and obviously enamored man whom she occasionally makes deleriously happy by allowing him to buy her a dinner. This suggestion ranks number one, by a wide margin, because it would allow Ziva to retire from business and, at the same time, would permit the world of commerce to return to its normal and tranquil orbit.

Ziva rejects the suggestion out of hand, crying: "Anything but that! I'd rather do 25 years in stir in San Quentin!—Its coeducational, isn't it?" she asks.

It isn't, Its a sexist male institution.

2. Elect to be a Subchapter S Corporation. This would reduce the cash flow requirements by $89,487. The suggestion is also rejected because Ziva's backer doesn't want ordinary income. "He has loads of ordinary income," Ziva informs us. "What he wants is unordinary income." (See Figure 14-10.)

3. That the $100,000 be borrowed. Financing the machine with borrowed money would reduce the cash flow requirement to $130,000, which is $148,974 less than if the machine were financed by equity capital. This suggestion has instant appeal. (See Figure 14-4.)

While Ziva is off putting on her sincere dress for her trip to the bank, let me explain Figure 14-5, Schedules I and II. A high school dropout, who hires PhDs, CPAs, and BSers, might ask you about it.

## How To Compute The Inflation Factor For Payment Of Dividends And Return Of Capital In Constant Value Dollars

Figure 14-5 repeats the wealth transfer problems of the infla-tax and the decline in the value of money that we have already discussed. But it also reviews how these problems affect the cash flow planning of an incorporated business. What is unique in planning the inflation-affected cash flow of a corporation, is that you must provide for two levels of infla-taxation. The inflation factor is taxed at both the corporate and stockholders' levels.

## How To Compute The Inflation Factor To Provide The Cash Flow For The Payment Of Dividends In Constant Terms

Figure 14-5, Schedule I, Column (3) illustrates the computation of an inflation factor that provides for the corporate infla-tax, as well as for the payment of dividends in constant value dollars. The formula for the computation of the inflation factor is:

$$\frac{1 + \text{the inflation rate}}{1 - \text{Corporate tax rate}}$$

Thus, if the inflation rate is 8%, and the tax rate is 50%, the inflation factor for computing dividends is:

$$\frac{1 + .08}{1 - .50} = \frac{1.08}{.50} \quad 2.16. \text{ See Year 1, Column (3)}$$

## Schedules Showing How A Corporation Must Compute Future Net Cash Flow To Stockholders To Provide For Inflation's Wealth Transfer Of Income And Capital

### SCHEDULE I

Corporate planning of net cash flow operation of a machine purchased for $100,000.* Required net cash flow to stockholders is 10% of invested capital computed in constant value dollars. Average inflation rate for five-year useful life of machine is 8%. Note that the dividend is computed on a declining balance—$20,000 capital returned each year.

**SCHEDULE SHOWING INFLATION ADJUSTED DIVIDEND PAYMENTS**

| Item | (1) Year | (2) Dividends to Be Paid. No Inflation | (3) Income Tax & Inflation Rate × 2 | (4) (2)×(3) Cash Flow Required to Charge for Infla-Costs | (5) Corporate Income Tax | (6) Inflation-Adjusted Dividend |
|---|---|---|---|---|---|---|
| (a) | 1 | $10,000 | 2.16 | $21,600 | −$10,800 | $10,800 |
| (b) | 2 | 8,000 | 2.3328 | 18,662 | − 9,331 | 9,331 |
| (c) | 3 | 6,000 | 2.519 | 15,114 | − 7,557 | 7,557 |
| (d) | 4 | 4,000 | 2.7208 | 10,884 | − 5,442 | 5,442 |
| (e) | 5 | 2,000 | 2.9386 | 5,878 | − 2,938 | 2,938 |
| (f) | | $30,000 | | $72,138 | −$36,069 | $36,069 |

*Purchase price of machine    $107,146
  Less: Investment Tax Credit    7,146 (Approximate)
  Firm's Investment in Machine    $100,000

**FIGURE 14-5**

---

## How To Compute The Inflation Factor For The Return Of Capital In Constant Terms

The problem in computing the inflation factor for the return of investment principal in constant value dollars is that we must provide for the income tax on illusory gains from the return of capital in excess of historic

*The Wealth Transfer of Inflation*

## SCHEDULE II
### SCHEDULE SHOWING RETURN OF $100,000 CAPITAL TO STOCKHOLDERS

**Corporate Cash Flow Planning**

| (1) Year | (2) Return of Capital. No Inflation | (3) Inflation Factor | (2)×(3) Cash Flow Required To Charge for Infla-Costs | (5) Corporate Income Tax 50% | (6) Capital Returned to Stockholders |
|---|---|---|---|---|---|
| 1 | $20,000 | 1.32 | $26,400 | −$ 3,200 | $23,200 |
| 2 | 20,000 | 1.665 | 33,300 | − 6,650 | 26,650 |
| 3 | 20,000 | 2.038 | 40,760 | − 10,380 | 30,380 |
| 4 | 20,000 | 2.4416 | 48,832 | − 14,416 | 34,416 |
| 5 | 20,000 | 2.8772 | 57,544 | − 18,772 | 38,772 |
|   | $100,000 |   | $206,836 | $53,418 | $153,418 |

**Stockholders' Cash-Flow Planning**

| (7) Year | (8) Return of Capital | (9) Income Tax on Infla-Profit | (10) Net Return of Capital | (11) Divide by Inflation Factor | (12) Return of Capital 19X0 $s |
|---|---|---|---|---|---|
| 1 | $ 23,200 | −$ 1,600 | $21,600 | 1.08 = | $20,000 |
| 2 | 26,650 | − 3,325 | 23,325 | 1.1664 = | 20,000 |
| 3 | 30,380 | − 5,190 | 25,190 | 1.2597 = | 20,000 |
| 4 | 34,416 | − 7,208 | 27,208 | 1.3604 = | 20,000 |
| 5 | 38,772 | − 9,386 | 29,386 | 1.4693 = | 20,000 |
|   | $153,418 | $26,709 | $126,709 |   | $100,000 |

**FIGURE 14-5 (cont'd.)**

---

cost, at both the corporate and stockholders' level. See Column (3), Schedule II.

The return of historic cost capital—here, $100,000—is not a taxable event, so the first number in inflation factor is 1. However, the payment of an additional amount of money to compensate for the decline in the value of the dollar, due to inflation, is taxable, at both the corporate and stockholders' levels. So we must produce an amount of cash that will pay the corporate and stockholders' income tax on the illusory gain from the return of capital.

The formula for computing the inflation factor for the return of capital in constant terms is:

$$1 + \frac{\text{Predicted Inflation Rate}}{\frac{1 - \text{Stockholders' Tax Rate}}{1 - \text{Corporate Tax Rate}}}$$

Assume an inflation rate of 8% and a tax rate of 50%, at both the stockholders' and corporate levels.

$$1 + \frac{.08}{\frac{1 - .50}{1 - .50}} = 1 + \frac{.16}{.5} = 1.32. \text{ (See year 1, Column (3), Schedule II)}$$

## The Wealth Transfer of Capital Must Be Provided For In Cash Flow, Even Though The Stockholders' Investment Is Not Returned

It would be a just criticism to say that I have overdrawn the inflation factor as it affects capital in the case of Fashions Incorporated, at Schedule II. Few corporations, if any, have a marginal tax rate of 50%, as I have shown, nor does the average stockholder. I have used the 50% tax rate because it is easy to compute and, therefore, assists the reader to comprehend the point being demonstrated.

However, a great many stockholders do have an effective tax rate of 40% or more—the maximum tax rate on dividends is 70%. So, while the Fashions case is overdrawn for some, it is not for a great many.

It might also be thought that the Fashions case is impractical because it is not customary for a corporation to return capital. May I disagree? I think the transfer of capital—whether to the government through the infla-tax, or by holding losses to debtors—is a real expense incurred in doing business during a period of price inflation. Like any other expense, it must be charged for, or the stockholders' investment will be transferred to the beneficiaries of inflation.

The argument that capital is not distributed to the stockholders and, therefore, need not be maintained in constant value dollars, is faulty on another count. Stocks are sold every day. The sale of stock is a return of

## Summary Of Cash Flow Required
## If Cutting Machine Is Financed By Equity Capital

| | Total Cash Flow | Cash Flows for Taxes |
|---|---|---|
| Corporate income tax on illusory income required to return capital in constant value dollars. Column (5) | $ 53,418 | $ 53,418 |
| Stockholders' income tax on illusory gain from return of capital in constant value dollars. Column (9) | 26,709 | 26,709 |
| Corporate income tax on funds required to pay inflation-adjusted dividends ($36,000 – $30,000, Column (5) | 6,069 | 6,069 |
| Total infla-tax requiring cash | | $ 86,196 |
| Additional payment of capital to compensate for the decline in the value of money. $126,709 – $100,000. Column (10)(r) minus (12) | 26,709 | |
| Return of historic cost capital Column (12)(r) | 100,000 | |
| Additional cash flow needed to pay dividends in constant value dollars $36,000 – $30,000. Column (6) – (2) (4) | 6,069 | |
| Dividend in historic cost dollars | 30,000 | |
| 50% income tax paid on $60,000 required to pay historic cost dividends | 30,000 | 30,000 |
| Total net cash inflow required | $278,974 | $116,196 |

**FIGURE 14-6**

capital. If the corporation has not generated a cash flow to offset the wealth transfer of inflation, it will be detected by the market. The company's stock will be bid down, as the stocks listed on the stock exchanges are being bid down as I write this.

Furthermore, if the firm has not provided funds to reimburse the stockholders for the infla-tax on the return of capital, then the price of the stock will be depressed even more. The intelligent investor, whether making an investment in a small or large firm, will value a firm's stock on the basis of the future after-tax net cash flows.

The return of capital in excess of historic cost dollar investment is taxed as ordinary income if it is received in liquidation of a firm. However, if the return of capital in excess of historic cost is received from the sale of stock held for more than one year, then the infla-excess over historic cost will be taxed at capital gains rates. But no matter how the stockholders' funds are returned, the illusory gain from return of capital will be taxed, either at capital gains rates or ordinary income rates. Therefore, the infla-tax must be provided for in cash-flow planning.

## Inflation Strategies "Fashions Incorporated" Might Use To Offset The Wealth Transfer Of Inflation

Possibly, Fashions Incorporated most productive strategy to provide both the cash flow to cover the dividends and the return of capital from the operation of the cutting machine would be to increase sales prices, increase sales volume, reduce costs, and, in general, employ all other means that managers use to produce a favorable net cash flow. However, the simplest strategy from an accounting point of view would be to finance the cutting machine with borrowed money instead of equity capital.

The use of borrowed money to finance the cutting machine would eliminate $148,974 of infla-expense created by equity financing. The computation of the savings is shown below:

If you borrow money, you eliminate the requirement that you pay dividends and capital in constant value dollars.

| | | |
|---|---|---|
| Infla-cost of returning equity capital of $100,000 in constant value dollars. ($206,836 − $100,000 Column (4) − (2) Figure 14-5, Schedule II) | | $106,836 |
| Additional cash flow needed to pay dividends in constant value dollars. Column (6)(f) minus (2)(f), Schedule I, Figure 14-5. | | 6,069 |
| Corporate income taxes on cash flow needed to pay dividends. Schedule I, Column (5)(f) | | 36,069 |
| Total infla-expense saved by borrowing | | $148,974 |

**FIGURE 14-7**

**Fashions Inc.**

### SCHEDULE SHOWING WEALTH TRANSFER FROM DECLINE IN VALUE OF INTEREST PAYMENTS

| (1) Year | (2) Nominal Interest Payments | (3) Inflation Factor | (4) (2) ÷ (3) Interest Payments in Constant $s | (5) Wealth Transfer |
|---|---|---|---|---|
| 1 | $10,000 | 1.08 | $ 9,259 | $ 741 |
| 2 | 8,000 | 1.1664 | 6,858 | 1,142 |
| 3 | 6,000 | 1.259 | 4,766 | 1,234 |
| 4 | 4,000 | 1.3604 | 2,940 | 1,060 |
| 5 | 2,000 | 1.4693 | 1,361 | 639 |
| | $30,000 | | $25,184 | $4,816 |

**FIGURE 14-8**

***Borrowed money will also produce a holding gain:*** The infla-expense savings of $148,974, is not the only reduction in wealth transfer costs that would be realized if the purchase of the machine were funded by borrowed capital. Holding gains would also be realized.

Assume Ziva borrows the $100,000 needed to buy the machine. Terms of the loan: 5-year pay back at $20,000 per year, interest at 20% per annum. Since interest costs are tax deductible, and since Fashions' tax rate is 50%, the effective rate of interest in nominal terms is 10%. Total interest cost over the 5-year term of the loan is, therefore, $30,000. See Figure 14-8, Column (2).

But Column (4) of Figure 14-8 shows that, in terms of constant value dollars, Fashions would pay only $25,184 of interest, for an infla-interest savings of $4,816. Column (5), Figure 14-8.

The cornucopia of debt has even more to offer. It spills forth a holding gain of $20,147. Figure 14-9, Column (5).

**Fashions Inc.**
### SCHEDULE SHOWING WEALTH TRANSFER FROM DECLINE IN VALUE OF LOAN PRINCIPAL

| (1) Year | (2) Annual Principal Payment | (3) Inflation Factor | (4) (2) ÷ 3) Principal Payments in Constant $s | (5) Holding Gain |
|---|---|---|---|---|
| 1 | $20,000 | 1.08 | $18,518 | $ 1,482 |
| 2 | 20,000 | 1.1664 | 17,146 | 2,854 |
| 3 | 20,000 | 1.2597 | 15,876 | 4,124 |
| 4 | 20,000 | 1.3604 | 14,701 | 5,299 |
| 5 | 20,000 | 1.4693 | 13,612 | 6,388 |
|   | $100,000 |  | $79,853 | $20,147 |

**FIGURE 14-9**

However, since the interest savings and the holding gain from the decline in the value of debt would appear in operating revenue and be taxed at 50%, only the after-tax portion of the interest savings and holding gain would be retained by Fashions Inc. Thus, the net wealth transfer would be:

| | |
|---|---:|
| Infla-interest savings, $4,816 − .50 tax = from Figure 14-8, Column (5) | $ 2,408 |
| Holding gain from debt, $20,147 − .50 tax = from Figure 14-9, Column (5) | 10,073 |
| Total After-Tax Wealth Transfer Realized | $12,481 |

*Summary of advantages of financing with debt:*

| | |
|---|---:|
| Infla-expense savings (From Figure 14-7) | $148,974 |
| Net Wealth Transfer from Debtor (above) | 12,481 |
| Total savings from financing with debt | $161,455 |

*Cash flow required to pay for cutting machine if financed by debt:*

| | |
|---|---:|
| Return of Loan Principal | $100,000 |
| Interest Expense (From Figure 14-8, Column (2)) | 30,000 |
| Nominal Cash Flow Required | $130,000 |
| Less After-Tax Wealth Transfer (above) | 12,481 |
| Net Cash Flow Required | $117,519 |

**Conclusions In The Case of Fashions Inc.**

The principal message of the Case of Fashions Inc. is that the planning of cash inflow must include a provision for funding the stockholders' infla-tax on return of capital. Schedule II, of Figure 14-5, instructs us that it is not enough just to maintain capital in constant value dollars at the corporate level. Cash flow planning must also provide for the infla-tax the stockholders will be required to pay on the return of capital in excess of historic cost dollars invested. The stockholders will realize a return of capital when they sell their stock or when the business is liquidated.

Can firms incease their cash incomes sufficiently to defray the total infla-cost? Not so long as business people are ignorant of these costs.

However, even if the firm were unable to charge for the wealth transfer, this would not detract from the vital need to know the amount and the source of the shortfall of cash inflow. Politicians, Price Control Proponents, financial managers, business persons, and accountants need to understand the costs inflation adds to the expense of doing business.

My experience, both in South America and in the United States, leads me to the conclusion that inflation's wealth transfer has persisted—almost without detection—because it has not been perceived and reported by accounting. One of the infla-costs that has totally escaped the attention of financial writers and accountants is the infla-tax on the return of capital in excess of historic cost.

We need to name inflation as a surreptitious wealth transfer, without the wealth owners' permisssion. To know this, offers the opportunity to report its consequences to inflations winners and losers. The report on the losers must include the infla-experience of the stockholders.

The second message—the contra-message—of the case of Fashions Incorporated is that the outflow of wealth from an enterprise to the governments and to the debtors, can be reversed by funding with borrowed money instead of equity capital. See Figure 14-11. The fact that borrowing money saves the great costs of inflation, validates the theory that inflation is a tax on savers.

## Strategy Of Electing To Be Taxed As A Subchapter S Corporation

If Fashions Inc. would elect to be a Subchapter S Corporation, it would eliminate the income tax and the infla-tax at the corporate level. This would effect a savings of $89,487.

## Savings From Electing To Be Taxed As A Sub S Corporation

| | |
|---|---:|
| Corporate income tax on dividends Column (4), Schedule I, Figure 14-5 | $36,069 |
| Corporate Income Tax on Return of Capital Column (5), Schedule II, Figure 14-5 | 53,418 |
| Total Subchapter S Savings | $89,487 |

**FIGURE 14-10.**

*Contrast of equity cash flow requirement with borrowed capital requirement:*

| | |
|---|---:|
| Cash Flow required if machine is funded by equity from Figure 14-5 | $278,974 |
| Cash Flow required if machine is funded by borrowed capital (from above) | −117,519 |
| Cash Flow savings from debt | $161,455 |

**FIGURE 14-11**

---

The Subchapter S tax savings arise from treating small business stockholders as partners, thus eliminating the corporate income tax.

Finally, we have urged that the corporate tax structure be avoided by electing to be taxed as a Subchapter S Corporation, if that is possible. Obviously, operating as a partnership, or a proprietorship, would have the same effect as a Sub S corporation—the corporate infla-tax would be avoided.

## HOW TO COMPUTE THE WEIGHTED INFLATION FACTOR FOR PLANNING THE CASH INFLOW FROM THE MANUFACTURE AND SALE OF A PRODUCT

Let's now study the more complex problem of how to compute a "Weighted Inflation Factor" to be used in planning the cash inflow from the manufacture and sale of Product X. Our primary concern is how the inflation factor should be charged for in setting the sales price of Product X. This is the first step in making a Cash-Flow Plan.

The mathematical procedure for computing the Weighted Inflation Factor for Product X is quite simple. See Figure 14-12.

**Step-By-Step Explanation Of How To Compute
The Weighted Inflation Factor For Product X:**

1. The first operation in the computation of the "Weighted Inflation Factor" is to list all the costs that will be incurred in the production of Product X and the amounts that were expended on these items in the prior year. Columns (1) and (2), Figure 14-12.

## HOW TO COMPUTE THE WEIGHTED INFLATION FACTOR IN THE PRODUCTION COSTS OF PRODUCT X[1]

**000 Omitted**

| (1) Item | (2) Prior Years' Costs 19X0 $s | (3) Weighted Factor | (4) Inflation Factor | (5) Weighted Inflation Factor |
|---|---|---|---|---|
| 1. Labor | $ 250 | .25 | .10 | .025 |
| 2. Material A | 150 | .15 | .48* | .072 |
| 3. Material B | 250 | .25 | .20* | .05 |
| 4. Depreciation | 100 | .10 | .60* | .06 |
| 5. Distribution | 50 | .05 | .10 | .005 |
| 6. Administration | 50 | .05 | .10 | .005 |
| 7. Interest | 100 | .10 | −.10** | (−.01) |
| 8. Holding Loss on Monetary Assets | 50 | .05 | .40* | .02 |
| | $1,000 | 1.00 | | |
| Predicted Weighted Inflation Factor | | | | .227 |

*The inflation factor is quadrupled to provide for the infla-tax on illusory gain produced to maintain capital, at the stockholders' level, in constant value dollars. This assumes that both the corporation and the stockholders have a 50% effective tax rate.
**The holding gain from debt will reduce interest costs.

**FIGURE 14-12**

---

2. Divide each cost in Column (2) by the total of all costs, to arrive at the "Weighted Factor." Example of the computation of the "Weighted Factor" for Labor: Divide "Labor cost" of $250 by $1,000, the total of all costs, to arrive at the Weighted Factor of 25%, as shown.

3. State the predicted percentage of price increase for each item of expense for the ensuing year, Column (4). More about this later.

4. Multiply Columns (2) by (3) by (4) to arrive at the "Weighted Inflation Factor," Column (5).

5. Add Column (5). The sum of Column (5) is the predicted "Weighted Inflation Factor" for Product X.

*The Wealth Transfer of Inflation*

*How to compute the selling price of product:* The objective of computing the "Weighted Inflation Factor" is to enable us to compute the inflation adjusted selling price of Product X for the year 19X1.

Facts needed to make the computation of the selling price of Product X:

The S Firm, which manufactures Product X, marks up its sales price at 50% of cost. The unit cost of Product X for the year 19X0 was $10. Therefore, the selling price of product X was $15 ($10 × 1.50).

The selling price of X for the year 19X1 is:

| | |
|---|---|
| Sales Price per unit of X as of 12/31/X0 | $15 |
| Multiply by Weighted Inflation Factor for year 19X1 + 1 | 1.227 |
| Selling price per unit of Product X, 19X1 | $18.40 |

The sales price of $18.40 per unit is the price that must be charged sometime during the year 19X1. It is useful only as an illustration of procedure for computing a sales price that charges for the inflation factors—the decline in the value of money and the infla-tax.

In practice, a Cash-Flow Plan is constructed on a monthly basis. We will demonstrate how to compute a "Weighted Inflation Factor" for each individual month in the year, and the inflation adjusted sales price of goods to be sold, at Figures 14-13 and 14-14. But, before we do, let me explain how the Inflation Factor shown in Figure 14-12, Column (4) was arrived at.

*Explanation of how to compute the inflation factor, Figure 14-12, Column (4). Separate the vital few from the insignificant many:* All costs have their individual rate of price increase. It is necessary to determine their inflation factor in order to compute the "Weighted Inflation Factor," which we use to compute projected income. However, it would be an arduous task to forecast the price rise of each item of expense a manufacturing firm will incur in the subsequent year. The solution to the price forecasting problem is to separate the vital few costs from the insignificant many. You will find that 10 to 15 percent of the items of expense will account for 80 to 90 percent of the dollars a firm will expend. These are the vital few costs, which weigh heavily in determining the accuracy of predicted future income. So it is worth our time to obtain the best information available as to their future price trend. Suppliers, members of the purchasing staff, and the economics departments of our banks or universities can all contribute informed forecasts of price trends.

## Forecasting The Price Trend For The Insignificant Many

We can use the predicted trend in the Consumer's Price Index to forecast the price increases of the insignificant many expenses. The economics department of your bank or university can provide you with the information.

## How Far Ahead Should You Plan?

Cash Flow Plans in excess of six months are of limited value because they have a low probability of accuracy. It is difficult enough to predict price trends three months in advance. Furthermore, small businesses and many medium-sized firms find it difficult to take the time to plan. So, since cash flow planning is a necessity in a period of inflation, I suggest a compromise: plan at least three months in advance on a continuing basis.

## Explanation Of Individual Inflation Factors Assigned To Items In Column (4), Figure 14-12

*Costs assigned the Consumer's Price Index inflation factor of 10%:*

*Item 1. Labor Expense:* Labor contracts are usually tied to the Consumer Price Index, so we have assigned the predicted 10% rise in the CPI to labor expense.

*Items 5 and 6. Distribution Expense And Administration Expense:* We have arbitrarily assigned the Consumer Price Index increase of 10% to these items. In our example, these items of expense are ranked as the insignificant many and, therefore, do not require individual estimates. This may not prove to be true in practice.

*Item 7. Interest:* The holding gain from debt reduces interest expense. Since interest costs usually rise at the rate of the CPI, we have assigned its value of 10% to the holding gain.

*Item 8. Holding Loss From Monetary Assets:* We have assumed that purchasing power of monetary assets will decline in value at the same rate as the CPI increases, i.e., 10%. In addition, we have quadrupled the inflation factor to provide for the infla-tax on capital maintenance. The quadrupling of the inflation factor will cause the inflation-adjusted selling price of Product X to rise sufficiently, to provide a cash inflow to fund the infla-tax at both corporate and stockholders' levels. The increase in the inflation factor to 40% was arrived at as follows:

Assume that both the corporation and the stockholders have an effective tax rate of 50%:

$$\frac{\text{Inflation Factor}}{1 - \text{Stockholders' Tax Rate}} = \frac{.10}{.50} = 40\% \text{ as shown}$$
$$1 - \text{Corporate Tax Rate} = .50$$

*Inflation factors assigned to the vital few costs:*

*Items 2 and 3. Materials A and B:* We have increased the inflation factors for items 2 and 3, in accordance with the formula shown above. The increase in the price levels of these raw materials will cause an illusory inventory profit to be reported, which will be taxed. The tax will be assessed regardless of the inventory method used. If the LIFO convention is employed, it may postpone the tax, but sooner or later the iron tooth of taxation will take its bite. Therefore, the infla-tax must be funded.

*Item 4. Depreciation:* Similarly, we have increased the inflation factor for depreciation also in accordance with the above formula. A study of future price trends for the vital few depreciable assets indicates that their prices will rise by an average of 15%. Therefore:

$$\frac{\frac{.15}{1-.50}}{1-.50} = \frac{.30}{.50} = .60 \text{ as shown}$$

**Example Of How To Compute
The Weighted Inflation Factor
For A Monthly Cash-Flow Plan**

Figure 14-13, the "Monthly Weighted Inflation Factor Worksheet," illustrates how to compile the inflation factor for each cost, for each month, in an orderly fashion.

In Figure 14-14, we have chosen to illustrate how to compute the Weighted Inflation Factor for the month of January 19X1. Please notice that we have introduced two new elements into the computation. The first is the separation of costs into fixed and variable categories, Column (1),

## MONTHLY WEIGHTED INFLATION FACTOR WORKSHEET

| Months | 1 | 2 | 3 | 4 | 5 | 6 | 7 | 8 | 9 | 10 | 11 | 12 | Total |
|---|---|---|---|---|---|---|---|---|---|---|---|---|---|
| Month's % of Sales | 10 | 10 | 5 | 5 | 10 | 5 | 5 | 5 | 15 | 15 | 10 | 5 | 100% |
| Units Sold Yr. X 0 | 100 | 100 | 50 | 50 | 100 | 50 | 50 | 50 | 150 | 150 | 100 | 50 | 1,000 |
| Add 10% Increase | 10 | 10 | 5 | 5 | 10 | 5 | 5 | 5 | 15 | 15 | 10 | 5 | 100 |
| Total Unit Sales 'X1 | 110 | 110 | 55 | 55 | 110 | 55 | 55 | 55 | 165 | 165 | 110 | 55 | 1,100 |

**Predicted Inflation Factor for Costs:**

| | 0 | 0 | 10 | 10 | 10 | 10 | 10 | 10 | 10 | 10 | 10 | 10 | |
|---|---|---|---|---|---|---|---|---|---|---|---|---|---|
| Labor | | | | | | | | | | | | | 10% |
| Material A | | | | | | | | | | | | | |
| 3% × 4* | 12 | 12 | 12 | 12 | 12 | 12 | 12 | 12 | 12 | 12 | 12 | 12 | |
| 6% × 4 | | | | | | | 24 | 24 | 24 | 24 | 24 | 24 | |
| 3% × 4 | | | | | | | | | 12 | 12 | 12 | 12 | |
| Total | 12 | 12 | 12 | 12 | 12 | 12 | 36 | 36 | 48 | 48 | 48 | 48 | 48% |
| Material B, 5% × 4 | 20 | 20 | 20 | 20 | 20 | 20 | 20 | 20 | 20 | 20 | 20 | 20 | 20% |
| Depreciation | | | | | | | | | | | | | |
| 10% × 4 | 40 | 40 | 40 | 40 | 40 | 40 | 40 | 40 | 40 | 40 | 40 | 40 | |
| 5% × 4 | | | | | | | 20 | 20 | 20 | 20 | 20 | 20 | |
| Total | 40 | 40 | 40 | 40 | 40 | 40 | 60 | 60 | 60 | 60 | 60 | 60 | 60% |
| Distribution | 5 | 5 | 5 | 5 | 5 | 5 | 5 | 10 | 10 | 10 | 10 | 10 | 10% |
| Administration | 5 | 5 | 5 | 5 | 5 | 5 | 10 | 10 | 10 | 10 | 10 | 10 | 10% |
| Interest | (5) | (5) | (5) | (5) | (5) | (5) | (10) | (10) | (10) | (10) | (10) | (10) | (10) |
| Holding Loss × 4 | 20 | 20 | 20 | 20 | 20 | 20 | 40 | 40 | 40 | 40 | 40 | 40 | 40% |

*Items increased by a factor of 4 to provide for 50% infla-tax.

**FIGURE 14-13**

The Wealth Transfer of Inflation

Figure 14-14. The second new element is the factor of an increase in production, Column (5). The management of the S Company, the manufacturer of Product X, has forecasted a 10% increase in the production and sales of their product.

The increase in unit production will affect variable expenses, but we are assuming that fixed expenses will not change. The computation of raw material A will increase by 10%, but the fixed expense, depreciation, will remain as it was in 19X0, but increase by the inflation factor column (3). The effect is to increase the relative weight of the variable expenses in the computation of the "Weighted Inflation Factor."

## COMPUTATION OF WEIGHTED INFLATION FACTOR—JANUARY 19X1

| (1) Item | (2)* Weighted Factor | (3) Inflation Factor | (4) (2)×(3) Total | (5) % of Production Increase | Weighted Inflation Factor |
|---|---|---|---|---|---|
| **Variable Expense** | | | | | |
| 1. Labor | .25 | 0 | 0 | 1.10 | 0 |
| 2. Material A | .15 | .12 | .018 | 1.10 | .0198 |
| 3. Material B | .25 | .20 | .05 | 1.10 | .055 |
| 4. Distribution | .05 | .05 | .0025 | 1.10 | .00275 |
| **Fixed Expense** | | | | | |
| 5. Depreciation | .10 | .40 | .04 | | .04 |
| 6. Administration | .05 | .05 | .0025 | | .0025 |
| 7. Interest | .10 | −.05 | −.005 | | (−.005) |
| 8. Holding Loss | .05 | .20 | .01 | | .01 |
| Predicted Inflation Factor for Month of January | | | | | .125 |

*Weighted Factor taken from Figure 14-12.

**FIGURE 14-14**

**Computation of Selling Price
And Cost Of Product X
For The Month Of January 19X1**

| | |
|---|---:|
| Sales Price, per unit of Product X as of December 31, 19X0 | $15 |
| Multiply by Weighted Inflation Factor for January 19X1 + 1 | 1.125 |
| Sales Price per unit for Month of January 19X1 | $16.875 |
| Unit Cost of Product X for Month of January 19X1, $16.875 × .666 cost factor | $11.22 |

**FIGURE 14-15**

*The timing of the sales price rise:* The correct computation of the selling price of a product is important because it determines the amount of cash inflow the firm will receive. For example, if the sales price of Product X is raised from $15 to $16.88, and 110,000 units are sold in January, then the total income from January sales will be $1,856,800. From this, we can plan a cash inflow of $1,745,392 (94% × $1,856,800), assuming a 6% bad debt rate. If the price of Product X is not raised from $15 to $16.88, there will be a shortfall of $1.88 per unit, for a total of $1.88 × 110,000 or $206,800. The shortfall in January income will have to be captured in future price rises, if the cash inflow plan is to be met.

Many factors will affect the timing and even the feasibility of the price rise:

1. The government may institute a program of price control which would prohibit, either partially or wholly, the scheduled 12.5% price increase.
2. Foreign and domestic competitors may not raise their prices as rapidly or to the extent that our costs dictate.
3. A rapid and large raise in prices may cause our customers to seek substitute products.

   If the firm is able to raise its prices it has several options:

(a) Raise prices in anticipation of rising costs. This is the preferred option because it will provide additional funds with which to pay the higher costs when they are incurred. Our example in Figure 14-15 is deficient in this respect. We should have computed the weighted inflation factor for February or March and used it to compute the unit price of Product X for January.

(b) Raise prices as costs rise. This is what we have done in Figure 14-15.

(c) Raise prices on a quarterly basis to cover either average, or mid-point, costs. For example, on January 2, raise prices to cover average or midpoint price increases. This probably will create an excess inflow the first month and an excess outflow the third month. In the second quarter, April-June, adjust for variances in the first quarter plan and add second quarter estimates. My expert on price changes warns me that monthly price changes may lose sales due to the customer's inability to plan.

(d) Delay raising prices until after costs have increased. The longer the delay, the more we shall have to raise prices when the action is taken.

No matter what alternative price strategy we adopt, it will have to produce the cash inflow planned.

## HOW TO PREPARE A CASH FLOW PLAN

*Step 1:* Prepare a Monthly Weighted Inflation Factor Worksheet, Figure 14-13, and Schedule, Figure 14-14. Using this data, make a sales forecast. On the basis of past experience, determine what percentage of monthly sales is received in cash and what percent is deferred into accounts receivable.

*Example:* Cash received from sales = 10%
Credit sales that are paid in the following months = 90%

*Step 2:* Analyze accounts receivable to determine the payment pattern.

*Example:* 70% of charges are paid in the first month after the sale is made.
20% are paid in the second month.
4% are collected in the third month.
6% are uncollectable.

*Step 3:* Add cash sales to receipts from accounts receivable and other cash to be received from nontrade sources. The total will represent the projected cash inflow for the month.

*Step 4:* Make a cash outflow budget for each month in the year. List when the cash will be expended for each item of operating expense and when each item of acquisition cost of fixed assets will be incurred.

*Note A:* No cash will be expended for depreciation.

*Note B:* The cash required to pay interest costs will not be decreased by the amount of the holding gain. The holding gain from monetary liabilities will appear in the cash inflow.

*Note C:* The holding loss from monetary assets is a cost that will require cash funding. The amount of cash on hand and in the bank will have to be increased to offset the loss of purchasing power. Accounts receivable will also require additional funding.

*Step 5:* Subtract total cash outflows from total cash inflows. If a cash deficit results, a decision will have to be made as to whether to finance the deficit by borrowing or by selling stock.

For a more detailed description of how to prepare a cash flow budget, I suggest you read *Budgeting: Profit Planning and Control,* by Glenn A. Welsch, Prentice-Hall Inc., Chapter 12. Mr. Welsch's presentation does not deal with the inflation factors which we have discussed in this chapter, it is excellent in all other respects.

For those who wish to obtain an in-depth knowledge of the impact of price changes on cash-flow budgets, I highly recommend that you read: *Impact of Relative Price Changes On One Year Budget*—Parts I, II, and III, by Professor G.H. Lawson, MA (Econ), MBA, FCCA, and R. Raimond, BA, MBA, ACA, *Management Accounting,* January, February, and March 1976. I have drawn heavily on Part III in writing this chapter.

*Summary of the five requirements for Product X:* The forecasting and planning of cash flow of an enterprise devoted to manufacturing requires:

1. That we forecast and plan cash inflow on a product-by-product basis.
2. That we make a reasonably accurate forecast of the number of product units that will be sold.
3. That we compute the weighted inflation factor on a monthly basis, as shown in Figure 14-14, and an inflation-adjusted sales price, as shown in Figure 14-15.

4. In addition, that we predict our ability to raise prices, taking into account the possibility of governmental price control which will not permit the capturing of the infla-costs. We must also consider the limits foreign and domestic competition and substitute products will place on our ability to raise prices.

5. We determine in advance how a shortfall in cash inflow will be funded. For example: we can increase unit sales, thus causing a decrease in unit costs. We can discontinue the manufacture and sale of products whose prices are inelastic so they cannot be increased enough to fund the infla-costs. We can concentrate on the marketing of those products that do produce a satisfactory net cash inflow. Should our efforts to find a method to increase income fail, we shall have to decide how we are going to finance the shortfall in cash inflow. We have several options: Increase cash inflow velocity by improving our collections procedures or finance the shortfall out of retained earnings, out of new equity, or out of borrowed money.

**Conclusion**

In this chapter, we have stated the maximum case for including the infla-costs in planning cash inflow. The argument has been exaggerated to make a point. Not everybody has an effective tax rate of 50%. Not every corporation needs to quadruple its inflation factors to arrive at an adequate selling price. But the point made is valid. There is an infla-tax on income and capital that is assessed at both the corporate and individual taxpayer's levels. There is a holding loss from monetary assets and a holding gain from monetary liabilities. These items must be factored into the computation of sales prices, into the computation of cash inflow.

To fail to recognize and to treat with these infla-costs and income, is to be deluded. It is to believe what Historic Cost Accounting would have us believe—that prices rise but the value of money is stable. The success of the wealth transfer of inflation is dependent upon this misperception—this miscomprehension of fiscal reality.

How successful the illusion of inflation is! As I write this summation, firms are issuing bonds in preference to funding by stock. These bonds are offering an interest rate that the gullible or uninformed public, and the media, believe to be fantastically high. But a cash-flow analysis, similar to the one illustrated in the case of Fred Jason, would illustrate how fantastically low the interest offered really is. The collapse of the bond market in early 1980 demonstrated that inflation has not caused the laws of mathematics to be suspended.

The forecasting and planning of cash inflow may seem of little worth if it informs you that you should be charging more than 30% interest for your money when the market's maximum yield is 15%. It may seem of no practical use to know that you should sell your product for a price 20% higher than the market will allow, or that the iron tooth of the infla-tax is gnawing on the vitals of your capital. But to lack knowledge is to lack options.

What is the point of manufacturing a product whose selling price will not recover its costs? What is the point of paying the government their infla-tax, and labor their high wages, if you have nothing for your work but the capital deficit you do not detect?

If you plan your income and costs on a cash flow basis, you will have foreknowledge and you will have options. You can plan to cut costs on the manufacture of Product Y. Or, if this is not possible, you can discontinue its production. In the alternative, you may want to concentrate on expanding the market for the highly profitable Product A. You can opt to buy back stock and to fund with borrowed money. You can avoid investments in those firms which are most heavily infla-taxed—the smoke stack, capital intensive, companies. You can calculate a firm's holding gain from debt.

It would also be ideal to elect to Congress people who would abrogate the ruinous infla-tax. But even the best-intentioned politician—and there are many—cannot act to correct an error that is undefined. The wealth transfer of inflation has been so successful, and so ruinous, because its effects have been so badly accounted for. There can be no options for a problem that has not been stated.

We have argued that the infla-costs should be funded by cash inflow. The only thing that will pay costs is cash—accrual entries will pay for nothing. In a time of inflation, accrual accounting gives an uncertain signal, even when accounts are supposedly adjusted for inflation. In contrast, cash basis planning and accounting, while not perfect, states the hard realities of cash, or lack of it. This is infinitely better than accrual accounting's reporting of illusory income.

## NOTES

1. John J. Hampton, *Handbook For Financial Decision Makers,* Reston Publishing Company Inc., A Prentice-Hall Company, Reston, Virginia, pp. 60-62.

# 15

## Infla-Accounting Solutions: Constant Dollar Accounting (CDA)* And Current Cost Accounting (CCA)

This chapter is divided into five parts:
1. Explanation of the different standards of measurement used by Constant Dollar and Current Cost Accounting;
2. A comparative financial statement which shows how Historic Cost, Constant Dollar, and Current Cost Accounting would treat the same set of fiscal facts;
3. An explanation of the Constant Dollar (CDA) and Current Cost (CCA) accounting adjustments made on the comparative financial statement;
4. A critique of CDA and CCA, explaining their virtues and their vices;
5. Finally, we show Mr. Chris Westwick's alternative solution to Constant Dollar and Current Cost Accounting—a solution that combines the better features of CDA and CCA.

At the very back of the book, Appendix D, we print the Financial Accounting Standards Board's Appendix E of FASB Statement Number 33, "Financial Reporting and Changing Prices".[1] While we take some exception to the treatment of holding gains and losses as shown in the ex-

---

*Constant Dollar Accounting has several synonyms: Historic Cost/Constant Dollar, General Price Level, and Price Index Accounting.

perimental "Statement," we think it is, on the whole, excellent—a long step in the right direction for accounting for the wealth transfer of inflation.

## WITH WHICH DOLLAR SHOULD ACCOUNTING MEASURE? CAN IT BE ADJUSTED TO PERFORM ITS ACCOUNTING ROLES?

With which dollar should accounting measure economic activity in an epoch of inflation? Should accounting measure with a Constant Value Dollar or with a Current Cost Dollar? Can either of these monetary units restore the long-term, accounting uses of money—a standard of value for long-term transactions and a store of value for savings and investments? This is the difficult question the Financial Accounting Standards Board (FASB) is attempting to answer.[1]

Constant Dollar (CDA) and Current Cost Accounting (CCA) attempt to correct the seven measurement errors of Historic Cost Accounting (HCA), detailed in Part Two of this book. These two infla-accounting systems try to measure income and acquisition costs with a monetary measuring rod that will correctly gauge the fiscal effects of inflation.

While HCA, CDA, and CCA measure economic activity with differing standards of measurement, they are quite similar in other respects. They all use the standard accrual accounting convention. They attempt to use the accounting roles of money.

### Different Units Of Measure Produce Different Statements of Income

The use of differing measuring rods gives radically different answers when applied to gauging the income of capital intensive firms. In 1979, the Westinghouse Corporation reported income from operations, using three different measuring units:

| | |
|---|---|
| Historic Cost Accounting reported: | 331.1 million, H$s |
| Constant Dollar Accounting reported: | 196.1 million, Consumer Price Index $s |
| Current Cost Accounting reported: | 193.9 million, CCA$s |

Which one of these systems of accounting most closely approximated the truth in its statement of operating income? I think you will agree that HCA probably erred substantially in stating the fiscal truth. But, as between Constant Dollar Accounting and Current Cost Accounting, it is difficult to say which one most accurately informs us of fiscal reality.

## COMPARISON OF ACCOUNTING SYSTEMS: EXAMPLES OF HOW THEY DIFFER

As a step toward understanding Constant Dollar Accounting and Current Cost Accounting, let's look at the different monetary measuring rods used by accounting:

(a) Historic Cost Accounting measures in units of money. The number of dollars you pay for an item is its eternal cost. No more. No less.

(b) Constant Dollar Accounting measures with units of current general purchasing power. Units of current general purchasing power are derived from price indexes, like the "Consumer Price Index For All Urban Consumers (CPI)."[2]

*Example:* You carry on your balance sheet a parcel of land you purchased in 1967 for $1,000. The Consumer Price Index stood at 100 in 1967. At what dollar value will you state the land in 1978, when the Consumer Price Index (CPI) is at 200?

*Answer:* 2,000 1978 Consumer Price Index Dollars.
200 / 100 × $1,000 = 2,000 1978 CPI Dollars.

*The Consumer Price Index Dollar does not measure the fair market value of an item:* Mind you, the 2,000 1978 CPI Dollars are not intended to express the fair market value of the land in 1978. If you were to sell the parcel of land in that year, you might get less or you might get more than $2,000. The 2,000 CPI dollar value only expresses the land's worth in terms of 1967 general purchasing power. According to the Consumer Price Index, 2,000 1978 dollars had the same command over 382 household goods and services as did 1,000 1967 dollars—the number of dollars you paid for the land.

Which is to say that Constant Dollar Accounting measures in terms of the price of household goods and services. If it sounds absolutely potty to suggest that we measure the value of a machine or an inventory of copper by a basket of household goods and services, let me assure you that, on the face of it, it is. But when the results of Constant Dollar Accounting are compared with those of inflation-blind Historic Cost Accounting, CDA appears to be fiscal sanity herself.

    (c) While Constant Dollar Accounting measures all economic activity with one constant dollar, Current Cost Accounting (CCA) operates under no such constraints. It employs not one, but several, standards of measurement. For example, Current Cost Accounting (CCA) measures monetary assets, such as cash and accounts receivable, with the Historic Cost Dollar, but fixed assets with the Current Cost Dollar (C$).

At the end of each accounting year, CCA requires us to determine the replacement cost of all tangible nonmonetary assets, such as machines and equipment, buildings, and land. Intangible nonmonetary assets, like good will and patents, are usually excluded from the year-end appraisal or determination of current cost.

CCA also requires us to establish the specific year-end cost of each significant, tangible, nonmonetary asset the firm possesses. However, if we find that the use of an asset is expected to recover less than its current replacement cost, then the recoverable amount is the value we use.

The use of the various fiscal units of measurement will become clear if you will review the Case of 12-B Corporation, Figure 15-1. This excellent and easy to understand model makes clear the measuring processes of Constant Dollar and Current Cost Accounting. The model was prepared by Mr. M.C. Westwick and appeared in the magazine *Accountancy* (London), December 1975, under the title "Sandilands PSSAP 7, But What Now?" I have modified Mr. Westwick's model somewhat—mostly to make the accounting terms agree with American usage, and to make the accounting treatment agree with American accounting texts.

The model gives an overview of the infla-accounting systems—Constant Dollar and Current Cost Accounting. It is not intended to be a complete explanation of these systems of accounting. But the model does provide as much general knowledge of Constant Dollar and Current Cost Accounting as most accountants and business persons will currently need.

There are several versions of Current Cost Accounting. We have used the version most often seen in textbooks, which does not have CCA accounting for monetary holding gains and losses. The Financial Accounting Standards Board, Statement No. 33, follows the opposite course. It requires that the approximately 1,000 very large firms, who are participating in the FASB's infla-accounting project, to report monetary holding gains and losses in suplementary CCA schedules. We shall later show that these monetary gains and losses are uncertain and that, if they are realized, they are an addition to, or a subtraction from, operating income.

On June 30, 19X1, the beginning inventory was sold for $800 and replaced at a cost of $440 (10% increase in cost). As of December 31, 19X1, the current cost of fixed assets was $600. Inventory prices did not rise during the second half of year 19X1. See Schedule III.

As of January 1, 19X1, the Consumer's Price Index stood at 100. At December 31, 19X1, it registered 116, or a 16% increase. Straight line depreciation on fixed assets is 10%. Interest on loan is ignored.

## Explanation Of Adjustments Appearing On Schedule I, The Beginning Balance Sheet

*Why it is important to identify the unit of measurement?* The heading of Schedule I announces the method of accounting used. It also informs us of the standard of measurement used to gauge economic activity. Historic Cost measures with the Historic Cost Dollar; Constant Dollar Accounting

---

**COMPARATIVE FINANCIAL STATEMENTS: HISTORIC COST, CONSTANT DOLLAR, AND CURRENT COST ACCOUNTING, 12-B INCORPORATED**

*Basis Data:* Business purchased on 12/31/19X0. As of 12/31/19X0, the firm's balance sheet was as follows:

| | |
|---|---:|
| Cash | $ 100 |
| Accounts Receivable | 200 |
| Inventory (FIFO) | 400 |
| Fixed Assets | 500 |
| Total Assets | $1,200 |
| | |
| Accounts Payable | 200 |
| Loans Payable | 400 |
| Capital Stock | 600 |
| Total | $1,200 |

**FIGURE 15-1**

measures with the Consumer Price Index Dollar; while Current Cost Accounting measures with the Historic Cost Dollar and the Current Cost Dollar. Each dollar measures a different quantity of value. It is as important to know the standard of measurement we are using to gauge economic activity, as it is to know the unit of measurement we are using to gauge distance—the inch, the centimeter, the mile, or the kilometer.

| Method of Accounting | HCA | CDA 12/31/X1 | CCA |
|---|---|---|---|
| Unit of Measure | H$ | CPI$ | C$ |

*Explanation of Constant Dollar Accounting Adjustments to the Beginning Balance Sheet—Schedule I:* The CDA heading informs us that all items on the 1/1 Balance Sheet are stated in December 31, 19X1, Consumer's Price Index Dollars. If you will look at the other Schedules II-IV, you will see that CDA consistently measures with only one standard of measurement. That is, the year-end Consumer Price Index Dollar. Consistency is one of the CDA's principal virtues.

The amounts shown in the CDA column were arrived at by multiplying the historic cost of each item by an inflation factor. The inflation factor was computed as follows:

$$\frac{\text{Consumer Price Index at 12/31/X1}}{\text{Consumer Price Index at 1/1/X1}} = \frac{116}{100} = 1.16$$

*Constant Dollar Accounting is a version of Historic Cost Accounting:* CDA does not change Historic Cost values. One hundred sixteen 12/31/X1 CPI dollars have the identical purchasing power of household goods and services as do 100 Historic Cost Dollars acquired on 1/1/X1. CDA attempts to express the historic cost of an item in terms of the current year's general purchasing power. To accomplish this objective, it measures historic costs with a CPI dollar. But that is not to say that the CDA's measurement is accurate. For example: Gold purchased for $150 in 1977 had a value in 1979 of $550. But CDA, using 150 1977 historic cost dollars as its base value, would inform us that gold had a value in 1979 of only $188, not $550.

$$\frac{\text{Average CPI, Year 1979}}{\text{Average CPI, Year 1977}} = \frac{.227}{.181} = 1.254 \times \$150 = \$188 \text{ 1979 dollars}$$

## COMPARATIVE FINANCIAL STATEMENTS

HCA = Historic Cost Accounting  CPI$ = Consumer's Price Index Dollar
CDA = Constant Dollar Accounting  C$ = Current Cost Dollar
CCA = Current Cost Accounting  N/A = Not Applicable
H$ = Historic Cost Dollar

**SCHEDULE I**

**Balance Sheet 1/1/X1**

| Method of Accounting | HCA | CDA 12/31/X1 | CCA |
|---|---|---|---|
| Unit of Measure | H$ | CPI $ | H$ |
| 1. Cash | $ 100 | $ 116 (a) | $ 100 |
| 2. Accounts Receivable | 200 | 232 (a) | 200 |
| 3. Inventory (FIFO) | 400 | 464 (a) | 400 |
| 4. Fixed Assets | 500 | 580 (a) | 500 |
| Total Assets | $1200 | $1392 | $1200 |
| 5. Accounts Payable | $ 200 | 232 (a) | $ 200 |
| 6. Loans Payable | 400 | 464 (a) | 400 |
| 7. Capital Stock | 600 | 696 (a) | 600 |
| Total Liability and Equity | $1200 | $1392 | $1200 |

*Notes:* (a) H$ × 1.16
(b) H$ × 1.08
(c) From Schedule II, Holding Loss on Monetary Assets
(d) CPI $232 − H$200 = $32
(e) CPI $464 − H$400 = $64
(f) Current Cost of 1/1 inventory at 6/30
  C$440 − 1/1 HS Cost, H$400 = $40
(g) 10% of Current Cost at 12/31/X1
(h) Current Cost C$600 at 12/31, minus Historic Cost H$500
(i) From line 14, Schedule II

*The Wealth Transfer of Inflation*

To state the value of gold in 1979 at $188 is to talk nonsense. Five hundred fifty 1979 dollars, the price of gold in 1979, will obviously purchase far more household goods and services than did $150 in 1977, the price of gold in that year. The error of Constant Dollar Accounting's valuation of gold in 1979 is derived from the fact that CDA is premised on the historic cost theory that the number of dollars paid for an item is its eternal cost. But the market value of commodities, marketable securities, and nonmonetary assets are not permanently fixed at the date of acquisition, as CDA erroneously premises.

In contrast, Current Cost recognizes that values change. It would report the value of gold at its 1979 current cost of $550. Constant Dollar Accounting is an historic cost attempt to account for inflation. Current Cost Accounting is not. It is a system of accounting quite distinct from Historic Cost Accounting. Its valuation of nonmonetary assets is not concerned with values obtained at the date of acquisition. It is concerned only with current cost values.

**SCHEDULE II**

**Computation of Holding Loss from Monetary Assets**

| Method of Accounting | HCA | CDA 12/31/X1 | CCA |
|---|---|---|---|
| Unit of Measure | H$ | CPI $ | H$ |
| 8. January 1, Cash Balance | $ 100 | $ 116 (a) | $ 100 |
| 9. 1/1 Accounts Receivable | 200 | 232 (a) | 200 |
| Total 1/1 Mon. Assets | $ 300 | $ 348 | $ 300 |
| 10. Cash Inflow from Sales | 800 | 864 (b) | 800 |
| Total | $1100 | $1212 | $1100 |
| 11. Cash Outflow—Purchases | −440 | −475 (b) | −440 |
| 12. 12/31 Monetary Assets Balance in CPI$s | | $ 737 | |
| *13. 12/31 Actual Monetary Asset Balance | $ 660 | $ −660 | $ 660 |
| 14. Holding Loss from Monetary Assets | N/A | $ 77** | N/A |

*From 12/31 Balance Sheet. Cash 460 + Accounts Rec. $200 = $660.
**Forwarded to Line 30, Schedule III, Holding Losses.

## SCHEDULE III
### Comparative Profit And Loss Statement

| Method of Accounting | HCA | CDA 12/31/X1 | CCA 12/31 |
|---|---|---|---|
| Unit of Measure | H$ | CPI $ | H$ & C$ |
| 15. Inventory 1/1 | $400 | $464 (a) | $400 |
| 16. Purchases 6/30 | 440 | 475 (b) | 440 |
| 17. Total | $840 | $939 | $840 |
| 18. Inventory 12/31 | −440 | −475 (b) | −440 |
| 19. Cost of Goods Sold | $400 | $464 | $400 |
| 20. Cost of Sales Adjusted | N/A | N/A | 40 (f) |
| 21. Cost of G.S. Adjusted | $400 | $464 | $440 |
| 22. Depreciation | 50 | 58 (a) | 60 (g) |
| 23. Total Operating Costs | $450 | $522 | $500 |
| 24. Sales (Made June 30) | 800 | 864 (b) | 800 |
| 25. *Operating Profit* | $350 | $342 | $300 |
| 26. Less Income Taxes | 140 | 140 | 140 |
| *27. Operating Profit A/T | $210 | $202 | $160 |

**Cost Savings (CCA Only)**

| | | | |
|---|---|---|---|
| *28. Realized Cost Savings From Inventory Sold 6/30 | N/A | N/A | $ 40 (f) |
| *29. Unrealized Cost Savings From Fixed Assets | N/A | N/A | 100 (h) |
| Total Cost Savings | | | $140 |

**Holding Losses and Gains**

| | | | |
|---|---|---|---|
| 30. Monetary Holding Loss | N/A | $ (77) (i) | $ N/A |
| 31. Monetary Holding Gains | N/A | 96 (d)(e) | N/A |
| *32. Total Holding Gain (Net) | | $ 19 | |
| 33. Total Operating Profit Cost Savings and Holding Gain | $210 | $221 | $300 |

*Forwarded to 12/31 Balance Sheet, Schedule IV

## Comparative Balance Sheet for Year Ended December 31, 19X1

**SCHEDULE IV**

| Method of Accounting | HCA | CDA 12/31/X1 | CCA 12/31 |
|---|---|---|---|
| Unit of Measure | H$ | CPI $ | H$ & C$ |
| 34. Cash | $ 460 | $ 460 | $ 460 |
| 35. Accounts Receivable | 200 | 200 | 200 |
| 36. Inventory | 440 | 475 (b) | 440 |
| 37. Fixed Assets | 500 | 580 (a) | 600 |
| 38. Depreciation | (50) | (58) (a) | (60) (g) |
| Total Assets | $1550 | $1657 | $1640 |
| 39. Taxes Payable | $ 140 | $ 140 | $ 140 |
| 40. Accounts Payable | 200 | 200 | 200 |
| 41. Loans Payable | 400 | 400 | 400 |
| 42. Capital Stock | 600 | 696 (a) | 600 |
| 43. Retained Earnings (from line 27, P&L) | 210 | 202 | 160 |
| 44. Realized Cost Savings (from line 28, P&L) | N/A | N/A | 40 (f) |
| 45. Unrealized Cost Savings (from line 29, P&L) | N/A | N/A | 100 (h) |
| 46. Net Monetary Holding Gain (from line 32, P&L) | N/A | 19 | N/A |
| Total Liability & Equity | $1550 | $1657 | $1640 |

### How CDA Items Are Carried Forward to Other Schedules

| Item | Schedule II | Schedule III | Schedule IV |
|---|---|---|---|
| 1. Cash | Item 8 | | |
| 2. Accounts Receivable | Item 9 | | |
| 3. Inventory | | Item 15 | |
| 4. Fixed Assets | | | Item 38 |
| 5. Accounts Payable | | Item 31 | |
| 6. Loans Payable | | Item 32 | |
| 7. Capital Stock | | | Item 43 |

*Why the Historic Cost and Current Cost columns show the same amounts in Schedule I:* Both Current Cost and Historic Cost Accounting measure monetary assets and liabilities with the Historic Cost Dollar. As a result, HCA's and CCA's statement of these items are identical. However, there is usually a difference between HCA's and CCA's reporting of the value of nonmonetary assets. There is no difference shown in Schedule I because of the unusual circumstance of 12-B Company being a new business, which commenced operating on 1/1. It is just coincidence that HCA's and CCA's statements of nonmonetary assets are the same.

However, in the subsequent year 19X2, CCA will value fixed assets at $600 on the beginning balance sheet, while HCA will list this item at $500. So, usually, HCA and CCA will list identical amounts for monetary items, but different amounts for nonmonetary assets.

## Explanation Of Adjustments Appearing On Schedule II, Computation of Holding Loss From Monetary Assets

In a period of inflation, the value of monetary assets held by a business declines in purchasing power. The objective of Schedule II is to measure the loss of value—the transfer of monetary wealth out of the company.

### Excerpt from Schedule II

| Method of Accounting | HCA | CDA 12/31/X1 | CCA |
|---|---|---|---|
| Unit of Measure | H$ | CPI $ | H$ |
| 12. 12/31 Monetary Asset Balance in CPI $s |  | $737 |  |
| *13. 12/31 Actual Monetary Asset Balance | $660 | −660 | $660 |
| 14. Holding Loss from Monetary Assets | N/A | $ 77** | N/A |

---

*From 12/31 Balance Sheet. Cash $460 + Accts. Rec. $200
**Forwarded to Line 30, Schedule III, Holding Losses

Item 12, of the CDA column, states that the 12-B Company should have had $737 in monetary assets on hand at December 31. However, the Company's December 31 Balance Sheet, Schedule IV, shows that the monetary assets balance amounted to only $660. Therefore, 12-B had a monetary holding loss of $77, as shown on Line 14.

**Explanation of Adjustments Appearing
On Schedule III, Comparative Profit
And Loss Statement**

*Comments on Constant Dollar Accounting's Holding Gains and Losses from Monetary Items. Items 30-32*

*Excerpt from Schedule III:*

| Method of Accounting | CDA 12/31/X1 |
|---|---|
| Unit of Measurement | CPI $ |
| **Holding Losses and Gains** | |
| 30. Monetary Holding Loss | $ (77) (i) |
| 31. Monetary Holding Gains | 96** (d)(e) |
| 32. Total Net Holding Gain | $ 19** |

\*Accounts Payable CPI $232 − H$ 200 = $32
Loans Payable CPI $464 − H$ 400 = 64
Total Holding Gain $96

\*\*Forwarded to 12/31 Balance Sheet, Line 46, Schedule IV

Note that the Holding Gains and Losses shown above are listed in a separate schedule, as something unrelated and apart from operating income and operating expense. This treatment implies that holding gains and losses have no tax consequences. Further note that monetary gains are offset against monetary losses. This assumes that a business has the ability to accomplish the netting of these items. The Financial Accounting Standards Board's Statement No. 33, page 118, (see Appendix D) and the accounting texts report monetary gains and losses in this manner. We think that holding gains and losses cannot be assumed. They do not occur simply because we hold monetary assets and we owe money.

It is true that a holding loss from cash can be offset against a holding gain from a loan used to finance money in the bank:

| | |
|---|---|
| Holding gain from $10,000 loan, for one year, during which inflation averaged 10% | $1,000 |
| Less: Holding loss from $10,000 cash acquired from above loan, and also held for one year during which inflation averaged 10% | − 1,000 |
| Holding gain offsets holding loss | $ 0 |

But this assumes the lender did not anticipate the 10% loss of purchasing power of money in the interest charge. In practice, we can make no such assumptions. Gain or loss from monetary items must be proven.

While it is possible to offset holding losses from cash against holding gains from debt with comparative ease, it is not that simple when we attempt to charge off a holding gain from debt invested in accounts receivable. Our holding gain from an investment of debt in accounts receivable will be realized if the cost of merchandise sold to us is paid for in dollars of less value than was anticipated by the vendor.

The holding gain from accounts payable is dependent upon whether the vendor does or does not charge us for inflation's erosion of the purchasing power of money. The value of the accounts payable will decrease between the period of delivery of merchandise and the time of our payment. If the vendor charges for the wealth transfer of inflation, then there will be no holding gain realized.

Furthermore, a holding gain from accounts payable must be received in cash if it is to have worth. It will be received in cash profits if we are able to raise the price of our goods in an amount which will capture the vendor's holding loss. The tooth fairy does not put holding gains under our pillow at night. The gain must be earned from trading.

We will gain inflation's wealth transfer from our vendors only if they do not charge for their holding loss. And our gain, like that of the heavily indebted Chrysler Corporation, is dependent upon our ability to sell our products at a price that will capture the vendor's holding loss from our accounts payable, in cash. If these conditions are met, we will realize a holding gain—but we must share it. Our gain will appear as taxable operating income. However, it will be reduced by the income tax. For this reason, it is erroneous to show a monetary holding gain as nonperating, nontaxable income. It may be, if it arises from holding cash that has been financed by a loan, but it won't be, if it arises from accounts receivable that were financed by accounts payable. Each case must be proven.

Inflation's wealth transfer from borrowed money will reduce the cost of depreciable assets. The holding gain from debt will cause the cost of depreciation to be reduced in real terms. The inflation-reduced cost of the asset will require a lesser depreciation charge than would be required if we had not received a holding gain.

But the gain is not automatic. It rests on the lender's failure to charge for inflation in its interest rate and on our ability to capture the holding gain in our selling prices. If a gain is realized, it will be a taxable gain, derived from operating income.

To summarize: With the possible exception of borrowed money invested in monetary assets, any holding gain realized will appear as a part of net taxable cash inflow. It is doubtful that the holding gain will be distinguishable from other operating income. Therefore, it is an error to report in financial statements information that would lead the reader to believe that the wealth transfer from the decline in the value of money is automatic, and that holding gains are something apart and distinguishable from taxable operating income.

*The double counting of holding gains:* If holding gains are reported in operating income, it follows that they should not again be counted in nonoperating income. Yet this is what is being done in both textbooks and the FASB Statement 33. The effect is to double count. The holding gain from monetary liabilities is first carried down into the balance sheet and shown as a part of retained earnings. Then it is again carried down into the equity section from the Monetary Holding Gain and Loss Schedule, where it is shown as a separate item. See lines 43 and 46, Schedule IV. (Also see paragraph 238 of FASB Statement No. 33, Appendix D.)

*The monetary loss shown at line 30, may be an illusion:* Whether the firm did or did not suffer a monetary holding loss of $77 depends upon whether the company was able to charge for the cost of the holding loss in the sales prices of merchandise sold. The holding loss from monetary assets is a cost that must be charged for, many firms do. If the expense of the wealth transfer from the decline in the value of monetary assets was included in the mark-up of goods sold, there will be no holding loss experienced. The revenue from the mark-up, for the holding loss, will appear in taxable operating income. However, the offsetting monetary holding loss is not a tax-deductible item. Therefore, it should be shown as a deduction from operating income after taxes. It is important to show the holding loss as a deduction from operating income because it is a normal cost of doing business in a period of inflation. Like any other operating cost, its amount should be plainly stated, so that it can be controlled. Even then it will be misleading, because there will be no information to inform the reader as to what extent it was charged for in the sales price of goods sold.

In a Supplementary Statement for the year 1979, the Westinghouse Corporation, in compliance with FASB Statement 33, reported a loss from the decline in the purchasing power of net monetary assets in the amount of 126 million dollars. We doubt that Westinghouse suffered so great a loss. The firm must have received interest, which partly charged for the inflation. It also seems likely that Westinghouse charged for the holding loss from accounts receivable and notes receivable in the sales price of its products. However, this information is nowhere given, so we do not know whether Westinghouse did or did not suffer a holding loss from monetary assets.

The reason that CCA does not report a holding loss from monetary assets is because it measures with an Historic Cost Dollar. The items "cash" and "accounts receivable" are held to have a stable general purchasing power. CCA will, however, report a holding loss from marketable securities, where market value is less than historic cost.

Our exclusion of monetary holding losses from CCA reporting is not in accordance with the FASB's Statement No. 33, "Financial Reporting and Changing Prices." This report requires that Current Cost supplementary financial statements record holding losses from monetary assets. (See paragraph 232 and 238 of FASB Statement No. 33, Appendix D.)

*Explanation of Current Cost Accounting Adjustments to the Profit and Loss Statement, Schedule III:*

1. Line 20, Cost of Sales Adjustment (f), adds $40 to the cost of sales for the purpose of reflecting the replacement cost of inventory sold on June 30.

    Inventory was purchased on January 1 for $400. It was sold on June 30. At the date of sale, the replacement cost of the inventory sold was $440. Adjustment (f) charges operating income with the $40 increase in the replacement cost of the inventory.

Adjustment (f) also carries the $40 down to line 28, where it is shown as an item of nonoperating income, entitled, "Realized Cost Savings From Inventory Sold 6/30."

2. Line 22, Depreciation (g), charges operating profit with a $60 depreciation cost. The $60 is 10% of the $600 December 31 replacement cost of the fixed assets.

*Are cost savings real? Lines 28 and 29, Schedule III:* A cost savings is the difference between the replacement cost of a nonmonetary asset and its historic cost. For example: The replacement cost of fixed assets at December 31, was $600, whereas their historic cost was $500. Therefore, there was a cost savings of $100 ($600 − $500).

English accountants use the more accurate and more descriptive term, "Capital Maintenance," in place of Cost Savings. The purpose of the Cost Savings adjustment is to maintain capital by providing for the replacement cost of used assets.

The cost savings of $40 from inventory is described as "Realized Cost Savings," because it is believed that $40 was realized in cash when the inventory was sold on June 30. However, the cost savings of $100 from fixed assets is described as "Unrealized" because the fixed assets have not yet been sold.

*It is doubtful that the cost savings from inventory were realized:* There is doubt whether the cost savings of $40 from the sale of inventory were realized. The cost savings, or capital maintenance charge, would be received in cash if the sales price of the merchandise sold was increased to provide for the $440 replacement cost of the inventory—that is, if the selling price of merchandise sold included a normal profit mark-up, plus a charge of $440 for the replacement cost of the inventory, plus an additional charge for the income tax on the $40 illusory inventory profit (C$440 − H$400), in that case we could conclude that there was a cost savings.

However, if the sales price of the inventory at June 30 was not raised sufficiently to provide for these various charges, then we would conclude there were no cost savings. The fact is that we do not have enough information to determine whether or not there was a savings of $40.

In any event, the cost savings, if there was one, must appear as a part of taxable operating income. For this reason, it is double counting to report cost savings first in operating income, and later in nonoperating income. Both the model and Statement 33 of the FASB make this error.

There is also the question of whether the cost savings is an illusion created by subtracting historic cost dollars from current cost dollars. Take the example of the gain reported from fixed assets:

| | | |
|---|---|---|
| Current Cost of Fixed Assets at 12/31 | 600 | Dec. 31 C$s |
| Less Historic Cost of Fixed Assets | 500 | Jan. 1 H$s |
| Cost Savings | 100 | ? dollars |

The $100 dollar gain appears to result from the mathematical manipulation of unlike quantities.

The FASB's Statement 33 resolves this problem by reducing all dollar amounts to a common term:

| | | |
|---|---|---|
| Current Cost of Fixed Assets at 12/31 | 600 | 12/31 CPI $s |
| Less Historic Cost $500 \times \dfrac{116}{100} =$ | 580 | 12/31 CPI $s |
| Excess of Increase in Specific Prices over Increase in General Price Level | 20 | 12/31 CPI $s |

The FASB's example in Statement 33 carries the $20 excess down to the equity section of the balance sheet, where it is shown as an addition to equity.

However, the cost savings, or whatever it is called, is certainly not a savings, nor does it represent income. Rather it is a charge against operating income. The basic concept of Current Cost Accounting is that the objective of a business is to provide for its continuity. A firm will continue in business only so long as it is able to recover the cost of the assets it consumes. If the replacement cost of an asset is in excess of its original cost or its prior year current cost, then operating profit must be charged for the difference. It is a capital maintenance charge. It should be shown as a deduction from operating income, and as an addition to the equity section of the balance sheet, as appropriated undistributed earnings.

## Summary of Discussion Of Monetary Holding Gains, Losses, And Cost Savings In Financial Statements

Monetary holding gains and losses are real. But we cannot assume that if a firm has monetary debt it will have a holding gain, or that if it has monetary assets it will have a holding loss. To compute a holding loss, we must first know whether the loss were charged for in the selling price of the firm's products. If it was charged for, there would be no holding loss. Financial statements do not provide the information. We think it is an error to show a holding loss from monetary items in a separate nonoperating schedule and as a charge against retained earnings when we do not know if a loss was, in fact, experienced.

Similarly, we cannot assume that a firm is certain to receive a holding gain from accounts payable and other monetary liabilities. First, we must know whether the creditors have charged for the inflation factor, either in interest or in cost of goods sold. Second, we must know if the debtor firm has been able to raise its prices to realize, in cash, the wealth transfer from the creditors. This information is also not available in financial statements. So we do not know if there was or was not a holding gain.

Finally, we must recognize that, if there is a holding gain from debt that is not invested in cash, it will appear as a part of operating income and will be carried to the balance sheet in that guise. Therefore, it is double counting to report holding gains as taxable operating profit and also as a phantom nontaxable, nonoperating income.

The so-called cost savings are an illusion. A firm that reports cost savings has no more assets after the cost savings than it had before. The 12-B Company had no more fixed assets when they were valued at 600 C$s than it had when they were valued at 500 H$s.

The idea of charging operating profit for capital maintenance is excellent. But it should be termed capital maintenance, not cost savings. It should be shown as a charge against operating income. It should not be labeled as an item of nontaxable, nonoperating revenue.

Furthermore, the charge for capital maintenance should include the income tax the stockholders, or owners, will have to pay on the capital maintenance reserve when it is distributed. See Chapter 14.

## ADVANTAGES AND DISADVANTAGES OF THE INFLA-ACCOUNTING SOLUTIONS

*What's good about Constant Dollar Accounting?*

1. The principal merit of CDA is that it attempts to measure the effect of inflation's wealth transfer on all items listed in the balance sheet and profit and loss statement. CDA attempts to measure inflation's effect on income and acquisition costs, on monetary and nonmonetary items. In this respect, CDA is more logical than

Current Cost Accounting which, at least in textbook presentations, does not attempt to account for monetary holding gains and losses.

2. CDA measures with one single unit of measurement, the constant value, Consumer's Price Index Dollar (CPI$). CDA could use other types of price index dollars, such as the Gross National Product Implicit Price Deflator dollar. But the Financial Accounting Standards Board has decreed that the CPI dollar will be used in preparing Constant Dollar financial statements. This is a good decision because the Consumer Price Index has wide distribution. Furthermore, it reports price changes more accurately than does the GNP Price Deflator. The GNP Price Deflator has the fault of not measuring all price changes in imported goods.

3. CDA is objective in its measurement process. The reporting firm's judgment as to the values of assets is not required. CDA's measuring rod, the CPI dollar, is neutral as to result. It cannot be influenced by the reporting firm. The objectivity of CDA in measuring economic activity is seen to have a substantial advantage, when compared to Current Cost Accounting's fairly subjective measurement process. Under CCA, the reporting firm determines the current cost of nonmonetary assets. Thus, the accuracy of CCA's reporting of income and financial condition is dependent upon the accuracy of the reporting firm's employee's determination of replacement cost. Constant Dollar Accounting's measurement process is mechanical. It uses historic cost multiplied by the CPI dollar. No personal judgment of value is involved.

*What's wrong with Constant Dollar Accounting?* The principal fault of CDA is that it reports a profit or loss and a financial condition that is a fiction. This unfortunate result comes from CDA's major premise that the number of dollars paid for an item is its eternal value. We earlier gave the example of gold whose value was $150 in 1977, but $550 in 1979. CDA would state the value of gold in 1979 at $188, which is the number of dollars paid for the gold in 1977, converted to 1979 Consumer Price Dollars. One hundred eighty-eight CPI dollars would purchase the same quantity of household goods and services as 150 1977 Historic Cost dollars would. But 188 1979 CPI dollars would not purchase an ounce of gold in 1979. It took $550 to do that.

The assumption that the average rise in the cost of household goods and services for an urban family of four will have relevance to the inflation experience of an operating company is not to be taken seriously. An operating company's costs are affected by specific price rises, not by the average general price rise for the entire United States. The cost of oil rose by 70% in 1979, not by 13.9%, the rise in the CPI. A firm using a substantial amount of oil in the manufacture of its products would have grossly understated its cost of goods sold if it computed inventory costs on the basis of the 13.9% rise in the Consumer Price Index. Each firm has its own specific price rise experience. This cannot be assumed to be replicated by the inflation experience of an urban family of four.

The cost of converting historic cost to Constant Dollars may not be worth the expense. The initial conversion of all Historic Costs to Constant Dollar cost can be exorbitantly time consuming for a small- or medium-size capital intensive firm. The conversion process requires that we search through old records to determine the date of acquisition of all significant nonmonetary assets. We then must refer to the Consumer's Price Index to learn the index number obtaining at that date. The index number becomes the base figure for computing the inflation index factor for all future Constant Dollar costs.

*Example:* Building purchased for $100,000 in 1975. What is its Constant Dollar value in 1979?

Average Consumer Price Index for 1975 = 161.2

Average Consumer Price Index for 1979 = 217.4

217.4 ÷ 161.2 × $100,000 = 134,863 − 1979 Average CPI $s (See Appendix C—Consumer Price Index etc.)

The time-consuming process of assigning a base index number to all nonmonetary assets can be expensive. Of course, there are short-cut methods for doing this but, even so, it does take a great deal of time. In my experience, where it has been tried, it has been found to produce information of little worth. Constant Dollar Accounting would be worthwhile for firms only in the event that the government would allow the income tax to be computed on the Constant Dollar Operating Profit. But see the Grady Method Chapter 9, Figure 9-1 to 9-4.

*What's right about Current Cost Accounting?*
1. CCA's basic concept is that a firm must provide for its regeneration before it counts its profits. Under CCA, there can be no profit before a firm's used-up productive assets have been charged for at current cost. CCA makes provisions for a firm's continuity by charging income for the consumption of assets on the basis of their current cost of replacement.
2. CCA's realistic statement of asset values and the income derived from these assets, provides valuable information for making predictions of future cash inflow.
3. CCA's additional virtue is that it matches current costs with current revenues with an acceptable degree of accuracy.
4. A principal and substantial virtue of CCA is that it states the replacement cost of nonmonetary assets in year-end dollars. Therefore, CCA's measurement of the depreciation cost of fixed assets and the cost of inventory consumed is quite accurate—far more accurate than that obtained by Constant Dollar Accounting, and infinitely better than that obtained from Historic Cost Accounting.

*What's wrong with Current Cost Accounting?*
1. Current Cost Accounting's substantial fault is that it measures with several standards of measurement. It measures monetary assets and liabilities with an Historic Cost Dollar. In those cases where it does attempt to measure holding gains and losses, it measures with a Consumer Price Index Dollar. It gauges nonmonetary assets with a Current Cost Dollar or with a Recoverable Amount Dollar, whichever produces the lesser amount. In addition, CCA may measure with an industrial index dollar, where an index is used, as a short-cut to determining replacement costs. The use of several standards of measurement affects the credibility of CCA financial statements. The reliability of CCA financial statements is also affected by the subjective nature of determining replacement costs. In many instances, it is the firm's employees who decide what that might be.
2. The cost of establishing the current cost of nonmonetary assets may be prohibitively expensive for smaller capital-intensive enterprises. The time just isn't available in most firms for the task of

obtaining the current costs of assets from catalogs, suppliers, or recent invoices. Nor is there the time required to estimate the current cost of assets that are no longer sold. Furthermore, few firms would want to bother with guessing what the recoverable cost of an item might be, where that would be less than the current cost. For small- to medium-sized firms, the rewards from Current Cost Accounting may not justify the expence. If the income tax were assessed on Current Cost results, then it would be clearly worth its cost of time and money.

3. A frequent complaint about Current Cost Accounting is that it fails to account for backlog depreciation. It is said that, if you

---

### AN EXAMPLE OF BACKLOG DEPRECIATION

*Assume:* Machine purchased on January 1, 19X1
Cost of Machine at January 1, 19X1 = $1,000
Useful life of machine = 5 years
Cost of machine will advance by $100 per year, so that in year 19X5 the machine will cost $1,500

| (1) Year | (2) Annual Replacement Cost at 12/31 | (3) Dep. Rate | (4) (1) × (2) Dep. Computed on Annual Current Cost | (5) Dep. Computed on $1,500 Year-5 Cost | (6) Depreciation Backlog |
|---|---|---|---|---|---|
| 1 | $1,100 | 20% | $ 220* | $ 300 | $ 80* |
| 2 | 1,200 | " | 240 | 300 | 60 |
| 3 | 1,300 | " | 260 | 300 | 40 |
| 4 | 1,400 | " | 280 | 300 | 20 |
| 5 | 1,500 | " | 300 | 300 | -- |
| Total | | | $1,300 | $1,500 | $200 |

*What is attempted here is to subtract 220 year 1 dollars from 300 year five dollars, to arrive at a backlog of $80. It is obvious that 1,100 year 1 dollars will purchase the same machine as 1,500 year 5 dollars. Therefore, it takes 1.3636 year 5 dollars to equal one year 1 dollar ($1,500/1,000 = 1.3636).

### FIGURE 15-2

compute replacement cost on a yearly basis, and that if inflation persists throughout the life of the asset, you will understate the depreciation costs. You will fail to account for backlog depreciation.

The argument is that, if an asset whose cost is $1,000 in year 0, will be replaced five years hence for $1,500, we must compute yearly depreciation on the year 5 cost of $1,500. If we don't, we will have backlog depreciation, as illustrated in Figure 15-2.

However, Figure 15-3 demonstrates that backlog depreciation is a phantom created by trying to mathematically manipulate different years' dollars.

If we multiply 220 year 1 dollars by the inflation factor of 1.3636, we will arrive at 300 year 5 dollars.

$220 × 1.3636 = $300 (See year 1 above)

To expand the example:

| Year | Dep. Computed on Annual Current Cost | Inflation Factor | Annual Dep. Cost as Adjusted | Dep. Computed on $1500 Year-5 Cost | Depreciation Backlog |
|------|--------------------------------------|------------------|------------------------------|------------------------------------|----------------------|
| 1    | $220                                 | 1.3636           | $300                         | $300                               | $0                   |
| 2    | 240                                  | 1.25             | 300                          | 300                                | 0                    |

etc. etc.

**FIGURE 15-3**

It can be seen from the above that the backlog depreciation problem is created by bad mathematics, not bad accounting.

## DO CONSTANT DOLLAR AND CURRENT COST ACCOUNTING CORRECT THE SEVEN MEASUREMENT ERRORS OF HISTORIC COST ACCOUNTING?

The objective of Constant Dollar and Current Cost Accounting is to solve the measurement errors of Historic Cost Accounting. That they only partially realize their objective can be seen in Figure 15-4.

| HCA Measurement Error | Corrects | Does Not Correct |
|---|---|---|
| 1. HCA understates income by not reporting holding gains from decline in dollar value of debt | CDA | CCA does not because it measures with H$* |
| 2. HCA does not recognize holding losses from monetary assets | CDA | " |
| 3. HCA understates the cost of inventory sold | CCA | CDA uses H$ × CPI$ not current cost |
| 4. HCA understates the cost of depreciation | CCA | " |
| 5. Sales may falsely appear to increase over the prior year | CDA | CCA measures with H$ |
| 6. Fixed Asset values are understated | CCA | CDA measures with H$ |
| 7. Retained earnings and capital may be overstated | | CDA CCA** |

*In the FASB's version of CCA, holding gains and losses are reported.
**CDA may overstate earnings and capital because it measures with an H$ × CPI. Actual replacement cost may exceed H$ × CPI. Holding gains reported may not be realized. CCA reports cost savings that are illusory.

**FIGURE 15-4**

## The Combination Of Constant Dollar Accounting With Current Cost Accounting—An Alternative Solution

Figure 15-4 delivers the depressing message that Constant Dollar Accouting and Current Cost Accounting do not correct all of the measurement errors of Historic Cost Accounting. Mr. Chris Westwick, Deputy Technical Director of the English Institute,[3] and others have suggested that if we were to combine the better features of Constant Dollar Accounting with Current Cost Accounting we would get a much better result. The system of accounting proposed bears various titles, such as Current Value/General Price Level Accounting. We shall simply call it CDA/CCA.

A demonstration of the effects of CDA/CCA accounting adjustments to the financial statement of 12B Corporation is shown in Figure 15-5, Schedules V and VI. The system has much to commend it. It more closely approximates fiscal truth than do Constant Dollar and Current Cost Accounting. Figure 15-5 is Mr. Westwick's model.

### Notes to Schedules V and VI, Figure 15-5.
(a) H$ × 1.16
(b) H$ × 1.08
(d) CPI $232 − H$200 = $32
(e) CPI $464 − H$400 = $64
(f) Current Cost of 1/1 inventory at 6/30
    C$440 − 1/1HS Cost, H$400 = $40
(g) 10% of Current Cost of Fixed
    Assets ($600)
(h) Current Cost C$600 at 12/31, minus
    Historic Cost H$500
(i) From line 14, Schedule II
(j) Constant Dollar Cost of Inventory Sold,
    $464, less replacement cost
    $440 = $24
(k) Current Cost of Fixed Assets $600,
    minus Constant Dollar Cost
    $580 = $20

## SCHEDULE V
## COMPARATIVE PROFIT AND LOSS STATEMENTS

| Method of Accounting | CDA 12/31 | CCA 12/1/X1 | CDA/CCA 12/31 | 12/31 |
|---|---|---|---|---|
| Unit of Measure | CPI $ | C$ | CPI $ | C$ |
| 15. Inventory 1/1 | $ 464 (a) | $ 400 | $ 464 (a) | |
| 16. Purchases 6/30 | 475 (b) | 440 | 475 (b) | |
| 17. Total | $ 939 | $ 840 | $ 939 | |
| 18. Inventory 12/31 | −475 (b) | −440 | −475 (b) | |
| 19. Cost of Goods Sold | $ 464 | $ 400 | $ 464 | |
| 20. Cost of Sales Adjustment | N/A | 40 (f) | − 24 (j) | |
| 21. Cost of G.S. Adjusted | $ 464 | $ 440 | $ 440 | |
| 22. Depreciation | 58 (a) | 60 (g) | 60 (g) | |
| 23. Total Operating Costs | $ 522 | $ 500 | $ 500 | |
| 24. Sales (Made on June 30) | 864 (b) | 800 | 864 (b) | |
| 25. Operating Profit | $ 342 | $ 300 | $ 364 | |
| 26. Less Tax on H/C Profit | 140 | 140 | 140 | |
| 27. Operating Profit A/T | $ 202 | $ 160 | $ 224 | |

**Cost Savings**

| | | | | |
|---|---|---|---|---|
| 28. Realized Cost Savings from Inventory Sold | | 40 (f) | 24 (j) | |
| 29. Unrealized Cost Savings from Fixed Assets | N/A | 100 | 20 (k) | |
| Total Cost Savings | N/A | $ 140 | $ (4) | |

**Holding Losses and Gains**

| | | | | |
|---|---|---|---|---|
| 30. Monetary Holding Loss | $ (77) (i) | N/A | $ (77) (i) | |
| 31. Monetary Holding Gains | 96 (d)(e) | N/A | 96 (d)(e) | |
| 32. Total Holding Gain Net | $ 19 | | $ 19 | |
| 33. Total of Operating Profit, Cost Savings, and Holding Gains | $ 221 | $ 300 | $ 239 | |

**FIGURE 15-5**

**SCHEDULE VI**

**COMPARATIVE BALANCE SHEET**
for Year Ended December 31, 19X1

| Method of Accounting<br>Unit of Measure | CDA<br>12/31<br>CPI $ | CCA<br>12/31/X1<br>C$ | CDA/CCA<br>12/31 CPI $ | 12/31 C$ |
|---|---|---|---|---|
| 34. Cash | $ 460 | $ 460 | $ 460 | |
| 35. Accounts Receivable | 200 | 200 | 200 | |
| 36. Inventory | 475 (b) | 440 | 475 (b) | |
| 37. Fixed Assets | 580 | 600 | 600 | |
| 38. Depreciation | (58) (a) | (60) | (60) | |
| Total Assets | $1657 | $1640 | $1675 | |
| | | | | |
| 39. Taxes Payable | $ 140 | $ 140 | $ 140 | |
| 40. Accounts Payable | 200 | 200 | 200 | |
| 41. Loans Payable | 400 | 400 | 400 | |
| 42. Capital Stock | 696 (a) | 600 | 696 (a) | |
| 43. Retained Earnings<br>(from line 28, P&L) | 202 | 160 | 224 | |
| 44. Realized Cost Savings<br>(from line 28, P&L) | N/A | 40 (f) | (24) (j) | |
| 45. Unrealized Cost Savings<br>from Fixed Assets | N/A | 100 | 20 (k) | |
| 46. Net Monetary Holding<br>Gain (from line 32,<br>P&L) | 19 | N/A | 19 | |
| Total Liab. & Equity | $1657 | $1640 | $1675 | |

**FIGURE 15-5 (cont'd)**

## NOTES

1. Copyright by the Financial Accounting Standards Board, High Ridge Park, Stamford, Connecticut 06905, U.S.A. Reprinted with permission. Copies of the complete document are available from the FASB.
2. *Consumer Price Index For All Urban Consumers (CPI)* published in "Monthly Labor Review," U.S. Department of Labor, Washington, D.C. The "Monthly Labor Review" can be subscribed to by writing to the Department of Labor.
3. "Sandilands PSSAP 7, But What Now?," M.C. Westwick, *Accountancy* (London Eng.), December 1975.

# 16

# In Conclusion: Accounting's Role In Inflation

To report semblance rather than fact has been the role of accountancy in our long epoch of significant inflation, which began in the year 1967. Accountancy continues to report what seems like income, but what is, in fact, something insubstantial—an illusion created by a faulty mathematical process—a process that attempts to manipulate unlike quantities.

Accountancy has added, subtracted, multiplied, and divided dollars of different years in the belief that the value of the dollar is fixed and immutable for all time. It has reported income and acquisition costs on the premise that the long-term uses of money are unimpaired by inflation.

But, as we all know, inflation has destroyed these roles. As a consequence, the value of money is no longer predictable. It can no longer act as a standard of value for long-term transactions nor as a store of value for savings and investments. As a further consequence, the theoretical basis for the type of accounting we all use, Historic Cost Accounting, has been destroyed—was destroyed way back in 1967.

When inflation's economic forces blew away the accounting roles of money, currency had but one remaining role to play in the economy. That is, to act as a medium of exchange for immediately completed transactions. The effect is to reduce accounting, which measures economic activity with money, to reporting income and acquisition costs on a cash basis. Cash-Flow Accounting recognizes this economic fact and, therefore, is the only valid system of accounting extant.

But commerce will not be satisfied with cash accounting alone. Cash-Flow Accounting does not produce a balance sheet. A list of assets, liabilities, and equity is indispensible to business. Furthermore, there is a need to smooth out the reporting of income and acquisitions costs, to match income with expense. The two infla-accounting systems, Constant Dollar Accounting and Current Cost Accounting, attempt to satisfy these requirements, while at the same time reporting the gain or loss from the wealth transfer of inflation. These systems try to meet these objectives by various adjustments which, in effect, are supposed to restore the accounting roles of money to accountancy. These infla-accounting systems are imperfect, as all accounting systems are, but they are an honest attempt to record fact in preference to illusion. They are much to be preferred over inflation-blind Historic Cost Accounting.

It is a matter of the greatest urgency that accountancy adopt one or the other of these infla-accounting systems for computing income for tax purposes. It is the infla-tax assessed on Historic Cost illusory profits that is decapitalizing industry.

# Appendix

**Appendix A:** Present Worth of One Dollar Table
**Appendix B:** Future Worth of One Dollar Table
**Appendix C:** Consumer Price Index for All Urban Consumers
**Appendix D:** Financial Accounting Standards Board's Appendix E of FASB Statement Number 33, "Financial Reporting and Changing Prices"
**Appendix E:** Examples of Consolidated Statement of Income Adjusted for Inflation as Required by FASB 33

*Explanation of Appendix A:* The table at Appendix A is a "Present Worth of One Dollar Table." It shows the decline in the purchasing power of one dollar at various rates of inflation.

*For example:* We buy a $10,000 bond in the year 0. The bond will mature 10 years hence. We estimate the inflation rate will average 7% during the term of the bond. We want to know what the purchasing power of the $10,000 will be when the bond matures.

The 7% column of Appendix A shows that, in the year 10, the value of the dollar will have declined to .5083 year 0 dollars. Thus, in the year 10, the $10,000 return of capital will purchase what $5,083 purchased in the year 0, the year the bond was purchased.

The important point to notice is that the table at Appendix A quotes values in year 0 dollars—that is, in today's dollars.

# APPENDIX A:

## TABLE SHOWING THE FUTURE WORTH OF A DOLLAR AT VARIOUS AVERAGE RATES OF INFLATION

| Year | 5% | 6% | 7% | 8% | 9% | 10% |
|---|---|---|---|---|---|---|
| 1 | 0.9524 | 0.9434 | 0.9346 | 0.9259 | 0.9174 | 0.9091 |
| 2 | .9070 | .8900 | .8734 | .8573 | .8417 | .8264 |
| 3 | .8638 | .8396 | .8163 | .7938 | .7722 | .7513 |
| 4 | .8227 | .7921 | .7629 | .7350 | .7084 | .6830 |
| 5 | .7835 | .7473 | .7130 | .6806 | .6499 | .6209 |
| 6 | .7462 | .7050 | .6663 | .6302 | .5963 | .5645 |
| 7 | .7107 | .6651 | .6227 | .5835 | .5470 | .5132 |
| 8 | .6768 | .6274 | .5820 | .5403 | .5019 | .4665 |
| 9 | .6446 | .5919 | .5439 | .5002 | .4604 | .4241 |
| 10 | .6139 | .5584 | .5083 | .4632 | .4224 | .3855 |

| Year | 11% | 12% | 13% | 14% | 15% | 16% |
|---|---|---|---|---|---|---|
| 1 | 0.9009 | 0.8929 | 0.8850 | 0.8772 | 0.8696 | 0.8621 |
| 2 | .8116 | .7972 | .7831 | .7695 | .7561 | .7432 |
| 3 | .7312 | .7118 | .6930 | .6750 | .6575 | .6407 |
| 4 | .6587 | .6355 | .6133 | .5921 | .5718 | .5523 |
| 5 | .5935 | .5674 | .5428 | .5194 | .4972 | .4761 |
| 6 | .5346 | .5066 | .4803 | .4556 | .4323 | .4104 |
| 7 | .4817 | .4523 | .4251 | .3996 | .3759 | .3538 |
| 8 | .4339 | .4039 | .3762 | .3506 | .3269 | .3050 |
| 9 | .3909 | .3606 | .3329 | .3075 | .2843 | .2630 |
| 10 | .3522 | .3220 | .2946 | .2697 | .2472 | .2267 |

*Explanation of Appendix B:* The table at Appendix B is a "Future Worth of One Dollar Table." It shows what the present purchasing power of the dollar will be worth in the future at various rates of inflation.

*Example:* We intend to invest $10,000 in a 10-year mortgage. We estimate that inflation will average 11% during the term of the loan. We want to know how many dollars the borrower must repay to return the present purchasing power of $10,000.

The 11% column of the table at Appendix B informs us that it will take 2.8394 year 10 dollars to equal the present value of one dollar. Therefore, it will require the repayment of 28,394 year 10 dollars to equal the value of 10,000 current year's dollars.

But we must not forget that the Federal and State governments will tax the $18,394 difference between $10,000 lent and $28,394 returned. So we must charge the borrower for the infla-tax. Therefore, assuming a 40% marginal tax rate, the borrower must return 40,657 year 10 dollars.

$$\frac{\$18,394}{1 - .40 \text{ tax rate}} + \$10,000 = \$40,657 \text{ (year 10 dollars)}.$$

# APPENDIX B:

## TABLE SHOWING THE NUMBER OF DOLLARS REQUIRED IN THE FUTURE TO MAINTAIN THE PRESENT VALUE OF A DOLLAR, AT VARIOUS RATES OF INFLATION

| Year | 5% | 6% | 7% | 8% | 9% | 10% |
|---|---|---|---|---|---|---|
| 1 | 1.0500 | 1.0600 | 1.0700 | 1.0800 | 1.0900 | 1.1000 |
| 2 | 1.1025 | 1.1236 | 1.1449 | 1.1664 | 1.1881 | 1.2100 |
| 3 | 1.1576 | 1.1910 | 1.2250 | 1.2597 | 1.2950 | 1.3310 |
| 4 | 1.2155 | 1.2625 | 1.3108 | 1.3605 | 1.4116 | 1.4641 |
| 5 | 1.2763 | 1.3382 | 1.4026 | 1.4693 | 1.5386 | 1.6105 |
| 6 | 1.3401 | 1.4185 | 1.5007 | 1.5869 | 1.6771 | 1.7716 |
| 7 | 1.4071 | 1.5036 | 1.6058 | 1.7138 | 1.8280 | 1.9487 |
| 8 | 1.4775 | 1.5938 | 1.7182 | 1.8509 | 1.9926 | 2.1436 |
| 9 | 1.5513 | 1.6895 | 1.8385 | 1.9990 | 2.1719 | 2.3579 |
| 10 | 1.6289 | 1.7908 | 1.9672 | 2.1589 | 2.3674 | 2.5937 |

| Year | 11% | 12% | 13% | 14% | 15% | 16% |
|---|---|---|---|---|---|---|
| 1 | 1.1100 | 1.1200 | 1.1300 | 1.1400 | 1.1500 | 1.1600 |
| 2 | 1.2321 | 1.2544 | 1.2769 | 1.2996 | 1.3225 | 1.3456 |
| 3 | 1.3676 | 1.4049 | 1.4429 | 1.4815 | 1.5209 | 1.5609 |
| 4 | 1.5181 | 1.5735 | 1.6305 | 1.6890 | 1.7490 | 1.8106 |
| 5 | 1.6851 | 1.7623 | 1.8424 | 1.9254 | 2.0114 | 2.1003 |
| 6 | 1.8704 | 1.9738 | 2.0820 | 2.1950 | 2.3131 | 2.4364 |
| 7 | 2.0762 | 2.2107 | 2.3526 | 2.5023 | 2.6600 | 2.8262 |
| 8 | 2.3045 | 2.4760 | 2.6584 | 2.8526 | 3.0590 | 3.2784 |
| 9 | 2.5580 | 2.7731 | 3.0040 | 3.2519 | 3.5179 | 3.8030 |
| 10 | 2.8394 | 3.1058 | 3.3946 | 3.7072 | 4.0456 | 4.4114 |

# APPENDIX C:

**U.S. Department of Labor**
**Room 1539**
**Bureau of Labor Statistics**
**Washington, D.C. 20212**
**Consumer Price Index**
**All Urban Consumers—(CPI-U)**
**U.S. City Average**
**All items**
**(1967 = 100)**

| YEAR | JAN. | FEB. | MAR. | APR. | MAY | JUNE | JULY | AUG. | SEPT. | OCT. | NOV. | DEC. | AVG. |
|---|---|---|---|---|---|---|---|---|---|---|---|---|---|
| 1946 | 54.5 | 54.3 | 54.7 | 55.0 | 55.3 | 55.9 | 59.2 | 60.5 | 61.2 | 62.4 | 63.9 | 64.4 | 58.5 |
| 1947 | 64.4 | 64.3 | 65.7 | 65.7 | 65.5 | 66.0 | 66.6 | 67.3 | 68.9 | 68.9 | 69.3 | 70.2 | 66.9 |
| 1948 | 71.0 | 70.4 | 70.2 | 71.2 | 71.7 | 72.2 | 73.1 | 73.4 | 73.4 | 73.1 | 72.6 | 72.1 | 72.1 |
| 1949 | 72.0 | 71.2 | 71.4 | 71.5 | 71.4 | 71.5 | 71.0 | 71.2 | 71.5 | 71.1 | 71.2 | 70.8 | 71.4 |
| 1950 | 70.5 | 70.3 | 70.6 | 70.7 | 71.0 | 71.4 | 72.1 | 72.7 | 73.2 | 73.6 | 73.9 | 74.9 | 72.1 |
| 1951 | 76.1 | 77.0 | 77.3 | 77.4 | 77.7 | 77.6 | 77.7 | 77.7 | 78.2 | 78.6 | 79.0 | 79.3 | 77.8 |
| 1952 | 79.3 | 78.8 | 78.8 | 79.1 | 79.2 | 79.4 | 80.0 | 80.1 | 80.0 | 80.1 | 80.1 | 80.0 | 79.5 |
| 1953 | 79.8 | 79.4 | 79.6 | 79.7 | 79.9 | 80.2 | 80.4 | 80.6 | 80.7 | 80.9 | 80.6 | 80.5 | 80.1 |
| 1954 | 80.7 | 80.6 | 80.5 | 80.3 | 80.6 | 80.7 | 80.7 | 80.6 | 80.4 | 80.2 | 80.3 | 80.1 | 80.5 |
| 1955 | 80.1 | 80.1 | 80.1 | 80.1 | 80.1 | 80.1 | 80.4 | 80.2 | 80.5 | 80.5 | 80.6 | 80.4 | 80.2 |
| 1956 | 80.3 | 80.3 | 80.4 | 80.5 | 80.9 | 81.4 | 82.0 | 81.9 | 82.0 | 82.5 | 82.5 | 82.7 | 81.4 |
| 1957 | 82.8 | 83.1 | 83.3 | 83.6 | 83.8 | 84.3 | 84.7 | 84.8 | 84.9 | 84.9 | 85.2 | 85.2 | 84.3 |
| 1958 | 85.7 | 85.8 | 86.4 | 86.6 | 86.6 | 86.7 | 86.8 | 86.7 | 86.7 | 86.7 | 86.8 | 86.7 | 86.6 |
| 1959 | 86.8 | 86.7 | 86.7 | 86.8 | 86.9 | 87.3 | 87.5 | 87.4 | 87.7 | 88.0 | 88.0 | 88.0 | 87.3 |
| 1960 | 87.9 | 88.0 | 88.0 | 88.5 | 88.5 | 88.7 | 88.7 | 88.7 | 88.8 | 89.2 | 89.3 | 89.3 | 88.7 |

| | | | | | | | | | | | | |
|---|---|---|---|---|---|---|---|---|---|---|---|---|
| 1961 | 89.3 | 89.3 | 89.3 | 89.3 | 89.3 | 89.4 | 89.8 | 89.7 | 89.9 | 89.9 | 89.9 | 89.9 | 89.6 |
| 1962 | 89.9 | 90.1 | 90.3 | 90.5 | 90.5 | 90.5 | 90.7 | 90.7 | 91.2 | 91.1 | 91.1 | 91.0 | 90.6 |
| 1963 | 91.1 | 91.2 | 91.3 | 91.3 | 91.3 | 91.7 | 92.1 | 92.1 | 92.1 | 92.2 | 92.3 | 92.5 | 91.7 |
| 1964 | 92.6 | 92.5 | 92.6 | 92.7 | 92.7 | 92.9 | 93.1 | 93.0 | 93.2 | 93.3 | 93.5 | 93.6 | 92.9 |
| 1965 | 93.6 | 93.6 | 93.7 | 94.0 | 94.2 | 94.7 | 94.8 | 94.6 | 94.8 | 94.9 | 95.1 | 95.4 | 94.5 |
| 1966 | 95.4 | 96.0 | 96.3 | 96.7 | 96.8 | 97.1 | 97.4 | 97.9 | 98.1 | 98.5 | 98.5 | 98.6 | 97.2 |
| 1967 | 98.6 | 98.7 | 98.9 | 99.1 | 99.4 | 99.7 | 100.2 | 100.5 | 100.7 | 101.0 | 101.3 | 101.6 | 100.0 |
| 1968 | 102.0 | 102.3 | 102.8 | 103.1 | 103.4 | 104.0 | 104.5 | 104.8 | 105.1 | 105.7 | 106.1 | 106.4 | 104.2 |
| 1969 | 106.7 | 107.1 | 108.0 | 108.7 | 109.0 | 109.7 | 110.2 | 110.7 | 111.2 | 111.6 | 112.2 | 112.9 | 109.8 |
| 1970 | 113.3 | 113.9 | 114.5 | 115.2 | 115.7 | 116.3 | 116.7 | 116.9 | 117.5 | 118.1 | 118.5 | 119.1 | 116.3 |
| 1971 | 119.2 | 119.4 | 119.8 | 120.2 | 120.8 | 121.5 | 121.8 | 122.1 | 122.2 | 122.4 | 122.6 | 123.1 | 121.3 |
| 1972 | 123.2 | 123.8 | 124.0 | 124.3 | 124.7 | 125.0 | 125.5 | 125.7 | 126.2 | 126.6 | 126.9 | 127.3 | 125.3 |
| 1973 | 127.7 | 128.6 | 129.8 | 130.7 | 131.5 | 132.4 | 132.7 | 135.1 | 135.5 | 136.6 | 137.6 | 138.5 | 133.1 |
| 1974 | 139.7 | 141.5 | 141.1 | 143.9 | 145.5 | 146.9 | 148.0 | 149.9 | 151.7 | 153.0 | 154.3 | 155.4 | 147.7 |
| 1975 | 156.1 | 157.2 | 157.8 | 158.6 | 159.3 | 160.6 | 162.3 | 162.8 | 163.6 | 164.6 | 165.6 | 166.3 | 161.2 |
| 1976 | 166.7 | 167.1 | 167.5 | 168.2 | 169.2 | 170.1 | 171.1 | 171.9 | 172.6 | 173.3 | 173.8 | 174.3 | 170.5 |
| 1977 | 175.3 | 177.1 | 178.2 | 179.6 | 180.6 | 181.8 | 182.6 | 183.3 | 184.0 | 184.5 | 185.4 | 186.1 | 181.5 |
| 1978 | 187.2 | 188.4 | 189.8 | 191.5 | 193.3 | 195.3 | 196.7 | 197.8 | 199.3 | 200.9 | 202.0 | 202.9 | 195.4 |
| 1979 | 204.7 | 207.1 | 209.1 | 211.5 | 214.1 | 216.6 | 218.9 | 221.1 | 223.4 | 225.4 | 227.5 | 229.9 | 217.4 |
| 1980 | 233.2 | 236.4 | 239.8 | 242.5 | 244.9 | 247.6 | 247.8 | 249.4 | 251.7 | 253.9 | 256.2 | 258.9 | 246.8 |

# APPENDIX D:

## Appendix E*
### ILLUSTRATIVE CALCULATIONS TO COMPUTE HISTORICAL COST/CONSTANT DOLLAR INFORMATION AND CURRENT COST INFORMATION
### INTRODUCTION

209. This appendix gives an example of the methodology that might be used in calculating the disclosures illustrated in Appendix A (Schedules A and B).

210. Computation of historical cost/constant dollar information and of current cost information could be based on a detailed analysis of all transactions and an updating of all revenues, expenses, gains and losses to reflect changes in purchasing power. However, the Board believes that the costs of preparing the information can be reduced with little loss of usefulness by simplifying the methods of calculation. The Board has therefore concluded that revenues, expenses, gains and losses except cost of sales and depreciation expense need not be adjusted from the amounts shown in the primary income statement and that approximate methods of computation are acceptable for adjusting cost of sales and depreciation expense (and the related asset measurements). The *measurement* of current cost is not illustrated in this appendix. However, enterprises may find it convenient to follow the methods of measurement illustrated for historical cost/constant dollar measurements, using specific price indexes in place of general price indexes.

211. The objective in making these calculations is to obtain a *reasonable degree* of accuracy—complete precision is not required. Preparers are encouraged to devise short-cut methods of calculation, appropriate to their individual circumstances. Some useful simplifications are described in the FASB Research Report, *Field Tests of Financial Reporting in Units of General Purchasing Power,* published in May 1977.

212. Where inventories and cost of sales are accounted for under the LIFO method in the primary financial statements the

---
*Copyrighted by the Financial Accounting Standards Board, High Ridge Park, Stamford, Connecticut, 06905, U.S.A. Reprinted with permission. Copies of the complete document are available from the FASB.

only adjustment normally required in computing income from continuing operations would be to eliminate the effect of changing prices on any prior period LIFO layer liquidation.

213. The following sample calculations illustrate the minimum required calculations (in paragraphs 223–237). A method of checking the arithmetic accuracy of the calculations is included in paragraphs 238 and 239.

214. Throughout this illustration $ indicates nominal dollars and C$ indicates average 1980 constant dollars.

215. The results of these calculations, summarized in paragraph 248, are reflected in the illustrative disclosures in Appendix A.

**STEPS TO RESTATE FINANCIAL INFORMATION**

216. Seven basic steps to restate nominal dollar information (either on a historical cost basis or a current cost basis) into constant dollars are illustrated in this appendix:

1. Analyze inventory (at the beginning and end of the year) and cost of goods sold to determine when the costs were incurred.
2. Restate inventory and cost of goods sold into constant dollars and current cost.
3. Analyze property, plant, and equipment, and related depreciation, depletion, and amortization expense to determine when the related assets were acquired.
4. Restate property, plant, and equipment and depreciation, depletion, and amortization expense into constant dollars and current cost.
5. Identify amount of net monetary items at the beginning and end of the period and changes during the period (Appendix D).
6. Compute the purchasing power gain or loss on net monetary items.
7. Compute change in current cost of inventory and property, plant, and equipment and the related effect of the increase in the general price level.

## Historical Cost/Nominal Dollar Financial Statements and Other Background Information

### Balance Sheets as at December 31, 1980 and 1979
(000s)

|  | 1980 | 1979 |  | 1980 | 1979 |
|---|---|---|---|---|---|
| Current assets: |  |  | Current liabilities: |  |  |
| Cash | $ 1,000 | $ 2,000 | Bank indebtedness | $ 35,000 | $ 22,000 |
| Accounts receivable | 36,000 | 30,000 | Accounts payable and accrued expenses | 12,000 | 10,000 |
| Inventories, at FIFO cost | 63,000 | 56,000 | Income taxes payable | 6,000 | 6,000 |
| Total current assets | 100,000 | 88,000 | Current portion of long-term debt | 5,000 | 5,000 |
| Property, plant, and equipment, at cost | 100,000 | 85,000 | Total current liabilities | 58,000 | 43,000 |
| Less accumulated depreciation | 56,000 | 46,000 | Deferred income taxes | 6,000 | 5,000 |
|  | 44,000 | 39,000 | Long-term debt | 34,000 | 39,000 |
|  |  |  | Total liabilities | 98,000 | 87,000 |
|  |  |  | Shareholders' equity | 46,000 | 40,000 |
|  | $144,000 | $127,000 |  | $144,000 | $127,000 |

220   *The Wealth Transfer of Inflation*

## Statement of Earnings and Shareholders' Equity

### For The Years Ended December 31, 1980 and 1979
### (000s)

|  | 1980 | 1979 |
|---|---:|---:|
| Sales | $253,000 | $220,000 |
| Cost of goods sold, exclusive of depreciation | 197,000 | 170,600 |
| Selling, general, and administrative expenses | 20,835 | 25,500 |
| Depreciation | 10,000 | 8,500 |
| Interest | 7,165 | 3,400 |
|  | 235,000 | 208,000 |
| Earnings before taxes | 18,000 | 12,000 |
| Income taxes | 9,000 | 6,000 |
| Net income | 9,000 | 6,000 |
| Shareholders' equity at beginning of the year | 40,000 | 37,000 |
|  | 49,000 | 43,000 |
| Dividends | 3,000 | 3,000 |
| Shareholders' equity at end of the year | $ 46,000 | $ 40,000 |
| Net income per share | $ 6.00 | $ 4.00 |

218. Inventory and Production

a. Inventory is accounted for on a FIFO basis and turns over four times per year. There is no significant amount of work in progress or raw material.
b. At December 31, 1980 and 1979 inventory consisted of 900,000 units and 1,000,000 units respectively—representing production of the immediately preceding quarter. Management has measured the current cost of inventory at $73 per unit at December 31, 1980 ($65,700,000) and $58 per unit at December 31, 1979 ($58,000,000).
c. Costs were incurred and goods produced as follows:

|  | 1979 | 1980 | | | | |
|---|---|---|---|---|---|---|
|  | 4th | 1st | 2nd | 3rd | 4th | Total |
| Historical Costs (000s) | $56,000 | $39,560 | $59,400 | $42,040 | $63,000 | $204,000 |
| Units produced (000s) | 1,000 | 618 | 900 | 618 | 900 | 3,036 |
| Units sold (000s) |  | 1,000 | 618 | 900 | 618 | 3,136 |

d. At December 31, 1980 the selling price per unit was $85.

219. Property, Plant, and Equipment

a. Details of fixed assets at December 31, 1980 are as follows:

| Date Acquired | Percent Depreciated | Historical Cost (000s) | Accumulated Depreciation (000s) |
|---|---|---|---|
| 1973 | 80 | $ 50,000 | $ 40,000 |
| 1974 | 70 | 5,000 | 3,500 |
| 1975 | 60 | 5,000 | 3,000 |
| 1976 | 50 | 5,000 | 2,500 |
| 1977 | 40 | 5,000 | 2,000 |
| 1978 | 30 | 5,000 | 1,500 |
| 1979 | 20 | 10,000 | 2,000 |
| 1980 | 10 | 15,000 | 1,500 |
|  |  | $100,000 | $ 56,000 |

b. Depreciation is calculated at 10% per annum, straight line. A full year's depreciation is charged in the year of acquisition.
c. There were no disposals.
d. Management has measured the current cost of property, plant, and equipment at December 31, 1980 and 1979 as follows:

(000s)

| Date Acquired | December 31, 1980 | | December 31, 1979 | |
|---|---|---|---|---|
| | Current Cost | Accumulated Depreciation | Current Cost | Accumulated Depreciation |
| 1973 | $120,000 | $ 96,000 | $110,000 | $ 77,000 |
| 1974 | 10,000 | 7,000 | 6,000 | 3,600 |
| 1975 | 15,000 | 9,000 | 7,000 | 3,500 |
| 1976 | 18,000 | 9,000 | 12,000 | 4,800 |
| 1977 | 12,000 | 4,800 | 10,000 | 3,000 |
| 1978 | 17,000 | 5,100 | 15,000 | 3,000 |
| 1979 | 12,000 | 2,400 | 10,000 | 1,000 |
| 1980 | 16,000 | 1,600 | – | – |
| | 220,000 | $134,900 | 170,000 | $ 95,900 |
| Accumulated depreciation | 134,900 | | 95,900 | |
| Net current cost | $ 85,100 | | $ 74,100 | |

e. The "net recoverable amount" has been determined by management to be in excess of net current cost.

220. Dividends
Dividends were paid at the rate of $750,000 per quarter.

*The Wealth Transfer of Inflation*

221. Consumer Price Index (All Urban Consumers)

| Average | 1973 | 133.1 | Average 4th Qtr. 1979 † | 210.0 |
|---|---|---|---|---|
| " | 1974 | 147.7 | Average 4th Qtr. 1980 † | 237.8 |
| " | 1975 | 161.2 | December 1979 | 212.9* |
| " | 1976 | 170.5 | December 1980 | 243.5* |
| " | 1977 | 181.5 | | |
| " | 1978 | 195.4 | | |
| " | 1979 | 205.0* | | |
| " | 1980 | 220.9‡ | | |

\* Estimated for illustrative purposes.
† Calculated by averaging the estimated monthly indexes for each quarter.
‡ Calculated by averaging the estimated monthly indexes for 1980. The index for the last month of the year may not be available at the time of preparing the supplemental disclosures and may be estimated by extrapolating the rate of change for the previous month.

## OBJECTIVE

222. The objective is to express the supplementary information in average 1980 dollars. As indicated in paragraph 210, nominal dollar measurements are to be used for all elements other than inventory, property, plant, and equipment, cost of sales, depreciation, and increases in current cost amounts of inventory and property, plant, and equipment.

### Inventory and Cost of Goods Sold

**Step 1: Analyze inventory and cost of goods sold.**

223. Inventory is assumed to turn over four times per year (paragraph 218). Therefore inventory with an historical cost of $63,000 at December 31, 1980 is assumed to have been acquired during the fourth quarter of 1980 and inventory with an historical cost of $56,000 at December 31, 1979 is assumed to have been acquired in the fourth quarter of 1979.

**Step 2: Restate historical cost of inventory and cost of goods sold into average 1980 dollars and at current cost.**

224. Inventory:

|  | (000s) | |
|---|---|---|
|  | Historical Cost Constant Dollars | Current Cost |
| $63,000† × 220.9 (average 1980) / 237.8 (4th qtr. 1980) | C$ 58,523 | $65,700‡ |

† From paragraph 218c.
‡ From paragraph 218b.

225. Cost of goods sold, historical cost/constant dollar:

| | Nominal Dollars | (000s) Conversion Factor | Average 1980 Dollars |
|---|---|---|---|
| Balance, January 1, 1980 | $ 56,000 | × 220.9 (avg. 1980) / 210.0 (4th qtr. 1979) | C$ 58,907 |
| Production during 1980 (paragraph 218c) | 204,000 | * | 204,000 |
| Balance, December 31, 1980 | (63,000) | × 220.9 (avg. 1980) / 237.8 (4th qtr. 1980) | (58,523) |
| Cost of goods sold | $197,000 | | C$204,384 |

226. Cost of goods sold, current cost:

| | |
|---|---|
| Current cost at the beginning of the year | $ 58/unit |
| Current cost at the end of the year | 73/unit |
| | $ 131/unit |
| Average current cost ($131 × ½) | $65.5/unit |
| Units sold during the year (000s) | 3,136 |
| Average current cost of goods sold (000s) | $205,408 |

* Assumed to be in average 1980 dollars.

*The Wealth Transfer of Inflation*

227. In applying the standard the historical cost/constant dollar and current cost amounts should be compared to the "recoverable amount." This is illustrated below:

| | |
|---|---|
| Market price/unit at year end (from paragraph 218d): | $85 |
| Restated to average 1980 dollars: | |
| $85 × 220.9 (average 1980) / 243.5 (Dec. 1980) | C$ 77.11 |
| Historical cost/constant dollar: | (000s) |
| Market value of inventory on hand at end of the year (77.11 × 900,000) | C$ 69,399 |
| Restated historical cost (paragraph 225) | 58,523 |
| Excess—no write down required. | C$ 10,876 |
| Current cost: | |
| Market value per unit at end of year | $85 |
| Current cost per unit of inventory on hand at end of year (paragraph 218b) | 73 |
| Excess—no write down required | $12 |

Property, Plant, and Equipment and Depreciation, Depletion, and Amortization Expense

**Step 3: Analyze property, plant, and equipment and depreciation, depletion, and amortization.**

228. An analysis of property, plant, and equipment was given in paragraph 219. It normally will not be necessary to restate the cost and accumulated depreciation for each asset individually in order to obtain an acceptable level of accuracy. Satisfactory results can normally be obtained by using annual totals of acquisitions and dispositions and the average index for the year of acquisition and disposal. Moreover, assets acquired many years before the balance sheet date might be combined into convenient groups where there is some doubt about the specific years of acquisition or where changes in the index for several years can be considered on an average basis. For example, the cost of all assets acquired between 1945 and 1950 could be measured by reference to an index representing an average of those years.

**Step 4: Restate property, plant, and equipment and depreciation, depletion, and amortization expense into constant dollars and current cost.**

229. Historical cost of property, plant, and equipment in average 1980 dollars:

| Date of Acquisition | (1) Historical Cost/ Nominal Dollars (000s) | | (2) Conversion Factor | | (3) (1) x (2) Historical Cost/ Constant Dollars (000s) | (4) Percent Depreciated | (5) (3) x (4) Accumulated Depreciation (000s) | (6) (3) — (5) Net |
|---|---|---|---|---|---|---|---|---|
| 1973 | $ 50,000 | × | 220.9/133.1 | (Avg. 1980 = 1973) | C$ 82,983 | 80 | C$ 66,386 | |
| 1974 | 5,000 | × | 220.9/147.7 | ( " 1980 = 1974) | 7,478 | 70 | 5,235 | |
| 1975 | 5,000 | × | 220.9/161.2 | ( " 1980 = 1975) | 6,852 | 60 | 4,111 | |
| 1976 | 5,000 | × | 220.9/170.5 | ( " 1980 = 1976) | 6,478 | 50 | 3,239 | |
| 1977 | 5,000 | × | 220.9/181.5 | ( " 1980 = 1977) | 6,085 | 40 | 2,434 | |
| 1978 | 5,000 | × | 220.9/195.4 | ( " 1980 = 1978) | 5,652 | 30 | 1,696 | |
| 1979 | 10,000 | × | 220.9/205.0 | ( " 1980 = 1979) | 10,776 | 20 | 2,155 | |
| 1980 | 15,000 | × | 220.9/220.9 | ( " 1980 = 1980) | 15,000 | 10 | 1,500 | |
| | $100,000 | | | | C$ 141,304 | | C$ 86,756 | C$ 54,548 |

*The Wealth Transfer of Inflation* 227

Historical cost/constant dollar depreciation expense for 1980 is calculated as follows:

C$ 141,304 (column (3)) × 10% straight line = C$ 14,130

**Property, Plant, and Equipment at Current Cost**

230. It will usually be appropriate to calculate current cost depreciation, depletion, and amortization expense by reference to average current cost of the related assets (current cost of assets at beginning of year and current cost of assets at end of year ÷ 2).

|  | Current Cost (000s) |
|---|---|
| Current cost, Dec. 31, 1979 (paragraph 219d) | $170,000 |
| Current cost, Dec. 31, 1980 (paragraph 219d) | 220,000 |
|  | $390,000 |
|  | ÷2 |
| Average current cost | $195,000 |
| Current cost depreciation: 10% straight line | $ 19,500 |

In this example, management has determined that the "recoverable amount" is greater than net current cost of property, plant, and equipment and there is no write down required.

Purchasing Power Gain on Net Monetary Items

**Step 5: Identify monetary items at the beginning and end of the period and change during the period.**

|  | (000s) Balance* | |
|---|---|---|
|  | Dec. 1980 | Dec. 1979 |
| 231. Monetary items: | | |
| Cash | $ 1,000 | $ 2,000 |
| Accounts receivable | 36,000 | 30,000 |
| Bank indebtedness | (35,000) | (22,000) |
| Accounts payable and accrued expenses | (12,000) | (10,000) |
| Income taxes payable | (6,000) | (6,000) |
| Current portion of long-term debt | (5,000) | (5,000) |
| Deferred income taxes | (6,000) | (5,000) |
| Long-term debt | (34,000) | (39,000) |
| Net monetary liabilities | ($61,000) | ($55,000) |

* Paragraph 217

### Step 6: Compute the purchasing power gain or loss on net monetary items.

232. The amount of net monetary items at the beginning of the year, changes in the net monetary items and the amount at the end of the year are restated into average 1980 dollars. The purchasing power gain or loss on net monetary items is then the balancing item as illustrated below:

|  | Nominal Dollars | (000s) Conversion Factor | Average 1980 Dollars |
|---|---|---|---|
| Balance, January 1, 1980 | $55,000 | × $\frac{220.9 \text{ (avg. 1980)}}{212.9 \text{ (Dec. 1979)}}$ | 55,338 |
| Increase in net monetary liabilities during the year | 6,000 | * | 6,000 |
|  |  |  | 63,067 |
| Balance, December 31, 1980 | 61,000 | × $\frac{220.9 \text{ (avg. 1980)}}{243.5 \text{ (Dec. 1980)}}$ | C$57,067 |
| Purchasing power gain on net monetary items |  |  | C$ 7,729 |

*Assumed to be in average 1980 dollars.

Increase in current cost of inventories and property, plant, and equipment

**Step 7: Compute change in current cost of inventory and property, plant, and equipment and effect of the increase in the general price level.**

233. Increase in current cost of inventories

|  | Current cost/ Nominal Dollars | Conversion Factor (000s) | Current cost/ Average 1980 Dollars |
|---|---|---|---|
| Balance, January 1, 1980 (paragraph 218b) | $ 58,000 | × 220.9 (avg. 1980) / 212.9 (Dec. 1979) | C$ 60,179 |
| Production (paragraph 218c) | 204,000 | * | 204,000 |
| Cost of goods sold (paragraph 226) | (205,408) | * | (205,408) |
| Balance, December 31, 1980 (paragraph 218b) | (65,700) | × 220.9 (avg. 1980) / 243.5 (Dec. 1980) | (59,602) |
| Increase/(decrease) current cost of inventories | $ 9,108 | | C$ 831 |

234. The "inflation component" of the increase in current cost amount is the difference between the nominal dollar and constant dollar measures. Using the numbers from paragraph 233:

|  | (000s) |
|---|---|
| Increase in current cost (nominal dollars) | $9,108 |
| Increase in current cost (constant dollars) | C$ 831 |
| Inflation component | 8,277 |

*Assumed to be in average 1980 dollars.

235. Increase in current cost of property, plant, and equipment

|  | Current cost/ Nominal Dollars | (000s) Conversion Factor | Current cost/ Average 1980 Dollars |
|---|---|---|---|
| Balance, January 1, 1980 (paragraph 219d) | $ 74,100 | × 220.9 (avg. 1980) / 212.9 (Dec. 1979) | C$ 76,884 |
| Additions (paragraph 219d) | 15,000 | * | 15,000 |
| Depreciation expense (paragraph 230) | (19,500) | * | (19,500) |
| Balance, December 31 1980 (paragraph 219d) | (85,100) | × 220.9 (avg. 1980) / 243.5 (Dec. 1980) | (77,202) |
| Increase in current cost of property, plant, and equipment | $ 15,500 | | C$ 4,818 |

236. The "inflation component" of the increase in current cost amount is the difference between the nominal dollar and constant dollars measures. Using the numbers from paragraph 235:

|  | (000s) |
|---|---|
| Increase in current cost (nominal dollars) | $15,500 |
| Increase in current cost (constant dollars) | C$ 4,818 |
| Inflation component | 10,682 |

Summary of increase in current cost amounts

237. Summarizing paragraphs 234 and 236 above:

|  | Increase in Current Cost | (000s) Inflation Component | Increase net of Inflation |
|---|---|---|---|
| Inventory | $ 9,108 | 8,277 | C$ 831 |
| Property, plant, and equipment | 15,500 | 10,682 | 4,818 |
| Totals | $24,608 | 18,959 | C$5,649 |

* Assumed to be in average 1980 dollars.

## Check of Calculations

238. A reconciliation of shareholders' equity, with changes in the amounts of net assets on a historical cost/constant dollar basis, and current cost/constant dollar basis although not required by this Statement, acts as a check on the arithmetical accuracy of the calculations.

Changes in shareholders' equity during 1980 in average 1980 dollars.

(000s)

|  | Source Paragraph | Historical Cost/ Average 1980 Dollars | Source Paragraph | Current Cost/ Average 1980 Dollars |
|---|---|---|---|---|
| Equity at Jan. 1, 1980 |  |  |  |  |
| Inventory | (225) | C$ 58,907 | (233) | C$ 60,179 |
| Property, plant, and equipment-net | (239) | 53,678 | (235) | 76,884 |
| Net monetary items | (232) | (57,067) | (232) | (57,067) |
|  |  | 55,518 |  | 79,996 |
| Loss from continuing operations | (App. A) | (2,514) | (App. A) | (8,908) |
| Dividends | (220) | (3,000) | (220) | (3,000) |
| Gain from decline in purchasing power of net monetary liabilities | (232) | 7,729 | (232) | 7,729 |
| Excess of increase in specific prices over increase in the general price level |  |  | (237) | 5,649 |
|  |  | C$ 57,733 |  | C$ 81,466 |
| Equity at December 31, 1980 |  |  |  |  |
| Inventory | (224) | C$ 58,523 | (233) | C$ 59,602 |
| Property, plant, and equipment-net | (229) | 54,548 | (235) | 77,202 |
| Net monetary items | (232) | (55,338) | (232) | (55,338) |
|  |  | C$ 57,733 |  | C$ 81,466 |

239. Historical cost/constant dollar property, plant, and equipment at December 31, 1979 in average 1980 dollars.

**(000s)**

| Date of Acquisition | Historical Cost/<br>Constant Dollars* | Percent<br>Depreciated | Accumulated<br>Depreciation |
|---|---|---|---|
| 1973 | C$ 82,983 | 70 | C$58,088 |
| 1974 | 7,478 | 60 | 4,487 |
| 1975 | 6,852 | 50 | 3,426 |
| 1976 | 6,478 | 40 | 2,591 |
| 1977 | 6,085 | 30 | 1,826 |
| 1978 | 5,652 | 20 | 1,130 |
| 1979 | 10,776 | 10 | 1,078 |
| Totals | C$126,304 | | C$72,626 |

| | |
|---|---|
| Accumulated depreciation | 72,626 |
| Net property, plant, and equipment at Dec. 31, 1979, carried to paragraph 238 | C$ 53,678 |

* Paragraph 229

240. Restated amounts

**Summary of Amounts Restated in Average 1980 Dollars**

**(000s)**

| | Source<br>Paragraph | Historical Cost/<br>Constant Dollars | Source<br>Paragraph | Current Cost/<br>Information |
|---|---|---|---|---|
| Cost of goods sold | (225) | C$204,384 | (226) | C$205,408 |
| Depreciation expense | (229) | C$ 14,130 | (230) | C$ 19,500 |
| Purchasing power gain on net monetary items | (232) | C$ 7,729 | (232) | C$ 7,729 |
| Increase in current cost of inventories | | | (234) | C$ 831 |
| Increase in current cost amount of property, plant, and equipment | | | (236) | C$ 4,818 |
| Inventory | (224) | C$ 58,523 | (233) | C$ 59,602 |
| Property, plant, and equipment-net | (229) | C$ 54,548 | (235) | C$ 77,202 |

## Appendix F
## THE CONSUMER PRICE INDEX

241. The table included in this appendix is the official Department of Labor Consumer Price Index—CPI (U), US City Average, All Items (1967 = 100). This table includes monthly indexes and the average index for the year from 1913.

Monthly updates to the table are published in the United States Department of Labor, Bureau of Labor Statistics, "News."

U.S. Department of Labor
Room 1539
Bureau of Labor Statistics
Washington, D.C. 20212

Consumer Price Index

All Urban Consumers—(CPI-U)

U.S. City Average

All items

(1967 = 100)

| YEAR | JAN. | FEB. | MAR. | APR. | MAY | JUNE | JULY | AUG. | SEP. | OCT. | NOV. | DEC. | AVG. |
|---|---|---|---|---|---|---|---|---|---|---|---|---|---|
| 1913 | 29.4 | 29.3 | 29.3 | 29.4 | 29.2 | 29.3 | 29.6 | 29.8 | 29.9 | 30.1 | 30.2 | 30.1 | 29.7 |
| 1914 | 30.1 | 29.8 | 29.7 | 29.4 | 29.6 | 29.8 | 30.1 | 30.5 | 30.6 | 30.4 | 30.5 | 30.4 | 30.1 |
| 1915 | 30.3 | 30.1 | 29.8 | 30.1 | 30.2 | 30.3 | 30.3 | 30.3 | 30.4 | 30.7 | 30.9 | 31.0 | 30.4 |
| 1916 | 31.3 | 31.3 | 31.6 | 31.9 | 32.0 | 32.4 | 32.4 | 32.8 | 33.4 | 33.8 | 34.4 | 34.6 | 32.7 |
| 1917 | 35.0 | 35.8 | 36.0 | 37.6 | 38.4 | 38.8 | 38.4 | 39.0 | 39.7 | 40.4 | 40.5 | 41.0 | 38.4 |
| 1918 | 41.8 | 42.2 | 42.0 | 42.5 | 43.3 | 44.1 | 45.2 | 46.0 | 47.1 | 47.9 | 48.7 | 49.4 | 45.1 |
| 1919 | 49.5 | 48.4 | 49.0 | 49.9 | 50.6 | 50.7 | 52.1 | 53.0 | 53.3 | 54.2 | 55.5 | 56.7 | 51.8 |
| 1920 | 57.8 | 58.5 | 59.1 | 60.8 | 61.8 | 62.7 | 62.3 | 60.7 | 60.0 | 59.7 | 59.3 | 58.0 | 60.0 |

234  *The Wealth Transfer of Inflation*

| Year | | | | | | | | | | | | | |
|------|---|---|---|---|---|---|---|---|---|---|---|---|---|
| 1921 | 57.0 | 55.2 | 54.8 | 54.1 | 53.1 | 52.8 | 52.9 | 53.1 | 52.5 | 52.4 | 52.1 | 51.8 | 53.6 |
| 1922 | 50.7 | 50.6 | 50.0 | 50.0 | 50.0 | 50.1 | 50.2 | 49.7 | 49.8 | 50.1 | 50.3 | 50.5 | 50.2 |
| 1923 | 50.3 | 50.2 | 50.4 | 50.6 | 50.7 | 51.0 | 51.5 | 51.3 | 51.6 | 51.7 | 51.8 | 51.8 | 51.1 |
| 1924 | 51.7 | 51.5 | 51.2 | 51.0 | 51.0 | 51.0 | 51.1 | 51.0 | 51.2 | 51.4 | 51.6 | 51.7 | 51.2 |
| 1925 | 51.8 | 51.6 | 51.7 | 51.6 | 51.8 | 52.4 | 53.1 | 53.1 | 52.9 | 53.1 | 54.0 | 53.7 | 52.5 |
| 1926 | 53.7 | 53.5 | 53.2 | 53.7 | 53.4 | 53.0 | 52.5 | 52.2 | 52.5 | 52.7 | 52.9 | 52.9 | 53.0 |
| 1927 | 52.5 | 52.1 | 51.8 | 51.8 | 52.2 | 52.7 | 51.7 | 51.4 | 51.7 | 52.0 | 51.9 | 51.8 | 52.0 |
| 1928 | 51.7 | 51.2 | 51.2 | 51.3 | 51.6 | 51.2 | 51.2 | 51.3 | 51.7 | 51.6 | 51.5 | 51.3 | 51.3 |
| 1929 | 51.2 | 51.1 | 50.9 | 50.7 | 51.0 | 51.2 | 51.7 | 51.9 | 51.8 | 51.8 | 51.7 | 51.4 | 51.3 |
| 1930 | 51.2 | 51.0 | 50.7 | 51.0 | 50.7 | 50.4 | 49.7 | 49.4 | 49.7 | 49.4 | 49.0 | 48.3 | 50.0 |
| 1931 | 47.6 | 46.9 | 46.6 | 46.3 | 45.8 | 45.3 | 45.2 | 45.1 | 44.9 | 44.6 | 44.1 | 43.7 | 45.6 |
| 1932 | 42.8 | 42.2 | 42.0 | 41.7 | 41.1 | 40.8 | 40.8 | 40.3 | 40.1 | 39.8 | 39.6 | 39.2 | 40.9 |
| 1933 | 38.6 | 38.0 | 37.7 | 37.6 | 37.7 | 38.1 | 39.2 | 39.6 | 39.6 | 39.6 | 39.6 | 39.4 | 38.8 |
| 1934 | 39.6 | 39.9 | 39.9 | 39.8 | 39.9 | 40.0 | 40.0 | 40.1 | 40.7 | 40.4 | 40.3 | 40.2 | 40.1 |
| 1935 | 40.8 | 41.1 | 41.0 | 41.4 | 41.2 | 41.1 | 40.9 | 40.9 | 41.1 | 41.1 | 41.3 | 41.4 | 41.1 |
| 1936 | 41.4 | 41.2 | 41.0 | 41.0 | 41.0 | 41.4 | 41.6 | 41.9 | 42.0 | 41.9 | 41.9 | 41.9 | 41.5 |
| 1937 | 42.2 | 42.3 | 42.6 | 42.8 | 43.0 | 43.1 | 43.3 | 43.4 | 43.8 | 43.6 | 43.3 | 43.2 | 43.0 |
| 1938 | 42.6 | 42.2 | 42.2 | 42.4 | 42.2 | 42.2 | 42.3 | 42.2 | 42.2 | 42.0 | 41.9 | 42.0 | 42.2 |
| 1939 | 41.8 | 41.6 | 41.5 | 41.4 | 41.4 | 41.4 | 41.4 | 41.4 | 42.2 | 42.0 | 42.0 | 41.8 | 41.6 |
| 1940 | 41.7 | 42.0 | 41.9 | 41.9 | 42.0 | 42.1 | 42.0 | 41.9 | 42.0 | 42.0 | 42.0 | 42.2 | 42.0 |
| 1941 | 42.2 | 42.2 | 42.4 | 42.8 | 43.1 | 43.9 | 44.1 | 44.5 | 45.3 | 45.8 | 46.2 | 46.3 | 44.1 |
| 1942 | 46.9 | 47.3 | 47.9 | 48.2 | 48.7 | 48.8 | 49.0 | 49.3 | 49.4 | 49.9 | 50.2 | 50.6 | 48.8 |
| 1943 | 50.6 | 50.7 | 51.5 | 52.1 | 52.5 | 52.4 | 52.0 | 51.8 | 52.0 | 52.2 | 52.1 | 52.2 | 51.8 |
| 1944 | 52.1 | 52.0 | 52.0 | 52.3 | 52.5 | 52.6 | 52.9 | 53.1 | 53.1 | 53.1 | 53.1 | 53.3 | 52.7 |
| 1945 | 53.3 | 53.2 | 53.2 | 53.3 | 53.7 | 54.2 | 54.3 | 54.3 | 54.1 | 54.1 | 54.3 | 54.5 | 53.9 |
| 1946 | 54.5 | 54.3 | 54.7 | 55.0 | 55.3 | 55.9 | 59.2 | 60.5 | 61.2 | 62.4 | 63.9 | 64.4 | 58.5 |
| 1947 | 64.4 | 64.3 | 65.7 | 65.7 | 65.5 | 66.0 | 66.6 | 67.3 | 68.9 | 68.9 | 69.3 | 70.2 | 66.9 |
| 1948 | 71.0 | 70.4 | 70.2 | 71.2 | 71.7 | 72.2 | 73.1 | 73.4 | 73.4 | 73.1 | 72.6 | 72.1 | 72.1 |

# APPENDIX E:

## Examples Of Consolidated Statement Of Income Adjusted For Inflation As Required By The Financial Accounting Standards Board (FASB) Statement No. 33

This is an analysis of the inflation-adjusted financial reports of the Pacific Gas and Electric Co. (Exhibits E-1 and E-2) and the Eaton Corporation (Exhibit E-3). These supplementary financial reports are found at the end of the analysis.

The two reports under review here were selected at random. They demonstrate how differently the infla-accounting systems, Constant Dollar and Current Cost Accounting, report financial results from that reported by conventional Historic Cost Accounting.

For example, the Pacific Gas and Electric Company (PG&E) "Consolidated Statement of Income, etc." Exhibit E-1, shows us that Historic Cost Accounting reported an income 45 times greater than that arrived at by Current Cost Accounting. This is valuable information for the users of financial statements and not heretofore available.

H$ = Historic Cost Dollar

C$ = Dollars having approximately the same purchasing power as the real dollar had in mid-1979.

|  | In Millions | |
|---|---|---|
|  | Income | Depreciation |
| Historic Cost Accounting | H$458 | H$251 |
| Constant Dollar Accounting | C$215 | C$494 |
| Current Cost Accounting | C$ 10 | C$699 |

It is obvious that the extreme differences in income reported by the three systems of accounting are attributable to the contradictory depreciation charges. Historic Cost Accounting computed depreciation expense at $251 million, whereas Current Cost Accounting reported the same expense at $699 million. The footnote at the bottom of the Consolidated Statement, etc. (Exhibit E-1) disclosed the reason for the dissimilar depreciation charges. Historic Cost valued PG&E's fixed asset at $8 plus billion. Current Cost valued the same assets at $17 plus billion.

The 8$ plus billion historic cost valuation of the property, plant, and equipment of PG&E is a nonsense figure. It was arrived at by totaling the number of dollars paid for the assets as they were acquired over many years. As we explained in Chapter 3, dollars of different years cannot be added because they measure different quantities of goods and services. Unlike quantities cannot be mathematically manipulated. We could as well add kopecs to wampam or bustles to blue jeans, as we could add the dollars of different years.

The $8 billion historic cost figure fails in another way to speak the truth. Money is a goods symbol. It can be nothing else. It is evident that $8 plus billion does not symbolize PG&E's fixed assets. Therefore, the figure has no meaning.

Since the value basis used to compute Historic Cost depreciation is invalid, it follows that the depreciation charge of $251 million and the net income figure of $458 million are also invalid.

Financial analysts regularly cite price-earnings ratios in their recommendations of stocks. The earnings they use to compute their P/E ratio are Historic Cost Accounting earnings. They would, for example, use the Historic Cost profit of $458 million in computing the P/E ratio of Pacific Gas and Electric stock. This is silly. No informed person would believe that PG&E had a profit of $458 million—was better off by $458 million at December 31, 1979 than it was at January 1, 1979.

All profits are expected to produce cash. Who would seriously argue that PG&E did realize, or would realize, cash in the future from its reported $458 million Historic Cost profit? Money is a goods symbol. Where can we find the goods symbolized by the $458 million? They are not to be found.

Also devoid of reality are the Constant Dollar Accounting reports of net income of $215 million and the depreciation charge of $494 million. The Constant Dollar depreciation charge of $494 million is computed on the historic acquisition costs of assets. These costs are increased by the percentage the Consumer Price Index advanced during the period the individual assets were held. The computation is predicated on the proposition that the cost of PG&E's assets advanced at the same ratio as did the cost of household goods and services for an urban family of four.

The Current Cost Accounting depreciation charge of $699 million gives lie to this supposition. It demonstrates that the cost of PG&E's fixed assets increased in price at a greater rate than did the Consumer Price Index. Since this is true, we can conclude that the Constant Dollar profit of

$215 million is invalid. It seems evident that PG&E could not spend $215 million during the year 1979 and still be as well off as it was at the beginning of 1979.

The $10 million profit reported by Current Cost Accounting is not 100% accurate, but it approximates fiscal truth as closely as accounting can measure. The logic of Current Cost Accounting is that all current costs of future operations must be provided for before a profit can be struck.

However, this is not to say that the Current Cost profit was earned from operations. It was probably financed by a holding gain from debt. PG&E is reported to have received a wealth transfer from its creditors in the amount of $634 million. This figure is reported under "General Information" at the bottom of Exhibit E-2, "Five Year Comparison . . . as Required By FASB Statement No. 33." Note that the item "Reduction of purchasing power lost through debt financing, $634 million" is not shown as an addition to profit. This is in compliance with instructions given in FASB's Statement No. 33.

We do not know what part of the $634 million wealth transfer entered the cash account of PG&E in 1979. We can surmise that some part of the wealth transfer was converted into cash, in the payment of debts and interest in amounts of less value than was originally contracted for.

However, we do know that the stockholders of PG&E were not the beneficiaries of the wealth transfer from the creditors. PG&E realized a loss of 79 cents a share after provisions were made for preferred stock dividends. Furthermore, the market value of PG&E's stock fell by 2.21 C$. See last line of Exhibit E-2. That is the market price per share of common stock fell from 23.85 C$ in 1978 to 21.64 C$ in 1979.

While it is certain that the creditors lost wealth, it appears that PG&E was merely the conduit for its transfer. Those who benefited from the wealth transfer were the customers of PG&E, who received utilities at less than their cost; the employees who received compensation in excess of standard; and the suppliers who raised their prices at a rate greater than the CPI.

We should mention here that the wealth transferred from the bondholders, PG&E's principal creditors, in any one year is an accumulation of wealth of several years. A bond issued in 1960 for $1000 would steadily decline in value over the life of the bond. But the wealth transfer from the decline in the worth of the bond would be realized in cash only in the year the bond was redeemed.

## Conclusion Of Review Of Pacific Gas And Electric Supplementary Financial Data

From our review of the supplemental financial data of the PG&E Company, a company well regarded in financial circles, we conclude that the firm was able to operate in the calendar year 1979, without serious financial difficulties, because the inflation caused the creditors to finance PG&E's losses from operations. This should give pause to the investors and creditors; to the employees and management; to the taxing authority and the utility rate setters. A review of almost any other utility would reveal the same lack of profit found in PG&E and the same massive transfer of wealth from the bondholders.


## The Supplementary Financial Data Does Not Reveal The True Loss Or Gain From Holding Stock

I have but one more item to discuss with you. That is, that you can be misled by the apparent amount of gain or loss that would be realized from the sale of stock, even though the stock quotation is given in constant dollars (C$). The misconception of gain or loss from the sale of stock arises from the fact that the out-of-pocket cost of stock, in real terms, must include the capital gains tax that is assessed on illusory income.

To illustrate the point, let's look at the Eaton Company's "Five Year Comparison of Selected Data, etc.," Exhibit E-3. This supplementary inflation adjusted financial report shows that the market price of the stock declined from 25 7/8 C$ in 1975 to 24 1/4 C$ in 1979.

From this we might conclude that an Eaton shareholder's loss was 1.63 in 1979 dollars per share. But this would understate the loss of a person who purchased Eaton stock in 1975 and sold the shares in 1979. This person's loss would be C$2.90 per share, not C$1.63. See Exhibit E-4.

The reason for the difference in the amount of loss, C$2.90 vs. C$1.63, is that the State and Federal governments compute capital gains and losses on historic cost, not on historic cost adjusted for inflation—that is, in constant dollars (C$).

Exhibit E-4 illustrates the issue we detailed in Chapter 14: The stockholders' cost of shares or the bondholders' cost of bonds is the value paid at date of purchase, plus the income tax that will be paid on illusory infla-capital gain at date of sale.

# EXHIBIT E-1

| | In Thousands | | | Earnings Per Common Share |
|---|---|---|---|---|
| | Operating Revenues | Operating Income | Net Income | |
| December 31, 1979 | $1,244,469 | $117,006 | $101,264 | $.71 |
| September 30, 1979 | $1,093,159 | $140,538 | $123,312 | $.98 |
| June 30, 1979 | $ 980,513 | $129,540 | $118,000 | $.94 |
| March 31, 1979 | $1,054,079 | $128,819 | $115,658 | $.92 |
| December 31, 1978 | $1,071,808 | $130,521 | $117,727 | $.95 |
| September 30, 1978 | $ 874,058 | $130,440 | $115,795 | $.94 |
| June 30, 1978 | $ 768,537 | $108,953 | $ 89,170 | $.70 |
| March 31, 1978 | $ 854,970 | $ 98,174 | $ 77,758 | $.60 |

For the quarter ended December 31, 1978, net income and earnings per common share were decreased $1,133,000 and two cents, respectively, from amounts previously reported to reflect restatement by a consolidated subsidiary (See Note 1).

## Supplemental Information Required by Financial Accounting Standards Board Statement No. 33 (unaudited)

For many years the purchasing power of the dollar, as measured by consumer and wholesale price indices, has declined each year. This decline in purchasing power of the dollar is commonly called "inflation."

Many complex theories have been proposed in an attempt to measure the impact of inflation on business, but no solution has emerged that commands general acceptance. In 1979 the Financial Accounting Standards Board (FASB) issued Statement of Financial Accounting Standards No. 33 requiring that certain supplemental financial information be furnished showing historical information converted to two bases—constant dollars and current cost—using specified techniques. Constant dollar amounts as reported herein represent historical amounts converted to dollars having approximately the same purchasing power as the real dollar had in mid 1979 as measured by the Consumer Price Index for All Urban Consumers.

Current cost amounts represent the price in constant dollars the Company would expect to pay for its assets if it could obtain them at today's prices.

Because regulation limits the recovery of inventory amounts to historical costs, the Company inventories are considered to have the same constant dollar and historical cost. Statement No. 33 requires that utility plant be repriced into constant dollars and that depreciation presented on both the constant dollar and current cost basis be calculated on the repriced amount. It was assumed that applying the Handy-Whitman Index of Public Utility Construction Costs for the Pacific Coast Division to historical cost of surviving plant would approximate current cost. The current year's provisions for depreciation on the constant dollar and current cost amounts of utility plant were determined by applying the Company's depreciation rates to the constant dollar and current costs.

As prescribed in Statement No. 33, income taxes were not adjusted.

PG&E has serious reservations as to whether the required supplemental financial information is appropriate for measuring the impact of inflation on a utility regulated, as PG&E is, on a cost-of-service basis. This information is presented solely because it is required to be presented. It should be clearly understood that the required information is complicated, difficult to understand and because of the permitted subjectivity inherent in developing this prescribed information unwarranted comparisons and inferences may result.

240 *The Wealth Transfer of Inflation*

## Consolidated Statement of Income from Continuing Operations Adjusted for Changing Prices As Required By FASB Statement No. 33
For the Year Ended December 31, 1979

|  | Conventional Historical Cost | In Thousands Constant Dollar | Current Cost |
|---|---|---|---|
| Operating Revenues | $4,372,000 | C$4,372,000 | C$4,372,000 |
| Operation, Maintenance and Other | 3,663,000 | 3,663,000 | 3,663,000 |
| Depreciation | 251,000 | 494,000 | 699,000 |
| Total | 3,914,000 | 4,157,000 | 4,362,000 |
| Income from continuing operations (excluding reduction to net recoverable cost) | $ 458,000 | C$ 215,000* | C$ 10,000 |
| Increase during the year in specific prices of property, plant and equipment** |  |  | C$1,850,000 |
| Reduction to net recoverable cost |  | C$ (779,000) | (255,000) |
| Effect of increase in general price level |  |  | (2,169,000) |
| Excess of increase in general price level over increase in specific prices after reduction to net recoverable cost |  |  | (574,000) |
| Reduction of purchasing power loss through debt financing |  | 634,000 | 634,000 |
| Net |  | C$ (145,000) | C$ 60,000 |

C$ – Dollars having approximately the same purchasing power as the real dollar had in mid 1979.

*Including the reduction to net recoverable cost, the loss from continuing operations on a constant dollar basis would have been C$564,000,000.

**At December 31, 1979, current cost of property, plant and equipment, net of accumulated depreciation was C$17,759,000,000 while historical cost or net cost recoverable through depreciation was $8,232,000,000.

*The Wealth Transfer of Inflation*

# EXHIBIT E-2

## Five-Year Comparison of Selected Supplementary Consolidated Financial Data Adjusted for Effects of Changing Prices As Required by FASB Statement No. 33

In Thousands (Except per share amounts)

| Years Ended December 31, | 1979 | 1978 | 1977 | 1976 | 1975 |
|---|---|---|---|---|---|
| Operating Revenues | C$4,372,000 | C$3,976,000 | C$4,352,000 | C$3,890,000 | C$3,159,000 |
| **Historical Cost Information Adjusted for General Inflation** | | | | | |
| Income from continuing operations (excluding reduction to net recoverable cost) | C$ 215,000 | | | | |
| Income per common share (after dividend requirements on preferred stock and excluding reduction to net recoverable cost) | C$ 1.19 | | | | |
| Net assets at year end at net recoverable cost | C$3,189,000 | | | | |
| **Current Cost Information** | | | | | |
| Income from continuing operations (excluding reduction to net recoverable cost) | C$ 10,000 | | | | |
| Loss per common share (after dividend requirements on preferred stock) | C$ (.79) | | | | |
| Excess of increase in general price level over increase in specific prices after reduction to net recoverable cost | C$ (574,000) | | | | |
| Net assets at year end at net recoverable cost | C$3,189,000 | | | | |
| **General Information** | | | | | |
| Reduction of purchasing power loss through debt financing | C$ 634,000 | | | | |
| Cash dividends declared per common share | C$ 2.38 | C$ 2.41 | C$ 2.40 | C$ 2.40 | C$ 2.54 |
| Market price per common share at year end | C$ 21.64 | C$ 23.85 | C$ 28.06 | C$ 28.86 | C$ 27.14 |

C$ – Dollars having approximately the same purchasing power as the real dollar had in mid-1979.

| Average consumer price index | 217.6 | 195.4 | 181.5 | 170.5 | 161.2 |
|---|---|---|---|---|---|
| Base year 1967=100 | | | | | |

# EXHIBIT E-3

## Supplemental Statement of Income Adjusted for Changing Prices
### Year Ended December 31, 1979

|  | As Reported in the Historical Income Statement | Adjusted for General Inflation (Constant Average 1979 Dollars) | Adjusted for Changes in Specific Prices (Current Costs) |
|---|---|---|---|
|  | (Millions of Dollars) | | |
| Net sales and other revenues | $3,394 | $3,394 | $3,394 |
| Costs and expenses*: | | | |
| Cost of products sold | 2,487 | 2,569 | 2,576 |
| Selling and administrative expenses | 453 | 456 | 457 |
| Research and development expenses | 67 | 68 | 69 |
| Interest expense | 87 | 87 | 87 |
| Exchange loss — net | 4 | 4 | 4 |
|  | 3,098 | 3,184 | 3,193 |
| Income Before Income Taxes | 296 | 210 | 201 |
| Income taxes | 142 | 142 | 142 |
| Net Income | $ 154 | $ 68 | $ 59 |
| Unrealized gain from decline in purchasing power of net amounts owed |  | $ 96 | $ 96 |

At December 31, 1979, current cost of inventories was $836 million (historical amount — $783 million) and current cost of property, plant and equipment, net of accumulated depreciation was $1,280 million (historical amount — $780 million). The excess of the increase in current costs of inventories and property, plant and equipment ($276 million) over the increase in general inflation on inventories and property, plant and equipment ($246 million) amounted to $30 million.

*The aggregate total of depreciation expense that has been allocated to the various expense categories amounts to $86 million on a historical cost basis, $130 million adjusted for general inflation and $155 million adjusted for changes in specific prices.

*continued*

As reported in the 1979 historical income statement, 48% of income before taxes was distributed to various worldwide governments as income taxes, 15% was distributed to shareholders as dividends, thus leaving presumably 37% of income before taxes for capital maintenance. Since current U.S. tax laws do not allow deductions for higher depreciation adjustments for the effects of inflation, the provision for income taxes in the statement of income adjusted for inflation is the same as reported in the historical income statement. Therefore, income before income taxes adjusted for the effects of general inflation was distributed as income taxes at the rate of 68%, to shareholders at the rate of 20%, thus leaving only 12% of income before income taxes adjusted for general inflation for capital maintenance. Income before income taxes adjusted for changes in specific prices was distributed as income taxes at the rate of 71%, to shareholders at the rate of 21%, leaving 8% for capital maintenance. As a result, taxes are actually levied in extremely high proportions to "real" distributable income.

**Five-Year Comparison of Selected Data Adjusted For Effects of Changing Prices***

| | 1979 | 1978 | 1977 | 1976 | 1975 |
|---|---|---|---|---|---|
| | (Millions of Dollars Except for Per Share Amounts) | | | | |
| Net Sales** | $3,360 | $3,105 | $2,528 | $2,306 | $2,102 |
| **Historical Cost Information Adjusted for General Inflation*** | | | | | |
| Net income | $ 68 | | | | |
| Primary net income per Common Share | 2.58 | | | | |
| Net assets at year-end | 1,270 | | | | |
| **Current Cost Information** | | | | | |
| Net income | $ 59 | | | | |
| Primary net income per Common Share | 2.24 | | | | |
| Net assets at year-end | 1,418 | | | | |
| Excess of increase in current costs of inventories and property, plant and equipment over increase in general inflation | 30 | | | | |
| **Other Information*** | | | | | |
| Unrealized gain from decline in purchasing power of net amounts owed | $ 96 | | | | |
| Dividends per Common Share | $ 1.61 | $ 1.68 | $ 1.60 | $ 1.58 | $ 1.63 |
| Market price per Common Share at year-end | 24¼ | 24⅞ | 28⅜ | 36½ | 25⅞ |
| Average Consumer Price Index | 217.4 | 195.4 | 181.5 | 170.5 | 161.2 |

*Certain information relating to years prior to 1979 is omitted, as it is impractical to obtain such information.
**Amounts are in average 1979 constant dollars by application of the average Consumer Price Index to historical data.

**EXHIBIT E-4**

## COMPUTATION OF PURCHASING POWER LOSS FROM HOLDING EATON STOCK

|  | Historic Cost $s | Constant 1979 $s |
|---|---|---|
| One Share of Stock Sold 12/31/79 | $24.25 | $24.25 |
| Cost of Share Sold at 12/31/75 | 19.18 | 25.88 |
| Real Purchasing Power Loss |  | $ (1.63) |
| Apparent Historic Cost Gain Subject to Capital Gains Tax | $ 5.07 |  |
| Capital Gains Tax at 25% | −1.27 | +1.27 |
| Historic Cost after Tax Gain | $ 3.80 |  |
| Real Purchasing Power Loss |  | $ (2.90) |

# Index

**A**

Accounts payable, definition of, 94
Accounts receivable, definition of, 94
Accounts receivable loss, 53, 54
Accrual accounting, 21, 69, 72, 89, 133-135, 138
Anticipated inflation, 25, 26, 28
Assets, 22
Asset index, 101

**B**

Bankruptcy, 29
Bin and pile inventory, 108
Bonds, 11, 42
Bookkeeping profit, 132
Borrowed capital, 35, 36

**C**

Capital equity base, definition of, 81
Capital gain, taxable, 124
Cash convention, 21
Cash-cycle, 29, 43
Cash-flow accounting, 5, 23, 81, 92, 129-145
   analysis, 133
   forecast, 148, 149
   planning, 92, 149, 170, 176
   statement, 87
   inflow, 96, 102, 139, 153, 168, 177, 178, 179
Cash management, 52
Cash profit, 132
Cash strategy, 49
CCA (*see* Current cost accounting)
CDA (*see* Constant dollar accounting)
Certificate of deposit (C.D.), 149
CFA (*see* Cash-flow accounting)

Chapter XI-(Bankruptcy), 29
Commodity index, 56
Common size analysis, 98-100
Constant dollar, 26, 27, 76, 81, 161, 163
   accounting, 5, 19, 23
   83, 128-139, 181-188, 191, 198-205
Constant value dollar, 182
Constant purchasing power, 36
Consumer price index, 9, 52
Consumer price index dollar, 199
Cost of equity capital, 35, 36
Cost savings, 196, 197
CPI (*see* Consumer price index)
CPI$ (*see* Consumer price index dollar)
Currency, 7, 8
Current cost accounting, 5, 19, 23, 81, 87, 128-139, 181-191, 200-205
   dollar, 182
Current ratio, 94, 95

**D**

Debt v. equity, 34
Debt-to-equity ratio, 36, 39
Deferred accounts payable, 41
Deferred tax, 39, 40
Depreciable assets, 19
Depreciation 21, 69-73
Dollar dating of, 15, 22
Dollar standard of measurement, 14, 15
Dollar value of, 5, 6, 9, 26, 27, 29, 31, 32
Double declining balance method, 40
Double taxation, 51

**E**

Economic activity, 13, 15
Economic gain, 13

Economic income, 22
Economic loss, 13
Effective rate of interest, 30
Equity, 50, 53
Equity capital, 33, 34, 35
Equity index, 101
Equity ratio, 36
Estate tax, 40

**F**
FIFO, 106-120
FIFO inventory convention, 97, 115
Financial analysis, 102
First-in, first-out, (*see* FIFO)
Fiscal reality, 20
Fixed asset value, 79
Fixed dollar asset, 149
Fixed dollar investment, 149, 153, 156
Foreign currency basket, 55, 56
Foreign money, 55
Free cash, definition of, 94
Funding by borrowing, 34
Funding by debt, 34
Funded by equity, 34
Funding by equity capital, 34

**G**
German mark, 20, 56
Gold, 55, 56
   coin, 56
   bullion, 56
Grady method, 81-83, 87

**H**
HCA (*see* Historic cost accounting)
HCA postulate, 61, 62
Hidden wealth transfer, 17
Historic cost accounting, 4, 61, 69
Historic cost accounting errors, 17, 23
Historic Cost accrual accounting, 8
Historic cost dollars, 33
Historic cost loss, 75
Historic cost profit, 75
Holding debt, 33
Holding gain, 18, 24, 28-32, 39, 42
   47-49, 113, 165, 171, 178, 194
   197, 198
Holding gain strategy, 48
Holding loss, 18, 25, 31, 47, 49-51, 178,
   197, 198

Holding loss formula, 50
Holding, loss nondedutible, 48
Holding loss strategy, 48

**I**
Illusory earning, 27, 51
   FIFO profit, 114
   gain, 61, 65, 154
   income, 149, 153, 155, 179
   infla-interest, 28
   infla-profit, 81, 133
   inventory profit, 61, 64, 66, 105,
     115, 172
   profit, 61, 71, 113
Imaginary profits, 106, 121
Income, definition of, 23, 123
Index trend analysis, 98, 100-102
Infla- (*see also* inflationary)
   accounting, 5, 129
   cost, 116, 178, 179
   expense, 51
   income, 27, 81
   interest, 28, 30, 31, 36
   loss, 71, 81
   mark-up, 61
   profit, 61, 115
   tax, 26, 27, 66, 81, 112, 114-116, 155,
     161, 171, 178, 179
Inflation, 3, 4, 5, 9, 11, 13, 15, 17
   22, 25, 28, 32, 39, 42, 50
   cost, 25
   definition of, 3
   double digit, 54
   factor, 95-97, 148-150, 158
   rate, 25, 28
   redistribution, 6
   strategy, 3, 6, 47, 53
Inflationary accounting systems,
   definition of, 19
Interest cost of, 29, 31, 64
   cost reduction, 49
   effective rate of, 30
   on loan, 26, 27, 29, 39
   rate of, 25, 26, 28, 30, 31
   real cost of, 31
   reduction of, 33
Interest-free debt, 39
   loan, 113, 121
Inventory, 19, 21, 29, 39, 40, 53,
   64, 105-120, 139

account, 20
 holding gain, 65, 66
 replacement, 61
I.R.S. disagreement with, 40

**L**
Labor index, 56
Last-in, first-out, (*see* LIFO)
LIFO, 39, 40, 105-121, 172
 inventory, 66, 81, 105-121
 layer liquidation, 110, 115, 118, 120
 profit, 117, 119-120, 125
Loans, 25, 26, 29, 31, 32, 41
Loan transaction, 4, 5, 25
Lock boxes, 54
Long-term debts, 19, 31, 94
 liability, 42
 loan, 42
Loss of wealth, 4, 17

**M**
Mixed dollar
 (*see* Dollar, dating of)
 (*see* Dollar, value of)
Monetary assets, 19, 47-49
 holding gain, 43, 47, 48
 income, 22
 holding loss, 47, 48
 inflation, 33
 liabilities, 29, 43, 44
 loss, 47, 194
 units, 13, 14, 15
Money, 7, 8, 11, 23, 62
 fund, 49
Mortgages, 42, 149

**N**
Newspeak, 124
Nonconvertible preferred stock, 42
Nondepreciable assets, 81
Nonfinancial analysis, 102
Nonfinancial factor, 93-95, 102

**O**
Obsolescence, 71
Opportunity cost, 49, 50

**P**
Preferred, nonconvertible stock, 42

Preferred stock, 42
Price control, 3
Producer price index, 76
Profit, definition of, 23
Profit from debt, 24, 29, 30
Profit and loss statement, 22, 23
Purchasing power, 5, 23, 26, 35, 42,
 47, 50, 83

**R**
Rack and shelf inventory, 108
Real income, 22, 26, 30
Real property, 42
Recoverable amount dollar, 201
Redistribution of wealth, 24, 33
Relative price stability, 33
Reversible asset, 43
Risk factor, 25, 31

**S**
Savings account, 149
SBA
 (*see* Small business administration)
Short-term cash flow, 94
 liquidity, 94
Small business administration (SBA),
 41, 42
Small business administration loan,
 41, 42
Subchapter S corporation, 167, 168
Swiss frank, 55, 56

**T**
Tax deferment, 39, 40
Tax forgiveness, 39
Tax liability, 32, 39
Taxation law, 125
Tax shelter, 40
TAXSPEAK, 124, 125
Transfer of wealth (*see* wealth transfer)

**V**
Value of debt, 24, 31
Value of dollar (*see* Dollar value)
Value of interest, 32
 loan, 32
Variables financial, 91
 nonfinancial, 91

## W

Wealth loss, 17
Wealth redistribution, **9**
   loss, 51
Wealth transfer, 4, 11, 13, 15, 17, 20,
   22, 28, 30, 32, 33, 35, 40, 42, 53
Wealth transfer of debt, 25, 33
   inflation, 20, 22
Weighted inflation factor, 168-170, 172,
   174, 177
Working capital, 42